Skills and Skilled Work

Skills and Skilled Work

An Economic and Social Analysis

Francis Green

OXFORD
UNIVERSITY PRESS

Great Clarendon Street, Oxford, OX2 6DP,
United Kingdom

Oxford University Press is a department of the University of Oxford.
It furthers the University's objective of excellence in research, scholarship,
and education by publishing worldwide. Oxford is a registered trade mark of
Oxford University Press in the UK and in certain other countries

First Edition published in 2013

Impression: 1

British Library Cataloguing in Publication Data

Data available

ISBN 978–0–19–964285–4

Printed in Great Britain by the
MPG Printgroup, UK

Preface

Every now and then I come across people who in their work can excel at something complex and meaningful, who not only are gaining immense satisfaction from a skilled job well done, but in addition are paid handsomely for their labours. Fortune favours this minority, and only a utopian would expect everyone in society to be so blessed. Yet a spirit of optimism about skills can be detected among those who contemplate the future beyond the current period of economic stagnation. The 'knowledge economy' has been generating the prospect that, even though not everyone can experience it, more people than ever can enjoy the benefits and privileges of learning and doing highly skilled work.

The aspiration has been sustained by the belief that raising skills is a 'win–win' resolution of the ever-present possibility for conflict between labour and capital, with employees gaining from higher pay and all-round job quality and employers from a rise in productivity large enough to improve their profits. Supporting the supply of skilled labour is also seen as providing a local escape from the pressures of global competition. Since labour power is a less mobile form of capital—compared with finance, technologies, materials, and equipment—regional agencies and nation states regard skills strategy as central among the few remaining policy options for economic growth, given that their monetary and fiscal choices have become so restrained by the open economy.

Even before the Great Recession hit the industrialized world in 2008, not all social analysts accepted this story. Doubts continued to be raised about how widely the demand for skilled labour was really growing, and about whether a skills policy could be successful unless accompanied by transformative industrial and social policies. As youth unemployment soared in the subsequent years of macroeconomic stagnation, education and training policies took second place in public discourse to the need for fiscal rectitude. The scarcity of work for young people became a huge setback for skills: with the immense importance of workplace learning, the young unemployed have been excluded from the knowledge economy.

In this book I consider skills and skilled work from a multidisciplinary perspective. From this vantage point, it is possible to accept some validity to the optimists' tenets, but to register concern about the many instances of naive idealism and parochialism about skills to be found in public discourse around the world. I have, for example, lost count of the number of well-meaning reports and papers I have seen, advocating that employers should all be supporting more training, or that employees must all be persuaded to devote a greater commitment to their organizations and to skills acquisition. I once heard a public official make the absurd claim that no amount of training could be considered too much. A common theme of many reports about skills and training is the need for enlightenment, yet this just seems too weak. Too many analyses and pieces of advice on skills emerge from a single disciplinary viewpoint, each ignoring those of other fields. Writing on skill is also often narrow in other senses, focusing, for example, on a restricted traditional definition of skill, as if all that mattered were the configuration of training institutions, or else exclusively on universities, as if only college education counts. Part of the problem is that 'skill' as a concept has a wide usage in both academic discourse and everyday life, but widely varying meanings. Very many people have opinions about skills, well honed and informed from experience, yet misconceptions are rife: the demand for skilled labour is conflated with the demand for learning, qualifications with skills, skill shortages with deficits, and so on.

Recognition is growing, nevertheless, that skill and skilled work have an important place in social scientific study of the possibilities for advancing prosperity in the twenty-first century, and that they will warrant a more central place in the curriculum and the agenda in coming decades. Travellers among a range of national and supra-national discourses are struck by their encounters with common problems and themes: with education systems, for example, concerns circulate about grade inflation, literacy standards, and excessive rote learning; with youth transitions, employers' complaints about the unpreparedness of students for work never cease. Each nation conceives itself to be in a skills race with others in the global economy, and wants to accept only highly skilled workers as immigrants. Concerns with social exclusion through skills poverty are widespread, and there is a general belief that skills are at least part of the way forward for economic development.

In effect, skills and skilled work are together becoming a cross-cutting sub-discipline of sufficient gravity suitable for study in itself. Yet the area lacks sufficient focus and consensus among the social sciences and within policy-making communities about how it should be analysed; correspondingly, a common understanding of how skills policies should be motivated and supported is missing. One intention of this book is to provide a synthesis that will be of value to readers who, whatever their intellectual homes, are thinking about skills and skilled work in the twenty-first century. This constituency will include those who may be charged with advising relevant actors in each nation's skill system.

The overall objective is to develop an analytical and empirical framework with common terms, thereby promoting the study of skills and skilled work in modern economies as a distinct sub-field. The focus is on the behaviour and decisions of key actors, principally employers and workers, and then on the roles of governments and other social actors. In particular, it will aim to establish the concept and measurement of skill in a multidisciplinary context, to set out a theoretical framework for skills analyses, and to investigate the roles of employers, workers, and other social actors. As well as hailing beneficial developments for skilled work in recent decades, several classes of skills problems are to be considered, as a prelude to an overview of how a social response from governments can be understood. The intention is to focus on common themes rather than the needs of any one country and to provide an understanding of recent techniques for analysing skills. Finally, it is hoped to assist readers to assess critically both the prospects and the limitations of what can be achieved for societies with a better emphasis on skills and skilled work.

Acknowledgements

While the usual disclaimers apply, very many thanks go to friends and colleagues who have helped me with the typescript for this book. Paul Auerbach helped me with thoughtful line-by-line contributions throughout, and very valuable comments have been gratefully received from Alan Felstead and Lorna Unwin. Special thanks are also due to Andy Green for allowing me to adapt and use in Chapter 9 some material from draft joint notes on national skill systems.

Contents

List of Figures	xii
List of Tables	xiii
Abbreviations	xiv
Note to Reader	xv

Part I. Skill Concepts and Framework

1. Skilled Work and Job Quality | 3
    Skills and skilled work as an embryonic field of study | 3
    The political economy of skills and skilled work | 5

2. What Is Skill? | 9
    The 'PES' concept of skill | 9
    Three disciplinary perspectives: economics, sociology, and psychology | 11
    Interrogating 'productive': the significance of value | 18
    Skill typologies and domains | 21
    An interdisciplinary appeal | 24

3. Framing the Analysis of Skilled Work | 27
    The articulation of two markets | 27
    Market outcomes: matches and mismatches | 30
    Markets or actors? | 32
    Collective actors | 35
    A framework, but no full theory | 37

4. The Measurement of Skill | 39
    Being measurable, quantifiable, and commensurable | 39
    Skills supply | 40
    Skills demand and job skill | 44
    Skill formation and loss | 48
    Mismatch | 51
    Skill measurement as a work in progress | 54

Contents

Part II. The Players

5. Employers and the Evolution of Skilled Work   57
    Why employers matter   57
    Employers' demand for skilled labour   58
    The role of evidence linking skills to performance   67
    How the demand for skill is changing overall   69
    Thinking about the future   77
    Appendix. The basic economic model of skills demand   78

6. Employers and Skill Formation   81
    The importance of work for skill formation   81
    A theoretical framework for skill formation by employers   83
    Collective skill formation   88
    The consequences of employers' dual functions   90

7. Skilled Workers for Skilled Work   93
    Sources of skills   93
    Skill and labour supply   94
    Framing workers' demand for skill formation services
      (the 'demand for learning')   96
    'Bounded agency' in the demand for learning   104
    Three themes: skills premia, youth transitions, and learning barriers   105
    Retreating to the middle range   113

Part III. Systems and Interventions

8. Skill Matching Processes, Problems, and Outcomes   117
    Prices or quantities?   117
    Classes of skills problems   121
    A tableau of skills outcomes and problems   124
    An optimism downgrade   135

9. Skill Systems and the Role of the State   141
    The need for a normative framework for skills interventions   141
    Reasons to be involved   142
    A critique of human capital theory's negative conclusions on
      training interventions   145
    The role of the state in promoting skilled work and skill
      formation: a restatement   150
    Skill systems and forms of state involvement   151
    The role for skills interventions in an institutionally
      constrained environment   160

10. Skills Analysis for Modern Economies 165
    Auditing skills 165
    Describing and projecting skills supply 167
    Describing and projecting skills demand 169
    The balance between supply and demand 172
    Measuring the private and social benefits of becoming
        more skilled 174
    Analyses to be done 177

11. Threads and Limits 179
    Threads 179
    Should governments worry about over-education? 180
    Limits of skills policies 183

Notes 187
References 195
Index 215

List of Figures

3.1. Skill formation and the deployment of skilled labour   28

5A.1. An isoquant for high-skilled and low-skilled labour   79

5A.2. Skill-biased technological change (SBTC) with fixed output   80

7.1. Framework for the formation of the demand for learning   101

8.1. Tertiary educational attainment of 25–64-year-olds, 1997 and 2009   125

8.2. Numeracy skills in the early–mid-1990s   126

8.3. Skills poverty: low-level literacy and numeracy skills in the early–mid-1990s   127

8.4. Past and expected occupational employment structure in the European Union   128

8.5. Changes in the use of generic skills in Great Britain, 1997–2006   129

8.6. Subjective skill matching in Europe, 2010   130

8.7. Trends in over-education in Great Britain and Germany   131

8.8. Participation in lifelong learning in the European Union   133

10.1. Proportion of the population that has attained tertiary education, 2009   168

List of Tables

4.1. Skills indicators   41

4.2. Job skills indicators   45

4.3. Skills change indicators   50

4.4. Mismatch indicators   52

8A.1. Educational attainment: % of 25–64-year-olds by level, OECD   136

8A.2. Quantitative literacy scores in the early 1990s   138

8A.3. Subjective skill matching across European countries, 2010   139

8A.4. Lifelong learning participation by education attainment and training costs, across Europe   140

10.1. Projections of the occupation structure in Europe   170

Abbreviations

ALLS	Adult Literacy and Life Skills Survey
BIBB/BAuA	Bundesinstitut für Berufsbildung/Bundesanstalt für Arbeitsschutz und Arbeitsmedizin
CEDEFOP	European Centre for the Development of Vocational Training
CME	Coordinated Market Economy
DE	Developmental Economy
DOT	*Dictionary of Occupational Titles*
EHEA	European Higher Education Area
EQF	European Qualifications Framework for Lifelong Learning
HIWP	High Involvement Work Practice
IALS	International Adult Literacy Survey
IEA	International Association for the Evaluation of Educational Achievement
ISCO	International Standard Classification of Occupations
ISCED	International Standard Classification of Education
LME	Liberal Market Economy
OSF	Official Statistics of Finland
PES	Productive–Expandable–Social
PIAAC	Programme for the International Assessment of Adult Competencies
PISA	Programme for International Student Assessment
RBV	resource-based view
SBTC	'skill-biased' technological change
TIMSS	Trends in International Mathematics and Science Study
VET	Vocational Education and Training

Note to Reader

This book ranges over disciplines and touches many subject areas. To minimize clutter, selected rather than comprehensive references, given in endnotes, are used as supportive evidence. Readers are thus spared the trials and weight of a lengthy literature assessment for all issues, but can follow trails as desired.

Part I
Skill Concepts and Framework

1

Skilled Work and Job Quality

Skills and skilled work as an embryonic field of study

As many social philosophers have attested, to do skilled work is to fulfil a fundamental need; to become more skilled in work is to respond to a basic desire for learning. By being allied to conscious thought, combining planning and execution, human work is distinguished from the intricate instinctive behaviours of other species. Through its greater productivity, more skilled work better meets our need for the means of living.

These connections between skills, work, and human needs are perennial, and can be used to frame the lives of workers in ancient eras as easily as those of today. Early political economists were not optimistic that fulfilment through skilled work was compatible with capitalism, or with industrial economic life in general, except for a tiny minority of the population. Yet what characterizes the modern era is the generally increasing salience of skill for many. No longer are education and training set for a small elite of upper-class professionals and privileged craft workers. Modern capitalist labour processes display considerable variation in the deployment of skills, and the humanist evocation of social philosophers has now been transformed to the proposition that more skilled work for the mass of the population is better and something feasible to strive for. It is an idea rooted both in materialist philosophy and in formal empirical evidence that links skilled work with indicators of well-being and with pay. The proposition emerges also as a child of affluence: the rise of living standards beyond recognition from those of just half a century ago fuels the desire for decent work.

Against this background, some of the largest questions in social science are being posed. How much are the skills of populations growing, and which types of skills? How do people make their choices about skills, and nurture their demand for learning as they go through life? How well are their skills being deployed in paid work? What are the effects on the growth and development of nations, and on the distribution of living standards? Can skills be a way out of poverty?

And, in the light of our answers, what if anything can governments do to enable modern 'skill systems' to perform more equitably and efficiently? With their macroeconomic policies hemmed in by the competitive global economy, many governments have come to assign an increasing economic importance to their education and training policies. With the presumption that raising skills has positive benefits for both employers and workers, promoting skilled work has become the quintessential 'win–win' strategy. There is a common belief that governments and other social agents can make a difference through skills policies in the twenty-first century, both to economic prosperity and to social cohesion. Heterogeneous interests have backed the promotion of skill formation as a cross-class objective; states that need the support of business groups typically present their skill formation policies as driven by their desire to improve 'economic performance' for all.

A large range of studies, across several fields, have been addressing these questions in recent decades: skills and skilled work are beginning to form a cross-cutting sub-discipline of social science. Much progress has been made with measurement protocols, broadening the perspectives on skill concepts, and delineating through empirical evidence some of the roles of skills in modern industrial economies. Lately analysts have been emboldened to develop forecasts of skills supplies and demands over a medium-term future. Given the centrality of the issues addressed, achievement of sub-discipline status is desirable, if it can facilitate the advancement of understanding and communication of findings, but it has not yet been realized. There remain large gulfs between perspectives in the understanding of some of the most basic questions surrounding skills, including the conceptualization of skills themselves, the importance of individual agency as opposed to economic and structural forces, and the significance of the demand side of the economy. Not infrequently, confusions arise stemming from differing terminology, or from a lack of appreciation of theories and methods from outside the home domain. Skills studies proceed in isolation from the learning of other literatures, cut off by jargon, techniques, or the urge to specialize. Sometimes differences reflect the reality among interested parties that, notwithstanding the win–win presumption, skills and their valuation are contested terrain in the workplace, given their close association with pay. In some disciplines, skill has assumed such great importance that discourse on skill is conducted with high stakes. In economics, skill is central to the story about the changing distribution of income. In sociology, skill underpins class, perhaps its most fundamental category. In psychology, competence analysis is at the heart of important branches of human resource practice. In each of these disciplines there is a large and ongoing literature, on which this book will draw.

The domains of skills and skilled work are, however, not self-contained. In particular, both the opportunity to do skilled work and the experience of a good learning environment are basic elements of good job quality. Job quality studies also incorporate other features that contribute to the satisfaction of human needs, including the other intrinsic aspects of the job, such as the climate of social support and the physical setting, and the extrinsic aspects such as pay, hours, and job security.[1] A good learning environment enables workers to become more skilled, potentially increasing their access to future jobs that are better quality in many dimensions. Job quality analyses therefore both contribute to, and draw from, studies of skills and skilled work.

The political economy of skills and skilled work

The intention of this book is to set out a political economy of skills and skilled work, a broad way of thinking about these issues that can serve as a basis for the further formation of this sub-discipline of social science. The term 'political economy' is consciously used here in the traditional sense characteristic of the eighteenth and nineteenth centuries, because it captures a synthesis of now-separated social science disciplines, especially economics, sociology, and political science. This classical reading contrasts with the modern, more specialized usage of the term, within political science and economics, as the study of the relation between economic interests and political forces, a branch that will be only briefly visited. A classical-type synthesis is desirable because of the inherently interdisciplinary nature of the subject, but in one respect it is insufficiently broad: the importance of occupational psychology also needs to be added in to the mix.

The first part of the book is devoted to the basics: concepts, framework, and measurement. Serious questions surround the classification of qualities as skills, yet there has been alarmingly little debate between schools of thought. An inclusive definition is proposed that may allow interdisciplinary discourse and analyses to proceed. Skills are thus viewed as personal qualities with three main features: they are productive of value, expandable, and social. The first of these features is key to the inclusiveness: the range of perspectives about skill reflect different perspectives and schools of thought about value. Chapter 2 uses the definition also to reveal the contested and ambivalent character of skill.

Chapter 3 sets out the essential economic framework that houses the generation and use of skills in the capitalist economy. At its heart are the two main actors, employers and workers, who participate in two interlocking markets: one for the demands and supplies of skilled labour, the other for the demands for and supplies of skill formation services. The term 'skill formation service' refers to any formal or informal opportunity to acquire skills, whether through education and training or through participating in a work environment that facilitates learning. The markets interlock, because the motives for skill formation relate to the future use of skills—a link that is especially direct when employers both supply and demand skill formation services, and then demand the skill-enhanced labour for their own companies. The framework is a simplification, since there are many types and levels of skills; it does not amount to a theory with predictions and explanations. Rather, it denotes a language to help describe how the system succeeds or fails, in terms of demands, supplies, matches, and mismatches; and it provides a gateway for some theories about aspects of the framework to be considered later in the book.

A recurring theme concerns the extent to which employers and workers can affect outcomes, or whether they are mere carriers of the large impersonal forces of technological change, enhanced international competition, or the structural imperatives of social class. The question is important, not least because it affects what governments and other social actors can and should do. If, for example, employers and workers have adequate foresight and capacities to be making privately 'rational' decisions about skills acquisition and use, then social intervention should be considered only when externalities and other market imperfections can be demonstrated. If, on the other hand, rationality of the sort assumed by economics is foreclosed by the deep uncertainty surrounding long-term skills decisions, and by the heterogeneous capacities and resources available to decision-makers, the potential case for social intervention is broadened.

Measurement has also been a troubling issue for skills analysts, in the past making it hard to test hypotheses and the sometimes opposing and contradictory grand narratives put forward to describe the directions that skills were moving in modern industrial societies. Yet there have been considerable advances in data collection since the early 1990s, chiefly through the use of high-quality representative surveys and skills testing vehicles, but also through the refinement of occupational and educational classification schemes. Clarity in linking empirical indicators to the skill concepts of the analytical framework has also improved. An overview of the current state of play, presented in Chapter 4, reveals that the measurement of skills is improving. Least well developed are measures of productive attitudes and dispositions, perhaps not surprisingly since they occupy an ambivalent place in the concept of skill.

Part II is devoted to the two main actors, employers and workers, including their collective embodiments in employers' organizations and in unions. Chapters 5 and 6 develop the employer's role in the demand for skilled labour and in the supply of skill formation services. Arguments are marshalled to support the view that the demand for skill has been growing for some time, linked to technological and organizational change, and to increased international competition. In several countries there has also been an asymmetric polarization of employment, with the largest increases coming in the high-skilled occupations, and relative falls in medium-skilled occupations, where disproportionately workers have been displaced by new technologies. Since work is an immensely important site for learning, the employer's role as a supplier of opportunities for learning is crucial: a worker in a job that is not designed to foster learning encounters a barrier that is hard to surmount without quitting and finding a better job. The dual roles of employers give them a great deal of influence over skills, and there are potentially two reasons why they may decide to invest too little in skill formation. On the one hand, lacking managerial capacities and the resources to see beyond the short term, some employers may, in an imperfect and dynamic world, nevertheless survive for considerable periods, even if with lower profits than they might otherwise have achieved. Recent evidence has revealed, for example, the extent to which the use of good managerial practices varies enormously within and across countries. On the other hand, employers acting rationally in their own interests may devote too few resources to training from the overall economy's perspective, since they do not want to pay for training when workers themselves and other employers gain the benefits. These reasons form the basis for a normative analysis of the state's role in Chapter 9.

Meanwhile, Chapter 7 considers the extent to which workers can make rational decisions in their role of supplying skilled labour and in their demands for learning new skills. For the supply of skilled labour, it takes only a straightforward piece of applied economics to show that, even though in theory the effect of being more skilled on the supply of labour is ambiguous, in practice skilled workers do supply more labour than low-skilled workers to the market. It is a demonstration—if it were needed—that doing skilled work helps to meet a need, more so than for someone who has only low-skilled work to contemplate. Indeed, the opportunity to use and develop a high level of skills is an important ingredient of intrinsic job quality.

The demand for learning, however, is a more complex process, about which there is much more to be investigated. Incentives matter for inducing learning, so one question concerns how large the incentive is. A great deal of research has been done in economics to try to estimate the skills premium in the labour market as accurately as possible. But incentives are not the only factor: individuals encounter a complex web of interactive and cumulative pressures and motives for their skills and learning decisions through their lives, with uncertain outcomes. A framework is presented that encompasses much of the research that is being undertaken, but this does not yet amount to a theory. Empirical studies document the increasingly problematic nature of young people's transitions between education and work. Throughout their lives workers can encounter barriers to their learning—that is, obstacles that prevent them from engaging in beneficial learning.

Part III turns to the skill system as a whole, comprising both markets and the institutions that support them, beginning with Chapter 8, which looks at the outcomes of the two markets' functioning. After documenting the successes, it classifies and illustrates the potential problems associated with skills inequalities and skills poverty, with the possibility of a low-skills equilibrium, and with poor matching processes in either market. Chapter 9 follows by setting the potential role for government in addressing these problems, in the context of different varieties of capitalist economy. Liberal market economy skill systems are contrasted with coordinated market economy systems (the latter divided among the social partner coordinated systems and the state-led coordinated systems), and the developmental economy skill systems of East Asia. For all countries and systems, the position advanced is that the arguments for and against intervention should be conducted both in terms of potential market failure (the conventional viewpoint) and in terms of the relative capacities and efficiencies of the actors—workers, employers, and government (the less-conventional managerial viewpoint). On the assumption that some forms of intervention may be advisable, Chapter 10 then sets out the sorts of analyses that are being developed to help governments and other agencies devise their strategies. All countries are different, and are changing, so analyses in support of policies have to be tailored to each country's needs. Some skills statistics—for example, occupational compositions—are relatively straightforward to collect for any state that conducts regular censuses of employment and has a decent classification system. Forecasts of skills supplies and demands, however, and measuring skills premia, need relatively complex analyses, the bases for which are described in the chapter. Just as the measurement of skills has been making progress, so the sophistication of the analyses has been growing, even if the study of skills remains only a science in construction.

The final chapter returns to a higher plane to consider the optimism about the possibilities for skills policy, and some of the pessimism espoused by critics. It turns to the question of the political and economic constraints, and how failure to recognize or tackle these can lead to false expectations and undue claims for what skills policy can achieve. It also builds on arguments about the demand side of the economy to review both sides of the debate about whether governments should be concerned in coming decades about skills mismatch.

2

What Is Skill?

The 'PES' concept of skill

Skilled work is the exercise of 'skill' at work, but what precisely is that? Widely regarded as a core object for policy interventions and analytical research in the modern global high-technology era, skills are claimed to have large economic effects for individuals, employers, regions and whole national economies. Yet there is no consensus among social scientists or among policy-makers about the meaning of the concept of skill. When economists, sociologists, and psychologists discuss skill, they often appear to be talking about different things. When their work is translated, scholars in different languages have still another take on the matter. Dialogue and discussion between disciplines and cultures are unusual, so similarities and differences are not made transparent or resolved. Disciplinary segmentation permits conceptual and semantic differences to persist; outsiders to academic discourse hear different approaches, depending on whom they are listening to. Nor does the scope for confusion end at the library door. Unlike constructs in the natural sciences, skill is one of those social science words in common parlance with many meanings, numerous synonyms such as 'ability', 'competence', 'knack', 'aptitude', and 'talent', and varied imprecise translations in other languages.

If skill is so important for economic progress, we had better be sure what we mean by it. It needs a careful and sufficiently broad definition to support a consistent analysis and a common dialogue. Narrow notions typically betray particular preferences, and intellectual tussles can themselves reflect conflicting interests. The consequences of the lack of clarity and consensus over the concept of skill are many. They include potential misconceptions such as the conflation of employers' demand for skill with workers' demand for skill formation opportunities, or of the subjective with the objective; unnecessarily narrow perspectives towards policy interventions; ill-informed critiques or ignorance of other disciplines' approaches; and difficulties with conceptualizing the role of work attitudes. The confusions impede the development of an integrated cross-disciplinary analysis of skill. Frequently researchers find it necessary to clarify the phrases they are going to use, often reinventing definitions and measurement concepts. It would be better if social scientists could agree terms.

This chapter advocates a functional concept of skill that builds upon some commonalities, and offers a prospect of dialogue and progress in interdisciplinary skills analysis. This is a field in which almost everyone has opinions, newcomers as well. There have been several distinguished scholarly contributions on the concept of skill, including a stimulating and much cited collection published in a 1990 issue of the journal *Work and Occupations*;[1] and countless glossaries annexed to public reports have paid obeisance to the need for definitions. But that 1990 issue left unfinished business, in so far as it was mainly addressed to an audience of sociologists, with only minor attempts to forge a dialogue with economics. Since then there have been substantial developments in measurement protocols that have forced rethinks of conceptual frameworks, including successive skill test surveys (national and international), the demise of the US Department of Labor's *Dictionary of Occupational Titles* (*DOT*) and its rebirth as O*NET, and the parallel development in Europe, the United States, and South-East Asia of a task-based (or 'job-requirement') approach;[2] while many volumes of research have turned to skill for their understanding of change in modern socio-economic life.

To try to progress beyond the 1990 positions within sociology, and the plethora of ad hoc glossaries, this chapter draws upon multiple traditions consulted over two decades' experience in designing, using, and teaching about skills measures for socio-economic research, in order to advance a concept of skill that encompasses critically the approaches of economics, psychology, and sociology. Ideally the concept should be capable of serving as a vehicle for theoretical and empirical scientific progress. It should aim to foster greater clarity in contemporary skills debates among those steeped in diverse traditions, and be an aid to interdisciplinary policy development. It should also be measurable in practice, though discussion of the principles and details of measurement is postponed until Chapter 4. The concept of skill proposed here is intended to be at once scientific, oriented towards human, social, and economic progress, and relevant for a discussion of social and economic action in twenty-first-century settings. The chapter thus situates skill within the classical tradition of political economy, yet in a modern setting.

Skills are personal qualities with three key features:

1. Productive: using skills at work are productive of value.
2. Expandable: skills are enhanced by training and development.
3. Social: skills are socially determined.

The above delineation—denoted hereafter the 'PES' concept of skill—has boundaries that make the concept functional for locating the role of skill in economic and social systems, and that afford it a place across the social sciences. Though broad and covering most common usages of the term, not all qualities are included. The focus on productive activity at work attends to qualities relevant for economic development, but excludes other qualities, such as those relevant to domestic labour, leisure time, or activities as citizens. These other spheres are indirectly connected to the domain of paid work, but are not part of this enquiry. Another delineation is that the concept is action centred, premised on how individuals and collective actors can change these qualities. Attributes that cannot by their nature be enhanced are not considered as skills.

The chapter first shows how far each discipline's concept of skill conforms to the PES concept, and uses the discussion to try to clarify the treatment of problematic aspects of skill, including the individualist methodology of human capital theory, the interpretation of complexity, and the characterization of work attitudes. These problematic aspects are related to familiar perspectives on valuation, and their implications are discussed in the following section. A robust conclusion is that skill has a normative aspect associated with the conceptualization of value. The two ways in which skills are socially determined are then described, and the stipulation that skills are expandable is elaborated. The chapter then shows how the PES concept of skill and the parallel concept of job skill give rise to common typologies used in the analysis of skills policies. The final section returns to the theme of communication blockage between social science disciplines and the expressed intention that the PES concept might enable debate to proceed in a more meaningful fashion. It defends the need for a broad but well-crafted concept of skill that will be usable for social and economic analysis.

Three disciplinary perspectives: economics, sociology, and psychology

In neoclassical economics, skill is one of the main ingredients of 'human capital', the other being health. With a strictly individualist connotation, human capital is the value of a person's stream of current and future prospective earnings discounted to the present.[3] Education and training are investments in the accumulation of human capital, with prospective if uncertain returns, which underpin rational individualistic decision-making about how much and which types of investment to make. As long as it is productive of a stream of earnings, nothing needs to be said about the content of skill, except to classify where it can be used, because this affects its financing. If skill is transferable between one workplace and many others, in a competitive market with no borrowing restraints workers pay to acquire their own skills. If there are labour market imperfections, or if the skills are firm specific, the costs and benefits of training are shared between worker and employer.[4] This approach to skill exhibits an attractive consistency and simplicity.

Nevertheless, the neoclassical concept of human capital reflects an objectification and alienation of workers in capitalism.[5] The scientific inadequacy, according to non-neoclassical critics within and beyond economics, is that, in regarding human capital as a thing to be acquired, like other capital, the neoclassical concept misses the social context of skill.[6] The incentives and outcomes are real, but what is found inadequate by critics are the assumptions that working people are islands of preferences and aspirations that are exogenous (that is, unaffected by socio-economic processes), that technologies also are exogenous and uniquely determine work organization, and that managers follow optimal policies. Rather, the acquisition, valuation, and utilization of skill are each socially determined processes.

The acquisition of skill is conditioned by attitudes and expectations that are imprinted with social norms, while opportunities for skill acquisition are circumscribed by social class. The value of skill lies in the value of the product, which itself is socially determined (unless one accepts all neoclassical premisses about individualistic consumers and producers). For example, the value of skill is perturbed by the 'social construction of skill', whereby social processes, including power, affect who can sport the label of 'skilled labour', and who can claim the rewards. The use of skill in organizations is affected by the quality of employment relations and by management strategy that is culturally determined. In all these ways, it proves to be a serious limitation to suppose, as the neoclassical model does, that individuals' skill decisions arise from maximizing some utility function that is purged of the social. In short, while the neoclassical perspective exhibits the first two features of the PES concept of skill, it does not incorporate the third, essential feature, that skill should be conceived as socially determined.

Within much of heterodox economics, by contrast, while education and training are still regarded as investments, issue is taken with the automatic equation of value to price. Heterodox economics is a loose configuration of several schools of economic thought, sometimes rooted in classical political economy, that have in common a rejection of the individualistic conceptions of neoclassical economics. While 'human capital' is a term often used as a shorthand for education and training even by heterodox economists, the individualistic methodology is contested. Market imperfections and information asymmetries (between consumers and buyers or between workers and bosses) lead prices to diverge from the levels that would prevail with perfect competition and full information. Hence, the values of individuals' skills diverge from their productive contribution of value to society. Heterodox economics includes as well the possibility of sustained mismatches between employees' skill and the skill required in the jobs they hold.[7] 'Rational' individualistic decision-making about educational investments is also taken to be a compromised assumption, in the face of much evidence and theory about the importance of context for learning and for decisions in uncertain situations.[8] Heterodox economics' accounts of skill can also incorporate social theories of how work skills are acquired.[9]

In several respects, heterodox economics draws on ideas from sociology, which, in contrast to neoclassical economics, looks inside the production process for its concept of skill; its discourse centres on the complexity of tasks. In this approach, to exercise greater skill is to carry out a more complex activity.[10] With activities bundled into jobs, much of the discussion within sociology has been about 'job skill' (the skill required to perform a job competently), which is seen as the primary determinant of social class. Workers can acquire the ability to do complex tasks, with greater complexity needing more learning and requiring greater reward. Thus sociology's perspective is encompassed in the PES concept of skill.

Challenging problems, however, lie at the heart of the proposition that complex activity is the substance of skill. How does one operationalize the notion of complexity? Measurement has come from expert systems, such as the *DOT*, its successor O*NET, or the lengths of required education, training, or related work experience. These compendiums yield loose proxies for a frankly fuzzy concept. And is complexity, even if it could be well defined and measured, always sensibly related to learning input and value? The most complex of tasks can become second nature, almost unconscious and seemingly easy. Walking might seem trivial for most adults, but it has proved a long and challenging journey for robotics engineers. Moreover, one can look for complexity in a choice of spaces, and be deceived by not opening the right doors. The discoveries of tacit or latent skills, especially emotional and aesthetic skills, are cases in point: the labour processes that utilize these complex tasks are not new, but it took the lens of feminist political economy to point them out after many years of invisibility in social science.

The ability to work autonomously, to exercise some discretion over work tasks, and thus to operate without close external direction is an important complement to complexity that normally requires a higher level of understanding. Complex tasks are likely to be less easily specified, more infused with contingencies, and subject to uncertainty; therefore greater task discretion is likely to be found in the organisation of complex work. Also, skill is likely to be needed in more autonomous situations that call for higher judgement. Skill is thus intimately associated with, though not constituted by, autonomy. For much of the sociology of labour, this association underpins the concept of skill, drawing on the Marxian concept of human labour. One strand of neo-Marxian thought even fuses autonomy into the very definition of skill; yet this conflates complementarity with identity, and misses the fact that even closely rule-bound operations can be complex.[11] For Marx himself it is the combination of conscious plan and action that defines human-specific labour.[12] Conversely, the subordination of labour and accompanying loss of control in capitalist workplaces is a central aspect of alienation. The retention of some autonomy by a skilled worker in the execution of complex tasks, however, suggests the preservation of an intrinsically human element even in a capitalist work context. Skilled and autonomous working, as in modern utopian accounts, is the heightened fulfilment of a need. Its archetype in Harry Braverman's influential account is the nineteenth-century craft worker before the advent of Taylorism in the twentieth century and the accompanying 'degradation' of work.[13]

Sociology's other main contribution to our understanding of the concept of skill is the recognition that skill can be 'socially constructed'.[14] A divergence can arise, through the exercise of social power, between a job's social status and its real level of job skill—in effect, through a distortion of the value generated. Social closure is the classical form that this adjustment takes—limiting entrants to an occupation, where the bar is set above the level that might be justified by complexity. The critique of occupation monopolies lies deep in the classical writings of the founders of modern sociology (Max Weber) and economics (Adam Smith). The attribution 'skilled job' then becomes a source of market power, while the association between high wages and 'skilled' seeps into tautology.

The theory of the social construction of skill provides a telling account of gender discrimination, whereby certain jobs predominantly held by women are conceived as low skilled, which self-justifies the consent to low pay, which then reinforces their perception as low skilled, and not suitable for men, and of lower value than men's work. This discriminating vicious circle can be broken by the dissection and exposure of job content, though even here the control of competency definitions and their link with comparable worth policies means that skills remain contested.[15] On occasion, technological change is radical enough to disrupt existing norms: the eventual exposure of print workers to skill reconstruction, when computer typesetting and offset lithography replaced linotype, is a case in point. In some versions of the theory, the social construction of skill goes beyond the disjuncture between 'real' and perceived skill, arguing that social processes such as gender determine real processes of value formation. Thus technology, in this account, cannot be assumed to be an exogenous determinant of values if the design of new technologies is driven by a gendered sensibility.[16] Skills might then differ according to sex, but the origin of the differentiation is a gendered, hence social, process.

The main practical lesson of social construction theory is that neither self-perceptions nor social classifications of skilled work can be taken as neutral concepts: both are subject to potential bias, to be revealed and potentially resolved by analyses of job content. Caution should be especially enhanced where a job has been subject to any form of class-based or gender-based social closure. The theory illustrates the significance of the link between skills and values: to question values is also to contest the skills that go into creating them. Social construction theory also reminds us that, since the 'skill' label is contested, it should not be regarded as an immutable, independent, quality of individuals.

Nevertheless, even though market values (hence skill labels and perceptions) can be distorted by unequal power, social construction theory does not imply that skills should be conceived independently of value, nor should it lead into a morass of relativism or untestable generalizations. Indeed, skill theory is not absolved from an engagement with theories of value. In this, the sociological approach to skill has been somewhat silent, tending to fall back on complexity of production as the true measure of skill. Some sociological accounts juxtapose objective and subjective concepts of skill, with the latter seen as somehow ephemeral or residing only in one person's opinions. But this dichotomy is false: all skills are social qualities, yet are rooted in real, objective, processes and not in perceptions. Moreover, the fact that skills are socially determined provides neither a valid argument against an empirically driven approach, nor a reason to reject quantitative measures that uncover trends and the relationships between skills and socio-economic outcomes. Some writers have rejected a positivist approach to the quantitative measurement of skill, but there is nothing in the concept itself to warrant such a stance. The practicalities of skills measurement—the pros and cons of various approaches—are discussed in Chapter 4. It will suffice for now to state that, while no strategy is ideal, the problematic issues are no more challenging than those of many other social and economic indicators.

The idea of skill also has a long lineage in occupational and educational psychology, being inherent in the study of learning processes. Well before skill entered central stage in public discourse, psychologists were studying the intricacies of, for example, sensory-motor skills, signal detection, and mental skills such as problem-solving, and then investigating how these faculties were best acquired.[17] The relevant modern concept in occupational psychology is 'competency', defined as the ability successfully to perform a range of tasks to a high level of performance; while the idea of 'competence' refers to the required standards needed to perform a job or set of tasks. In practice the two ideas, competence and competency, have merged and are often used interchangeably. The competence movement has played a significant role in the evolution of vocational education, and in the rise of human resource management. Human resource functions for which a competence framework has been used include recruitment, personal development, performance management and wage-setting; and competence frameworks have been used as the basis for systems of qualifications.

Through these functions, psychology joins with sociology in evaluating the social context in which skills are learned and used, and through its development of job content analysis provides material for revealing the deceptive character of socially constructed skills and provides support for comparable worth policies within organizations. Yet psychology's views of skills inside the organization do not necessarily endorse a sole emphasis on complexity; and, indeed, ethnographic studies tend to show up the complexities of activities normally not rated as skilled.[18] Job analysis, built upon competence frameworks, delivers the normative valuation process that occupational psychology substitutes for market valuation. Heterogeneous jobs are made comparable through commensurate grades using expert judgements about the competence levels involved, while in the education sphere qualifications are similarly ranked with descriptions of the competences they certify. This principle stands in contrast to that used in mainstream economics, where judgements of equivalence are delivered through the revealed preferences of those who demand skilled labour in a free market.

Competence is a widely used concept, both in education and in the management of labour, and it has proved relevant to break it down into three components, termed 'knowledge', 'skills', and 'attitudes' in Anglo-Saxon discourse. Yet both the components and the totality remain as somewhat problematic concepts. In France, the Vocational Education and Training (VET) system distinguishes, similarly, between *savoir*, *savoir-faire*, and *savoir-être*, but these categories do not exactly correspond to their apparently similar Anglo-Saxon translations. Occupational psychologists have trouble, in particular, arriving at a consistent and precise definition of skill, and there are serious difficulties when comparing across countries with different VET cultures.[19] 'Skill' is sometimes used to refer in a narrow way to whether someone can do a specific set of tasks. It came to be conceived and socially recognized in this restricted sense within the United Kingdom's market-oriented system of National Vocational Qualifications, partly as a means for government to audit the work of training providers. In the corporatist system of competence recognition found in Germany, the meaning of 'skill' encompasses the knowledge needed to exercise a somewhat broader range of functions within the *Beruf* (occupation). In France skill (*compétence*) is characterized, not just through the tasks that can be performed, but also by accounts of the mental processes of doing skilled work, and of ergonomic and employment relationships. Such conceptual differences across nations imply substantive difficulties for the cross-country harmonization of standards.[20]

By contrast, the need to sub-classify the components of competence in this way is not fundamental within economics, where skill, as human capital, is defined to embrace knowledge and attitudes as well. Thus 'skill' in economics is similar to 'competence' in psychology. The difference between the two disciplines lies rather in their analytical subject: in psychology, the focus is on the generation and function of competence, while in economics the interest is primarily in market valuations of skills and their implications for distribution and growth. In economics, any expandable quality that makes a worker more productive can count as a skill; for human resource specialists it is more important to unpack the concept into its components.

The economist's more inclusive use of the word 'skill' is sometimes closer than that of psychology to the concept that drives much of the policy discourse. When employers complain of skill shortages, if pressed they may mention technical skills but they also frequently refer to shortages of workers with what they consider to be the right attitudes and values, such as conscientiousness and reliability.[21] And the educational implications of job requirements extend to the need, not just for relevant cognitive and academic skills, but also for corresponding attitudes and values.[22] On the other hand, 'skill' is also sometimes used in both professional and common parlance in the narrower sense of ability to do something, often with reference to the 'skilled trades'. A still further variation is found in some policy discourses where skills are all channelled into the domain of vocational education and training, as if universities had nothing to do with it. Finally, it can also be the meaning of competence that is squeezed. For example, the language of competences has been used in the United Kingdom to define skills at the lower end of the spectrum in especially narrow terms, within the national qualifications framework.

In other usages, the principle of specifying competences is at the heart of recent 'task-based' approaches to the measurement of job skills, for use in economic analysis. Deployment of the psychology-driven O*NET content model describing occupations in the United States is a case in point: in addition to 'Abilities', 'Knowledge', 'Skills', and related contextual measures, analysts carefully delineate the 'Work Styles'—personal attributes such as self-control that are related to work performance. Other task-based, competency-inspired measurement strategies have been developed in Britain, Germany, Italy, Spain, Singapore, and elsewhere.[23]

Does economics have an attitude problem?

Even though economics writers have embraced a broad definition of skill, economics itself is not exactly at ease when it does turn to the components of competence. Applied economists have recently contributed with rigorous quantitative evidence about the effects of different skill types. They have found that attitudes—typically captured by the curious phrase 'non-cognitive' skills—can have large impacts alongside cognitive skills on educational and economic achievement.[24] Whether directly, or indirectly through enabling the development of cognitive skills, intervention programmes to improve certain behavioural traits are being found to yield substantial returns, private and social, notably for socially disadvantaged children. Yet economic theory—in contrast to applied economics—will have some conceptual angst in treating attitudes as skills. Preferences (rankings among choices) are typically conceived as individualistic and exogenous. While it is possible to model the formation of preferences, this tends to nullify most of economics' normal welfare conclusions, including its privileging of market-based solutions.[25] The importance of attitudes in the capitalist workplace thus points up again the problem with the neoclassical conception of skills as individualistic qualities. If preferences, attitudes, dispositions, and expectations concerning work are affected by social and economic context, then these 'skills' are, on the contrary, socially determined. If, alternatively, preferences are taken to be fixed, unable to be expanded, then they should not be seen as skills.

Interrogating 'productive': the significance of value

This conceptual overview has revealed that the three disciplines of economics, sociology, and psychology have developed fruitful and partly overlapping concepts of skill. The neoclassical economics' approach is centred on value, but its methodological individualism has abstracted its concept of skill from social processes. Sociology's approach, through its analysis of the social construction of skill, points up the potential distortions from the use of market values and centres the measurement of skill upon its concept of complex production; it has, however, only an incomplete alternative approach to skill valuation centred on social power. Psychology has a well-developed analysis of job competences, gauged in grades or levels, and thus orients educational achievement towards the development of competences. Even more exclusively it seems than in the case of sociology, valuation is derived from inputs to the production process. In this, psychology distantly echoes the perspective of economics for most of the nineteenth century, when the 'labour theory of value' held sway.

The PES concept of skill, by putting 'being productive of value' at its core, should facilitate communication between these perspectives. The conceptual differences are not abolished, but they are revealed as differences over theories of value. The centrality of value in skills discourse is what makes skill central to social science, and allows it to acquire a major role in socio-economic policy formation. Improving or raising skill can be construed as desirable if skill is by definition productive of value. If different disciplines can agree that skills are qualities that produce value, then dialogue on skill might be facilitated.

The question here, however—what is the source of value?—locates the problem of the concept of skill at the centre of social science. To illustrate, occupational psychology supported by sociology deploys a concept of job competence levels to develop a normative theory of pay. Linking pay to complexity holds out the prospect of equity within jobs, complementing policies to ensure open access to learning opportunities. If job competences are properly and fully defined, and their levels made commensurate across occupations and sectors, the intention is that skills can be fairly and efficiently rewarded. A quality is a skill if at work it generates value, which it does if the production process is complex; its quantitative value is measured in principle by the degree of complexity.

In contrast, economics proposes that the value of skilled labour derives from the values generated in production. In a competitive labour market the value is the wage rate, which equals the value of the extra services generated by the least productive worker that it is just profitable to employ. In so far as more complex processes generate services that are more scarce, hence having a higher price than services produced with less complex processes, there will be a convergence between the economics and psychology approaches: wages and complexity come in practice to be similar skill indicators, even though they are conceptually distinct.

Yet, if the number of workers with a particular quality come to be high relative to the demand, and if therefore their outputs are in abundance, no matter how complex is the labour process its value will fall; if the value falls to zero, it will no longer be regarded as a skill in economics. Conversely, a quality that is relatively scarce might be seen as a skill, even when the process is simple. With this intimate connection between skill and value, it follows that whether a quality is termed a skill is context and time dependent.

Even in economics, however, the value of skilled work need not always be equated with its market price. In countless cases, not least in voluntary unpaid labour, in caring labour, or in any employment where work has significant inherent interest and fulfilment, the value lies not just in the price but also in the direct satisfaction of needs.[26]

Ambivalent conceptions of skill also reflect the cleavage between private and social value, the difference being an 'externality'. Whose perspective should one use in deciding how a skill is valued? To put it starkly, suppose that the social value of an output is negative: society would be better off without it. Who wants a skilful murderer? And how should one assess the skills of the drug-dealer? Such questions illustrate how, contrary to common discourse, skills can in principle be negative quantities. To countenance this fact is not merely to entertain an intellectual curiosum. It is as valid for social policy to reduce negative skills as to promote positive ones. The acquisition of criminal skills, for example, through peer-group learning in poorly resourced prisons, is a known social problem and a deterrent to the use of custodial sentencing. Policies to counterbalance this process are in essence skills policies. Whether a social value is negative or positive may be contested: the skills of a great soldier are, to a pacifist, an affliction, not something to be applauded; for others they can make him a national hero.

Conversely, the private value of a skill could be negative, while the social value is positive and contested. Possession of skills might carry obligations that are unwelcome—for example, where a worker in a conflictual employment relationship declines training that would entail taking on additional duties.

The case of negative skills is but one example of the general issue that occurs when private and social values diverge. Another relates to the case of activities that create positional goods or services that are valued by their rank rather than their absolute magnitude. Education is sometimes argued to be, in part, a positional service.[27] Analogously, positional skills are qualities that contribute to positional outputs (for example, an advertiser's ability to elevate one brand at the expense of others). Similarly, rent-seeking skills that merely enable one business to thrive at the expense of another have only a private value. Conversely, there are numerous instances in which positive external benefits mean that the social value exceeds the private: when the skilled medic treats her patients with infectious diseases, others also gain. So the valuation of skills depends on one's perspective—private or social.

For a social perspective on valuation and skill, a normative account is called for, as was explicit in the example of the skilful soldier. Such an account is essentially both a philosophical and a political statement of the skills needed for the good life. An interesting multidisciplinary attempt to frame the key skills required for a successful life in all cultures converged upon three main categories: 'interacting in socially heterogeneous groups', 'acting autonomously', and 'using tools interactively'.[28] These are higher-level skills that are conceived as taking different forms across social and cultural contexts. Whether these particular foci command widespread acceptance depends not just on an intellectual argument about human and social needs but also on widespread adherence to a democratic political process. Skills may be personal qualities, but they are inherently embedded through their values in social structures.

The normative content of skill is especially evident in the consideration of work attitudes and dispositions as skills, but here the contradictions of value in the capitalist work relation come to the surface. Should one value attitudes and dispositions at market prices, and if not how else? A curious example arises in the context of repetitive, dull, or oppressive jobs. Is subservience to be regarded as a skill? Employees with monotonous working conditions are said to have 'boredom coping skills', which are positively associated with their well-being.[29] Yet, while it is personally useful to be able to deal well with adversity, in situations of conflict the classification and valuation of skills become a feature of the conflict itself. The need for coping is embedded in employment relations and the associated job design of workplaces. Policy implications might depend on which side you take: should one teach coping skills or resistance? The balance of power relations is important for the determination of the value of such attitudes as skills. Skills policy discourse unsurprisingly rarely debates the conflictual nature of skills determination, even though a suitable disposition is an acknowledged aspect of skill.

The social determination of skill is additionally evident in another way, to be framed in some detail in Chapter 7—namely, that the acquisition of work skills is inherently social. Work environment, class, and culture condition the dispositions, resources, and beliefs that interact to generate the demand for learning.[30] The motivation to gain new skills depends on aspirations, expectations, social networks, and social and financial support, all of which impinge on calculations of cost and future benefit. The acquisition of skill is like an investment, as the neoclassical framework tells us, in that resources are deployed in the present for future gain, but it may not be able to be reduced to an individualistic calculation.

The 'expandable' part of the PES concept of skill may be its least contentious aspect. Most accounts treat skill as something that can be acquired, building upon existing faculties, up to some limit that will vary among individuals. Yet some personal features that help to generate value are nevertheless largely fixed. A person's height might convey a labour market positional advantage, but, since there is nothing in the way of training or other investments that can add to it, this advantage is an economic rent that cannot be competed away. Though one can improve the next generation's height through the better nutrition of parents, it seems best not to include height within the definition of skill. Other personal but non-expandable features of value can be imagined too—for example, the aristocratic connections of family background. Nevertheless, few features are in practice entirely excluded in this way from the PES notion of skill: most productive qualities, if one thinks about it, are amenable to enhancement.

Skill typologies and domains

The concept of skill has thus far been examined at its most general level. Yet skill has often been categorized, reflecting ideas about how different types are generated and about the effects they have. The dissection of types has been an important feature of occupational psychology and recently of applied economics. The different components of competence are likely to be acquired in varying ways, and from different sources and contexts—home, school, work, and elsewhere. Formal education and training, for example, is the main generator of scientific knowledge, while work attitudes are moulded in multiple sites.

The various ways in which skills are productive of value—their uses—yield other typologies. One important type is the domain of activity in which the skill-type acts: literacy, technical processes, communication, and so on. Domains can be mapped at varying scales, with descriptions that summarize the complex functions involved in daily work. Such maps can resemble fractal graphs, where the description encompasses the same level of detail, however far you drill down. Analysts must choose levels of detailed disaggregation appropriate to other purposes. Moreover, domain types are never pure single processes: even low-skilled tasks, such as the collection of garbage cans, involve multiple physical and mental faculties.

Several task domains are 'generic': they can be described by indicators that are commensurate across a wide range of (though not necessarily all) occupations. IT tasks, requiring the use of generic IT skills, are a prominent modern example. In contrast, technical skills that are used in one or just a few types of occupation cannot be described with general indicators. Such 'occupation-specific' skills are commensurate with each other only with regard to general education, training, or work experience.

The significance of the various generic skills domains is that they may be supplied from differing sources and at different life stages. In addition, the drivers of changing skills demand may be affecting some skill domains more than others. Some domains have been more visible than others (again, the social construction of skill). The domains may also have different effects. The contemporary favoured typology is between cognitive, interactive, and physical skills. In education psychology, 'cognitive skills' are synonymous with learning skills, but the concept of cognitive skills used here, in economics, in sociology, and in the policy literature, is broader: it is the term applied to areas requiring thinking activities—reading, writing, problem-solving, numeracy, IT, learning new skills, and so on. 'Physical skills' comprise forms of strength and dexterity. 'Interactive skills' cover all forms of communication (including many types of management activities and horizontal communication with co-workers, clients, and customers), and other activities needed to elicit cooperative working and engagement with customers and suppliers, including emotional and aesthetic labour. Emotional labour involves the use of one's own emotions and working to manipulate the emotions of others, while aesthetic labour is looking and sounding good, in both cases for the benefit of the employer. Perceived beauty, which has a substantive association with pay, appears to be a skill worth developing.[31]

Cutting across these generic domains are further categorizations directly relevant to policy and analyses. One typology relates to finance. Focusing on the economic question of who pays for, and who benefits from, employees acquiring skills, the distinction (noted above) between firm-specific and transferable skills is significant. Generic skills are, *ipso facto*, transferable, while occupation-specific skills may not be.

Another policy-related typology concerns the level of complexity involved. At the lower end of the spectrum, 'basic skills' refer to a low threshold level of cognitive skills. Sometimes the threshold is said to be that level of skills needed for everyday life; other times it is the level normally needed for getting a low-skilled job and to be able to acquire further skills. Using the classic notion of poverty as constituting a relative deprivation, the citizen without basic skills can be said to be in 'skills poverty'. It is largely taken to be a responsibility of government to try to ensure that all citizens acquire basic skills.

At the other end of the complexity scale is the concept of 'talent', used to describe those with especially high skills. Though 'talent' is rarely properly defined by those who would use this concept, it broadly characterizes those qualities thought to be needed for leading the major private and public institutions of modern life, or for reaching the top in artistic or sporting arenas. Part of the problem, in respect of 'talent', is that it risks being identified only by its outcome of brilliant achievement, leading analysts up a tautological cul-de-sac.

The significance of the distinction between 'routine' and 'non-routine' derives from the link between tasks (generic or occupation-specific) and new technologies. Routine activities are argued to be more likely to be programmable and hence displaced by computers, unlike non-routine and unpredictable types of activity.[32] Closely related, domains may also be categorized according to how easily they can be outsourced to cheaper production sites in developing countries.[33] These classifications have implications for understanding the changing structures of employment and earnings in developed nations.

All these skill typologies have considerable relevance for the analysis of how skills fit with the structure of modern societies. Yet there are some typologies scattered around the skills discourse that are less functional because they have come to be defined in starkly inconsistent ways. One such is the idea of 'core' and 'non-core', a loose invention sometimes used in policy contexts. 'Core skills' have been variously defined to comprise the generic skills required for employability, or those required by an organization, or those needed for life in general. Another typology to be avoided is the distinction between 'hard' and 'soft' skills. Leaving aside the macho overtones to this terminology, the meaning of 'soft' varies between referring to work attitudes, personality types, or interactive activities such as communication. Such activities and attitudes may be no more difficult to capture that many cognitive or detailed technical skills, and are found to have substantive outcomes. So 'soft' reasonably characterizes neither the precision of indicators nor their salience for social analysis. The vocabulary of 'soft skills' will not reappear in this book.

Finally, it is useful for some purposes to define a concept 'overall skill' (alternatively 'broad skill') as an aggregate of all the separate skills that an individual possesses or that a job requires. Summing different skill types presupposes, however, an implicit value-driven weighting of the different components that is better made explicit. When a judgement is made that person A is more skilled than person B, it need not indicate that A has more of every quality, and indeed B could be more skilled in some dimensions. Rather, it is that the sum of the values that A's skills can create is greater than that from B's skills. But it should be made transparent that the judgement rests on acceptance of the valuation, which might then be contested. It is as well, therefore, to keep in mind the latent value-laden aspect of such phrases as 'high-skilled work' or its opposite 'low-skilled work'. Empirical indicators for overall skill, to be reviewed in Chapter 4, are especially loose.

An interdisciplinary appeal

It might seem strange, to any newcomer to the topic, that skill is held to be a pivotal object for modern social and economic life, even when there is no consensus as to what exactly it is. We are dealing with a slippery concept, whose meanings vary among writers from different disciplines, and among common usages. The concept has also evolved with the changing economy. Half a century ago skill was reserved in policy discourse for technical qualities, usually in craft and related occupations, and had a distinctly manual overtone. In the 'knowledge economy' its meaning is a great deal broader.[34]

There seems little doubt that part of the reason for this lack of consensus is the segmentation of fields—economics, sociology, and psychology—that have not been good at communicating with one another. In each of these disciplines there is a large and ongoing self-citing, inward-looking, literature. Moreover, in each subject, skill has assumed a considerable importance, if for rather different reasons, so that discourse is conducted with high stakes. In economics, skill is central to the story about the changing distribution of income, and to debates about the sources of economic growth. In sociology, skill underpins class, perhaps its most fundamental category, and is a crucial concept in the analysis of the labour process. In psychology, competence analysis is at the heart of important branches of human resource practice. An additional reason for potential disagreement in public discourse is that the determination and valuation of skills lie in contested terrain. Labour market actors vying for advantage are likely to follow their own convenient definitions and analyses.

It might be objected that the PES concept of skill advocated here involves conceptual evolution from a purer, classically rooted, notion of skill, and that with this comes a looser analysis. Yet set against this nostalgic viewpoint are two observations: in practice, 'skill' has acquired a much broader usage in common parlance and in scholarly and policy discourse; secondly, the problematic of the knowledge economy and skill-biased technological change, in the context of VET and labour market policies, necessitates a wider perspective. The need, then, is for a more encompassing approach to skill than a half-century ago, though one that is still conceptually precise.

The PES concept of skill set out in this chapter may not be the only 'right' concept of skill, and may indeed offend some scholars and practitioners in unanticipated ways. Yet it is broad enough for analysis of capitalist processes of skill formation and use, and of the possibilities for social action. It suggests that skills are personal qualities that can produce value at work, are expandable, and are socially determined. This framework suits the purposes of this book and, hopefully, many further analyses. All paid work activities entail qualities that potentially generate values; virtually no job should be called 'unskilled', since work almost always entails the exercise of qualities that have been, or can be, enhanced. It is practical only to make distinctions along the spectrum between low-skilled and high-skilled work.

The definition also encompasses the central features of the concepts adopted by the three main social science disciplines that periodically debate these matters—namely, economics, sociology, and psychology. Each of these disciplines has contributed insights on skill, but none on its own is up to the tasks being set for skills in modern economies. Mainstream neoclassical economics contributes in modelling the ideal investment processes that lurk beneath the acquisition and use of skill, but it is individualistic and does not incorporate the social determination of skill. Applied economics has the methodologies to make substantial inputs to the understanding of the empirical importance of skill. Sociology emphasizes complexity, though it has not fully successfully defined it, as being the real content of skill, with autonomy its bedfellow. Through social construction theory it critiques but only partially redevelops skill's association with value. Psychology, by contrast, is keen on measuring and categorizing levels and domains of skills, even though it uses another term, competency, and develops theories about how skills are acquired; and for valuation counterposes to the labour market and the economy a normative process centred on job content.

All modern skills analyses and policies need to be debated and improved using the best endeavours of several social sciences. The PES concept of skill is sufficiently broad and flexible to allow dialogue and engagement between disciplines without imposing an artificial veneer of theoretical convergence.

3

Framing the Analysis of Skilled Work

The articulation of two markets

If skills are seen as personal qualities defined by people's relationships to work, as delineated in the PES concept described in the previous chapter, a suitable framework is needed within which analyses of skill and skilled work can be located. The framework needs to house some key questions concerning the factors that shape the types and levels of skills that people acquire, and the extent to which these skills are exercised in contemporary workplaces. As with all social science, the analysis should then enable a way of thinking about social and individual actions that lead to improvement. What, for example, do the social partners (unions and employers acting together) do to help raise skill levels, and what might they consider doing instead? The same questions can be asked of other collective actors and of governments.

A focus on skilled work requires a framework that encapsulates *both* skill formation services and the deployment of skilled labour: not one, but two interacting markets. 'Skill formation services' refers broadly to all the activities provided to enable someone to learn, including teaching, training, learning resources, and access to the environment of a learning organization; while the word 'market' here refers to a circuit of value, not to any specific institution. The framework of the two markets is illustrated in Figure 3.1, organized around key actors who operate as demanders or suppliers or both. The three actors depicted are employers (including the government itself), skilled workers, and external providers of training. Other actors (such as social partners) and other institutional features lie behind the framework and will be considered later in the book. Each market comprises in practice many sub-markets corresponding to multiple skills and spaces: the diagram is therefore a simplification.

On one side of the market for skilled labour, depicted in the lower half of the diagram, is employers' skills demand. The concept of employers' skills demand (composed of the desired jobs and the job skill of each) refers to the

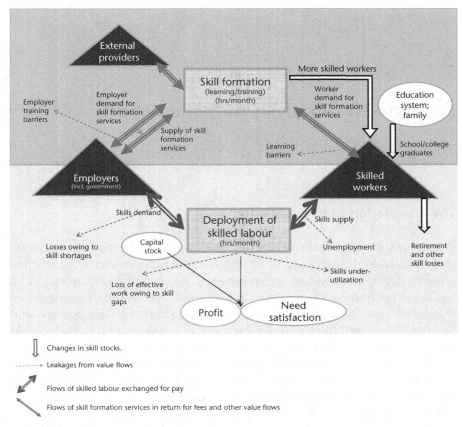

Figure 3.1. Skill formation and the deployment of skilled labour

hours of work that employers would choose to deploy of people with skills of various types and levels, given the productive environment and wages. Changes in technology that are complementary with skilled work, evolving forms of work organization and employer human resource policies, product market strategies, industrial restructuring, demographic trends and expanding trade with (and outsourcing to) less developed economies, are the factors that underpin employers' skills demand—to be considered in Chapter 5.

On the other side of this market lies skills supply, which refers to the hours that people with various skills would like to work, given the wage rates and other relevant working conditions. Education, new technologies for domestic labour, and cultural norms are the main sources of change in skills supply. Education not only leads to a more skilled population, but commonly raises the willingness to participate in the labour market. These sources of change are considered in Chapter 7.

The 'stock of skills' is a commonly used but imprecise phrase that tries to capture the totality of skills held by the population, or sometimes more narrowly by the economically active population (those able and willing to do paid work). This totality is a multidimensional concept, reflecting the many different types of skills that people have. The stock of skills in the economically active population is the net result of actions taken in the past—processes of skill formation, minus any losses of skills. School or college graduates join the labour force, while others retire; the existing workforce gains and loses skills. Since gaining skills does not come for free, there is also a market for this activity. Parallel to the demand for and supply of skilled labour, therefore, are the skill formation services for which there is also a demand and supply, which are depicted in the top half of Figure 3.1. The accumulating or declining stock of skills forms the analytical link between the two markets. Another link is that each of the actors, employers and workers, plays in both markets with related strategies. For example, an employer with a high demand for skills may—but need not—also have a high demand for skill formation services.

The demand for skill formation services comes from two sources: employers and workers (or potential workers). Employers have a demand because they want their workers to become more skilled, hence more productive. Workers also have a demand for skill formation services—to be termed here in short-hand the 'demand for learning'—derived from the many-sided rewards of doing skilled work and from the consumption benefits linked to learning. The supply is delivered by employers themselves and by education and training institutes. The providers in this market are frequently owned by governments or subsidized. The factors underpinning employers' demand for skill formation services include their benefits and costs, the uncertainties of the economy and labour market (including the mobility of workers), and managerial culture, capacities, and beliefs—all of these are discussed in Chapter 5. In a similar fashion, beliefs about incentives, decision-making resources, and preferences or dispositions are the factors affecting workers' demand for learning, discussed in Chapter 7, set in the framework of the life course that learners follow. Employers' supplies of skill formation services (Chapter 6) depend especially on their own demands.

Thus, in the skills framework there are two articulated markets: one for skilled labour hours, the other for hours of skill formation services. Workers are suppliers of skilled labour and demanders of skill formation services. The metric is time: each can be measured in units of so many hours service per month. Employers are the demanders of skilled labour, but both suppliers and demanders of skill formation services.

Market outcomes: matches and mismatches

'Equilibrium' occurs in each market when supply matches demand, and the term 'skills equilibrium' can usefully be reserved to describe the state where both markets are in equilibrium. The outcome in the skilled labour market is, for business, the deployment of skilled work, leading to the generation of value. This outcome is what makes it possible to characterize those personal qualities as skills. However, economic performance for employers in terms of profit depends also on the deployment of physical and financial capital, as well as on the management of labour—that is, securing the commitment of, and control over, workers, so that they work as effectively as possible while employed. For workers the outcome is the extent to which the qualities of the job, including its opportunities for doing skilled work and its learning environment, are meeting people's needs—the ultimate human objective for work.

The outcome of the skill formation market is the potential learning that augments the stock of skills for the next period. It is workers who acquire these additional skills, with employers benefiting indirectly from workers' greater productivity. The magnitude by which skills are increased depends on the effectiveness of the learning environment and on the capacity and readiness of people to learn. The net change in the stock of skills is the difference between this increase and skills loss through time, or through retirements, or through skills obsolescence (which refers to qualities that become devalued through structural changes in the economy).

However, supplies do not necessarily match demands. As with any markets, matching mechanisms for skilled labour and for skill transformation services can be a mixture of price and quantity adjustment processes. According to the classical mechanism, when skilled labour is scarce, its price will rise; similarly, the price of training services rises when they are scarce. Matching also requires that training providers respond positively to price increases (offering more courses, and so on) and/or that workers and firms reduce their demands. The supplies and demands in the two markets are connected, both through the increases in skills that are the outcomes of the skill formation market, and through the incentives anticipated (a higher price of skill induces greater demand for learning). Given price rigidities, the long-term aspects of skill formation, and the context of deep uncertainty, however, the process of adjustment of supply to demand via the price mechanism may be very slow. Alternative adjustment occurs via quantities. For example, firms that cannot recruit enough skilled workers may, rather than raise their wage offers, scale down their demands for skilled workers. Or employers might, through collective foresight, anticipate shortages and have planned ahead.

Mismatches between supplies and demands are the consequences of imperfect adjustment, whether through prices or quantities. They may be conceived as leakages from the two value circuits—that is, reductions in the values exchanged and generated. These are indicated by dotted lines on Figure 3.1. The potential consequences of mismatch are lost productivity, lower pay, and reduced well-being, all of which have begun to enter the radar of public discourse on skills policies. The leakages come in several forms:

- *Skills shortage* describes the situation where a job vacancy is hard to fill because of a lack of applicants with the needed skills. Since vacancies depend on demand, the level of skills shortages in the economy tends to rise and fall with the economic cycle. This definition excludes vacancies that cannot be filled because of unattractive wages or working conditions, but it is not confined to technical skills: shortages can also occur, because of a lack of applicants with 'suitable' attitudes and commitment. Employers' reports of skills shortages can expect to be coloured by the social construction of skill.

- *A skills gap* occurs where an employee's competence to do the job is called into question (typically by his or her manager). This phenomenon is relatively uncommon in cases where employers are free either to train or to dismiss incompetent workers: in England, only 7 per cent of workers are judged by their managers to have a skills gap.[1]

- *Skills under-utilization* is the opposite case, occurring where a worker has work-related skills not used (or used at too low a level) in the job. This phenomenon is loosely related to 'overeducation'—sometimes alternatively termed 'overqualification'—where someone has achieved education at a level higher than needed to get the job he or she is doing. Educational mismatch can also arise where a job requires a knowledge base different from that of education subject majors.[2]

- *Unemployment*, where workers are not employed yet available and looking for a job, indicates that all their skills are unused, thus leaking from the circuit of value. Under-employment, where workers are employed but for fewer hours than they desire, is the fractional equivalent. Sometimes, the phrase 'under-employment' has a more encompassing meaning that includes skills under-utilization. Unemployment may lead to skills obsolescence, a lasting loss to the stock of skills.

- *Worker training barriers* (also termed learning barriers) occur when individuals are unable to form and achieve a demand for learning that would be best for them, given their circumstances. An example would be where learning demand fails to surface owing to low self-efficacy, or to a lack of information about available opportunities and incentives, or to insufficient capacity to evaluate these alternatives. Another instance might be constraints arising from restricted access to loan funds for supporting a period of learning. (The term 'learning barrier' is taken, in some circles, to refer more narrowly to situations where an unusual impediment prevents someone from succeeding on a course of learning: the broader sense used here includes this narrower concept.) Worker training barriers are shown in Figure 3.1 as a leakage from the workers' demand for learning.

- *Employer training barriers* occur where employers lack sufficient information or capacity adequately to assess the benefits of training for their organization, or if external providers are unavailable. Such barriers can result in too little training, reducing the organization's performance in the long term. Such barriers are both hard to detect and difficult to surmount when the best strategy would involve a more wide-ranging shift in management practices, not just a revised training budget in isolation. Genuine employer training barriers are less commonly discussed than worker training barriers, for fear of intruding on the autonomy of private business.

All these concepts of mismatch between supply and demand are quite distinct from the widely used notion of a *skills deficit*, which refers to the state of a system where the levels of skills both supplied and demanded are below some desirable level. Where there is a skills deficit, it is quite possible for supplies and demands to be balanced, and hence for none of the above mismatch concepts to be a problem. What determines the desirable but unseen skill level is rarely specified, even theoretically, by users of the skills deficit concept, but a practical guide is often taken to be the superior levels exhibited by similar organizations or economies. In this vein, policy advisers have developed a strong interest in benchmarking with inter-regional and international comparisons of skills. Parallel is the notion of a *training deficit*, where both the demand for, and access to, training are set too low.

Whether via prices or quantities, the adjustment of supplies and demands in skills markets is imperfect and problematic. Chapter 8 discusses some of the generic issues and outcomes surrounding the failure of skills markets to be efficient and equitable. The potential roles for governments in trying to remedy these deficiencies is considered in Chapter 9.

Markets or actors?

The central players in these two linked markets are employers, workers, and the training providers (who are commonly also employers, sometimes also acting as recruitment agencies). To what extent does it matter who these actors are, what they think about, or how they make their decisions about skill formation and skill use?

One way of framing the skill system sees the two circuits as simply markets where actors follow determined logics: employers and providers maximizing the profits of their shareholders, workers their utilities, each well informed about the state of the world. The actors, in this perspective, are followers of rules. It does not concern us who they are, and the evolutionary logic of competition ensures that they must adhere to the objective of profit maximization or else be expelled from the system. The logic of markets also provides a simple yet powerful set of explanations for the things we are interested in—how much skill formation takes place, how it is used, who by, and so on. Technology and consumer preferences are the ultimate determining factors, along with market context. Such a framework works best when markets are assumed to be competitive, since their logic typically implies unique outcomes. Realistic imperfectly competitive contexts are nevertheless easily added.

To follow a system-level, 'actor-free', logic would suggest organizing the discussion and analysis of skilled work explicitly around the two markets and how they interact. The core of the theoretical framework would concern how supplies and demands in each market are related to price incentives, including the market interaction (whereby the incentive for demand for learning depends on the price and productivity of skilled labour), and how prices change to ensure that each market is in equilibrium. With this framework, it is possible to make testable predictions about how system variables shift in response to significant impulses such as technological changes. In this vein modern economics has developed a canonical model to help explain transformations in the distribution of wages that are related to changes in the relative values of skills. The effects of detailed forms of technological change can be captured in this framework when it is focused on the job tasks affected by new technologies and the consequent skill requirements.[3]

In using a system logic, however, depicting actors as receptacles embodying system imperatives, having neither room for manœuvre nor a separate identity, it becomes hard to account for heterogeneity among actors or between groups of actors. While neoclassical economics favours a deterministic explanation of the behaviour of the rational representative actor, such a view may therefore be less than scientific if it does not have a way of capturing varieties of skills and learning behaviour, other than in an ad hoc manner by resorting to residual unobserved variables. A notable feature is the complexity and substantial variation of the patterns of skill use and skill formation, across and within economies. Within Europe, for example, training participation is found to vary by a factor of as much as 6 to 1 between countries, and by the same large ratio between regions inside some countries.[4] There is much variation within industries, too, among similar-looking enterprises, and among similar individuals. Sometimes some of this variation can be explained by external features such as age or company size. In the system framework, country and regional variations might be ascribed to differences in both supply and demand for skill formation services, but such large differences are rarely predicted or discussed. A large amount of variation remains unaccounted for by deterministic behaviour models. Technologies and capitalist imperatives being ubiquitous, one could expect more convergence across and within countries than is observed.

The complexities in skilled work and in skill formation services need, therefore, to be framed instead by models that allow for considerable bandwidth in actors' behaviours, and are therefore consistent with the sort of variation in skills behaviour just described. The framework is even better if it can help to account for some of the persistent complexities. There are two reasons for conceiving that actors have leeway in their decisions and behaviours: 'deep uncertainty' and endogeneity of preferences.

The phrase 'deep uncertainty' characterizes the multidimensional and layered elements of uncertainty that both employers and workers are faced with when making decisions about skill formation. There is uncertainty over its effects. An employer can sometimes know quite precisely what skills a training course offers, but frequently the benefits are perceived to be in terms of greater effort and commitment, which are less well defined, while the quality of training programmes varies. Less formal learning, though arguably just as important, is harder again to measure. The value of these effects is a further element of uncertainty, especially if, as with many skills investments, the pay-off is long term. This uncertainty is then compounded by the possibility that the trained workers may not stay with the company. If one of the arguments for training is that firms need to cooperate to generate a stock of industry-specific skills, there is additional 'strategic uncertainty' about whether other firms in the industry will also cooperate by training their workers. And there is yet more 'analytic uncertainty' about the value of that cooperation.[5] From the individual's perspective, the uncertainty of training programmes reflects the ubiquitous problem that they have potential pay-offs that are generally quite long term, but must be evaluated with limited information, typically historical rather than future oriented.

Where there is deep uncertainty, we do not have a consensual theory or rules for actor behaviour that generate determinate outcomes. Expected utility theory underpins much of economics' formal understanding of behaviour with uncertainty, which typically presupposes known probability distributions; yet many of its predictions have been undermined by experiments and by the alternative of prospect theory.[6] Deep uncertainty entails true uncertainty in the sense of US economist Frank Knight, where probability distributions are unknown and where confidence and agency hold sway.[7] In such situations many outcomes are possible, and consequences hard to predict. For the skills decisions of companies, deep uncertainty elevates the importance of strategy and of managerial capacity, as will be discussed in Chapter 5. For individuals, 'identity' helps to delineate the options that are perceived to be available and their pay-offs, and to foreclose others. In this context, there is scope for wide variation in managers' and workers' beliefs about the efficacy of skills and training, and hence for the substantively heterogeneous behaviours that are seen in practice.[8] For both managers and workers, behaviour follows a 'bounded rationality', in that decisions and behaviours are built on limited information and on finite and heterogeneous capacities. Decisions are taken in real time—that is, through an individual's life course, or a firm's expansion path; they are accordingly hard to reverse.

The second argument for shunning a deterministic model is that preferences, beliefs, and technologies are themselves endogenous. Workers' and employers' demands, in both markets, are affected by norms and beliefs, which are learned or acquired through experiences, and, if experiences are affected also by mobility barriers and by varying managerial cultures, then biographies diverge and initial conditions matter a great deal, making it hard to predict a determinate path of skill development. The divergence of behaviours may be further entrenched by deep uncertainty.

For both these reasons, in the framework of this book actors follow conventional objectives, but in a context where preferences are interdependent because they are embedded in identities, and where behaviour additionally is loosely determined, because it involves unpredictable responses to the uncertainties each perceives. The lack of decisive predictability does not imply that behaviour has no bounds, or that economic imperatives do not bite. Employers and workers can be expected to respond to incentives, but are not uniquely determined by them. This book is therefore organized primarily around employers and workers as the two central actors—their contexts, behaviours, and effects. It then goes on to consider how the principal institutions of collective actors—namely, the social partners and government—affect employers' and workers' behaviour. It is only at that point that we can return to consider the operation of the two markets together in a 'skill system'.

Collective actors

Individual employers and workers are not the only types of actors in the markets for skilled work and for skill formation. Also involved are the external providers of training shown in Figure 3.1 and, hidden behind the diagram, the schools and colleges of the education world, and the families underpinning social reproduction systems. The activities of these will be picked up from time to time but are not the focus of this book. The spotlight will, however, be thrown on some collective institutional actors that occupy the environment in which individuals and employers operate. Their importance for skilled work is heightened by the indeterminacy of behaviour noted above. Specifically, employers' associations or chambers of commerce, regional clusters of employers within technology 'eco-systems', trade unions, and governments at various levels can each change behaviours through their effects on beliefs, expectations, and incentives.

Employers, by grouping together within industries or clusters, can economize on training costs, something that is likely to be especially valuable in sectors where high levels of initial training are necessary, and where good infrastructure and intelligence enables training to keep right up to date (see Chapter 6). Collectives of employers may also facilitate forms of cooperative behaviour among employers, making it easier to encourage employers to commit to transferable training. Employers' interactions may also run to learning about good practice and about the pay-offs from cooperation in training. Nevertheless, such cooperation is fragile, with incentives for employers to free-ride on others' commitments; it may require specific political conditions to sustain it.[9]

Trade unions also pursue a range of practices that affect decisions about skilled work. Through their collective voice they may reduce turnover, and with a more stable workforce there can be a greater incentive for employers to train (Chapter 6). In some cases—principally the dual systems of northern Europe—unions also make a collective contribution to curriculum design, typically aiming to ensure breadth of content, hence transferability. Through their bargaining function they might raise the pay of trained adult workers, which would stimulate a demand for more skilled labour and a greater contribution to training; alternatively, they might raise the pay of trainees/apprentices, which would lower employers' demand for skill formation services, and hence in the long run reduce skill levels. Union success at compressing wages in enterprises and within occupations stimulates greater training, since it allows employers to recoup the costs of their investments in workers by paying skilled workers less than their increased productivity warrants. Through their brokerage function, unions may stimulate workers' demands for skill acquisition, informing and persuading workers to dip into training, thereby lowering learning barriers (see Chapter 7). Dialogue between the social partners—unions and employers' groups—is a key part of the model for skill formation and utilization in many European countries.

Finally, governments have wide and intensive effects in both markets. They may regulate skill acquisition—for example, through centralized certification systems, occupational licences to practise, or indirectly through industry standards. They may subsidize training directly with grants, or distribute cheap and guaranteed loans. Calls on government are especially important for the retraining of unemployed people. As employers, governments are also large demanders of skilled labour, and providers of learning in their own workplaces. All such functions are potentially relevant policy vehicles for national and sub-national governments. Their rationale is examined in Chapter 9.

A framework, but no full theory

It is necessary to conclude this framework chapter in a wistful but honest tone: what has been described is not a full theory of skills and skilled work; nor does it presage an aspiration to find or develop one in this book.

Incompleteness arises not just from the indeterminacy of outcomes in the face of deep uncertainties. It is also because there are important feedbacks that render many of the elements of the framework endogenous, and as yet these feedbacks remain unspecified. Economics deals with feedbacks through its development of general equilibrium theories. From this perspective, the markets for skilled labour and for skill formation services interact with all other markets in the economy. For example, changes in the stocks of skilled workers in a particular economy may affect the distribution of wages, thus affecting consumer demand; both these outcomes in turn condition the demand for skill, the returns to skill acquisition, and thence future skill stocks. Feedbacks also include the possibilities that abundant skills might stimulate rational technological progress, or that technology becomes socially constructed through gender relations.[10] Although no full theory (equilibrium based or otherwise) is available, it is advisable to take account of such feedbacks at relevant stages where possible or where something is known about their importance. One framework simplification that takes feedbacks into account is the concept of the 'high-skills'/'low-skills' equilibrium developed to explain the comparative stability of skills outcomes in different institutional regimes; it will be reviewed in Chapter 9.

In setting out this framework no special claim is made to originality in any of its constituents: the framework builds on a considerable literature. Yet one deliberate feature may not receive universal assent: its inherently interdisciplinary quality. This is a framework for an understanding of skilled work using the PES concept of skill. It calls for analyses of skills markets that are alive to the social determination of skill, that set skilled work in a realistic frame of value creation, and that entertain a broad range of skill types.

Research approaching skilled work solely from the point of view of any one of the existing social science disciplines is almost bound to get things wrong in some important respects. An understanding of what actors in the skills markets actually do seems to call for sophisticated econometric methods and framing of incentive problems, a sociological contribution concerning the social and structural determinants of skills institutions, a psychological analysis of learning processes and competences, and political science to disinter the development of cooperation.[11] However, an interdisciplinary approach should not just be a matter of adding up the contributions of the different disciplines: each may need to adapt in the light of contributions from others. When building a house, one needs electricians, plumbers, and builders of many trades, yet an architect has to design the totality, which must require many adaptations. One must ask each discipline neither to suppose that it has sway, nor to talk only to its own. Social scientists studying skilled work should reason, neither as just-economists, nor as just-sociologists, nor indeed as just-anything.

4

The Measurement of Skill

Being measurable, quantifiable, and commensurable

If we want to understand skilled work, and if states should ever want to promote it in their domains or alter its qualities, knowing how to measure what one is aiming for is a mundane prerequisite. This chapter discusses some acceptable principles and practices of measurement. Back in 1990 it was charged that 'positive economists' had 'allowed the gap between the operationalization of skill and the theoretical concept to grow too wide'.[1] Whether or not that charge was valid at the time, the defence against it now would be a great deal more robust. Some, though not all, of the problems of measurement that occupied the earlier discourse have begun to be resolved. Progress has been made on both methodological and practical grounds, since these issues were being systematically visited within sociology more than twenty years ago. Economics, which largely waited outside earlier debates, has also broadened its scope and joined in, driven by a desire better to evaluate the impact of human capital on economic growth.

While it will be asserted that skills are measurable and can be quantified, there should not be an expectation of highly precise indices of skill. There are, moreover, no universal units of skill in which one quality can be objectively compared with another. We can say who is best at tennis by who wins the tournament, but how does one compare the skills of a top tennis star, a leading footballer, and a chess grandmaster, or those of a plumber and an electrician? One skill is only made commensurate with another in a different field when the outputs generated are expressed in values, but then the questions arise: which and whose values? Typically one settles on market values, yet this is hardly a robust prescription when social values diverge from what the free market throws up. With many ordinary jobs, recourse is had instead to the comparative judgements of experts, who assess the difficulties, responsibilities, and complexities of jobs. Social and economic power, encompassing employment relations and gender, impinge upon the judgements of both marketplace and expert.

With these caveats, however, there is no doubt that the PES concept of skill is measurable, that skill rankings are possible, and that, provided one recalls their dependence on values, different skill domains can be compared. An understanding of how measurement is done is an important ingredient of healthy scepticism when one is presented with skills-related statistics; at the same time, appreciating that it can be done is an antidote to the spread of untested narratives about skills masquerading as social science. Together with the previous chapters' conceptual discussions, this chapter is also designed as a source to be referred back to, supporting indicators that are cited later in this book and elsewhere. Tables 4.1 to 4.4 present organizing lists of skill indicators in common usage and the concepts to which they relate, together with examples of studies that deploy them. The chapter proceeds in turn to consider indicators for skills supply, skills demand, skill formation and loss, and mismatch.

Skills supply

Educational attainment has been the most commonly used measure for the overall skill levels of individuals and populations (see Table 4.1). Years of education are a common currency, and with the widespread development of modern statistical systems it became possible to compile data sets from many countries.[2] The average number of years of completed education was found to be a predictor of economic growth, and the individual relationship between pay and years of education (sometimes expressed in quadratic form) became the staple specification for one of the most widely recurring estimations in the history of economics.[3] Nevertheless, years of education are a very loose proxy for overall skill. On the one hand, the qualities that education generates are diverse and many job skills bear little relation to prior education. On the other, the extent to which each year of education generates skills depends on its efficiency and intensity, both of which are also highly variable.[4]

Measuring educational attainment by the achievements of standards or stages, as certified by academic or vocational qualifications, can begin to reduce the education-year-quality problem. Provided those standards are stable, the achievements over time of a population can be gauged by measures of the proportions of the population gaining each standard. In recent years, such measures have been the central ingredient of analyses assessing the progress and development of the stock of skills in national populations. It is reported, for example, that in 2008 some 28 per cent of the adult population in OECD countries had achieved tertiary education levels, up from just 21 per

Table 4.1. Skills indicators

Indicators	Concepts	Advantages	Disadvantages	International comparability	Example(s) of use
Years of education	Overall/broad skill	Objective; long-term trends available	Variable quality of education; loose link with skill	Yes	Barro and Lee (1996, 2001)
Educational qualifications or certificates	Overall/broad skill; occupation-specific/technical skill; generic skills	Objective; long-term trends available	Loose link of some qualifications with skills; variable quality; possible grade inflation	Some, via ISCED; difficult task for EQF	Giret and Masjuan (1999); Steedman and McIntosh (2001); OECD (2010)
Literacy, numeracy, and other tests	Generic skills	Objective; some trends will be available	Limited range of testable skills; outside work context; expensive to administer	TIMSS; IEA; PISA; for adults, IALS, ALLS, PIAAC	OECD and Statistics Canada (1995); Hanushek and Kimko (2000); Freeman and Schettkatt (2001)
Self-assessed skill	Generic skills	Wide range of skills	Self-reported assessments of skill likely to be biased, linked with self-esteem	No	Bynner (1994); Finnie and Meng (2005)
Behavioural indicators	Work attitudes	Grounded	Behaviour and attitudes are contested	No	Heckman (2008); Blanden et al. (2008); Borghans et al. (2008)

cent in 1997 and still growing.[5] Vocational certificates and qualifications also provide a way of measuring the attainment of some generic skills—for example, in computing, and for occupation-specific knowledge. Analysts are commonly interested in attainments in science, technology, engineering, and medicine, because many industries at the forefront of innovation call on these bases of knowledge.

Nevertheless, the general connection of educational qualifications with work skills remains loose, and the multiplicity of qualifications of variable quality can sometimes make it hard to link them to standards. Moreover, there are serious doubts as to whether standards have held stable over long periods during which education participation rates have increased. Grade inflation is often suspected, though rarely proven, especially where schools and colleges are penalized for failure rates.

The international comparability of qualification levels is also far from an exact science.[6] Qualifications are mostly country specific. Ongoing attempts to assert comparability from above, such as the 1999 Bologna Declaration for promoting a European Higher Education Area (EHEA)[7] through a framework for higher education qualifications, or the European Qualifications Framework for Lifelong Learning (EQF)[8] are slow moving and face complex problems associated with the social construction of skills and qualifications, which differs across cultures. The EQF and the framework for the EHEA both use competence levels as a convertible currency, thus potentially linking education more closely to the world of work. The EQF is a meta-framework into which each national government is asked to map its own nation-specific framework. Yet the comparability exercise can be compromised when the meaning of the different levels varies across countries. There are cross-national differences in the scope and breadth of the required learning for each level. Squeezing each nation into one framework is likely in some cases to be a painful political exercise.[9]

International comparability of educational attainment is largely served by the broad International Standard Classification of Education (ISCED) system, last revised in 2011, which classifies educational achievements into seven educational programme levels broadly in terms of their complexity and length, ranging from pre-primary to doctoral. Classification assignments of national programmes are made by member countries, a process that does not guarantee equivalence, but that appears to deliver practical and reasonably reliable solutions.[10]

The development of standardized skills tests for school pupils represents an attempt to sidestep the variability and instability of certification standards. From 1965 exercises such as the Trends in International Mathematics and Science Study (TIMSS) were developed by the International Association for the Evaluation of Educational Achievement (IEA); from 2000 the OECD's

Programme for International Student Assessment (PISA), was applied to representative samples of 15-year-olds. Together the tests provide a picture of pupils' skills in the literacy, science, and numeracy domains in many countries. Analyses with these data show a wide variation in the extent to which each year of education enhances literacy and numeracy, and the test scores are found to be substantially better predictors of economic growth than measures of educational attainment.[11] Skills tests for adults were a natural progression, and, following national-level developments within the United States during the 1980s, the early 1990s saw the development of the International Adult Literacy Survey (IALS), led by the OECD. The exercise was extended with the Adult Literacy and Life Skills Survey (ALLS) in a small number of countries in 2003. Individual countries have sporadically conducted their own surveys. It was not until 2012, however, that the testing of adult skills took off on a very wide scale, via the Programme for the International Assessment of Adult Competencies (PIAAC). This programme widens the range of skills tested to include problem-solving ability in 'technology-rich environments', yet allows comparisons for some items with those in the IALS programme for countries that took part in both.

These test programmes have made enormous progress in the quest for measures of skills for analytical purposes. It is through them that concepts such as skills poverty and the problems of insufficient basic skills can be measured. Yet significant gaps remain. Even after their expansion in scope, they still cover only a limited range of generic skills used in workplaces. Inevitably, they assess skills outside the work context—they are constructed as autonomous capacities, rather than as socially determined in accordance with the PES concept. Performance in context, like learning, differs from test outcomes.[12]

Finally, the testing of adult populations is costly. Large-scale survey and testing exercises are among the most expensive types of research (though minor in comparison to national investments in natural science research). Fiscal constraints and public distrust of social science will limit the frequency of such data-gathering exercises until such time as large-scale benefits can be demonstrated. It is cheaper to include questions in surveys asking respondents to self-assess their skills, thereby also enabling a wider range of skills to be tested. Unfortunately, the reliability of self-reports of skills is highly questionable, because they are strongly affected by esteem bias; indeed, self-reports of skill might be thought more acceptable as indicators of self-esteem than of the reported skill. A Canadian study that included tests and self-assessments of literacy found, for example, that the two measures were not highly correlated, and that the literacy tests were more strongly related than the self-assessments both to labour market outcomes and to education antecedents.[13]

Possibly the most difficult aspects of skill to measure are relevant work attitudes or dispositions. One supportable principle is that attitudes may be well proxied by reports of behaviours, if possible by other observers (for example, teachers or parents): actions and behaviours are better anchored than subjectively told attitudes. Both behavioural indicators (such as sleep difficulties or disobedience in children) and attitudes (such as time preference or personality factors) have been used in recent research. These utilized indicators tend to score well for both construct and predictive validity.[14] Yet the research has still to converge on a determination of which types of work attitudes should be regarded as skills, and of the parallel conceptual distinction between 'bad' attitudes and protest. This imprecision is hardly surprising, given that attitudes inhabit contested terrain, that their theoretical location is ambivalent, and that the research showing their sensitivity to interventions and their diverse effects on performance outcomes is recent and ongoing.

Using any of the above measures of skill in the population, indicators for *skills supply* can be obtained by multiplying the numbers of economically active persons with each skill level by their usual work hours. The indicator should also incorporate an adjustment for under-employment or over-employment, whereby workers' hours differ from what is desired.

Skills demand and job skill

It is quite common to take hours of employment in jobs at each level of job skill as an indicator for *skills demand*. Yet, if employers are unable to recruit as many skilled workers as desired, the quantity employed is less than demand. Thus, this indicator should be seen as a lower bound estimate for skills demand. A more precise indicator would include a measure of skill shortages.

The biggest challenge, however, has been to find satisfactory indicators for job skill. Occupational classification is the most widely used measure of job skill, if only because there are many data sources in all countries that collect job titles and descriptions and classify them into occupations (see Table 4.2). Occupations are given detailed codes (4-digit or 5-digit), then grouped successively into fewer 'major groups'. Key criteria defining the major occupation groups are the level of their overall job skill and their specialization, as judged on the basis of the length and type of education, training, and work experience required to do the job. Allocation to one or other major group gives an easily available proxy indicator for overall job skill, permitting comparisons over time and, with the use of the latest version of the international coding system ISCO08, international comparisons.

Unfortunately, the benefit of easy availability must be set against the fact that the validity of occupational group as an index of skill is far from

Table 4.2. Job skills indicators

Indicators	Concepts	Advantages	Disadvantages	International comparability	Example(s) of use
Occupation classification in major groups	Overall job skills	Easily available from labour force surveys or censuses	Skills change within occupations; occupation skill needs measurement, is contestable and changing	Via ISCO08	Machin and Van Reenen (1998); Gregory et al. (2001)
Occupation classification at 4-digit or higher level	Occupation-specific job skills	As above	As above	Via ISCO08	O*NET, see National Research Council (2010)
Prior education, training, and experience levels required to do job	Overall job skills and occupation-specific job skills	Available from social surveys	Loose connection of academic qualifications with job skills; variable quality; credentialism	Via PIAAC	Felstead et al. (2007a)
Wage rate	Overall job skills	Easily available	Loose proxy as other factors affect wages; risk of tautology	No	Goos and Manning (2007)
Generic tasks performed	Generic job skills	Wide range of skills; intimately connected to jobs	Subjective reports; construction of indices lacks consensus as yet	Via PIAAC	Howell and Wolff (1991); Cappelli (1993); Holzer (1998); Autor et al. (2003a); Dickerson and Green (2004); Felstead et al. (2007a); Handel (2008, 2013); Goos et al. (2010); F. Green (2012); Lindley (2012)
Domain/subject of training and education requirement	Occupation-specific job skills	Available from social surveys	Only some occupations use a subject-specific knowledge base	Some	Allen and van der Velden (2007)

perfect. The skill levels that emerge are defined rather imprecisely in just a few bands; in some occupation classification systems the character of employment relations, or labour market status, are additional factors in deciding the classification. The skills needed for occupations are not necessarily the same in different countries, since similar work may be carried out in dissimilar ways. Over time job skills within occupations evolve. Jobs and occupation codes sometimes need to be reclassified as their content changes. The changing composition of occupations over time has been found to capture only part—often no more than half—of the changing skill requirements.[15]

To capture overall job skill, analysts therefore typically look further than just the major occupational group. One alternative is to measure explicitly and directly the education, training, and experience requirements of jobs, which can then act as input proxies for overall job skill. These measures correlate as expected with occupation measures, and through successive surveys can pick up changes that take place within occupations as well as the evolution of the occupational structure of the economy; they can also be used to compare across countries. They are, therefore, arguably better than occupation as indicators of overall job skill. Nevertheless, their availability is much more limited. Moreover, education, training, and experience are each subject to the same caveats as are made above with respect to educational attainment of individuals: education is only loosely related with job skill, and all of these inputs are of variable quality. For example, work experience raises skills up to a certain point, but the quality of workplace learning environments is highly variable. An additional issue with respect to the education requirement is the possibility of credentialism at a time of rising supply of educational achievement in the population: employers may stipulate higher education levels for job applicants without redesigning jobs, because they wish to recruit from the same relative pool.[16] Thus, some measures distinguish the education level required for recruitment to a job from that required to do it competently.

A less satisfactory alternative is to proxy overall job skill via wages, the assumption being that greater skills are necessarily rewarded more highly. Such a proxy is occasionally used, justified by the economic prediction that the wage equals the value of the marginal product in a competitive environment. The main advantage is the relatively easy availability of wages data. Wages over the life course have been combined with education data to generate estimates of the stock of human capital.[17] Yet, other factors (regulation, employment relations, gender, labour market competition, location) that have little or no correlation with skill also affect wages. International pay comparisons would be especially misleading as proxies for skill. Moreover, since the analytical purpose to which skills measures are often put is to explain labour market rewards, this whole class of analyses would be ruled out by such a measure if they entail the tautology that wages account for wages. If taken as a measure of skill, wage data have to be put to other uses.

It is in the measurement of generic job skills that most progress has been made in recent decades. This has been achieved primarily through what is variously known as 'task-based' analysis, or the 'job requirements approach'. The underlying measurement principle of task-based research is that the use of skills can be reliably observed through reports about the tasks that workers perform. The measures are therefore grounded in behaviour and activity, rather than subjective judgement of qualities. Individuals are seen as the most informed reporters of their own work; especially where there is greater autonomy, jobs are partly moulded by job-holders, so that outsiders would be misinformed by written job descriptions. Possible reporting biases are recognized but thought to be less serious and less likely than for self-assessment of skills. The advantages of task-based data include the ability to capture a wide range of job skills, and the fact that reports come from the workplace (not the classroom).

Task-based measurement, however, is neither a finished product nor an ideal answer to the problems of skills measurement. A consensus is still to emerge as to how best to characterize skill domains and fit them into theoretical categories. It is hard, for example, reliably to classify tasks as routine or non-routine.[18] By no means all activities at work can be easily described with items fit for large-scale surveys. Since skills need also to be measured in context, task items should ideally be accompanied by work organization indicators. For some domains of skill, one might need to investigate with in-depth qualitative interviews, or to research through participation, even if in these cases the focus of study has to be at the micro level. Finally, generic job skills can only ever be proxy indicators for the generic skills of workers themselves: individuals' skills can exceed their jobs' requirements, or even for a while fall short of them.

The principle of establishing skill requirements in occupations through surveys and detailed expert judgements comes from occupational psychology. There are a number of substantial questionnaires, some proprietary, that measure and classify tasks, and hence skill requirements—for example, the Job Components Inventory.[19] An increasing number of employers have deployed competence frameworks, based on the complexity levels of generic task requirements, and used them to support appraisals, training needs analysis, career management, and organizational effectiveness. At the national level the approach began in 1939 with the US *Dictionary of Occupational Titles* (*DOT*), the aim of which was to provide information for the US Employment Service. It evolved through stages until it was replaced by the modern O*NET system, with the intention that it should also be an aid to individual education and training decisions, and support business needs.[20] O*NET provides detailed information on the average characteristics of over 900 occupations. A simpler system, though with similar aims, had meanwhile been developed independently in Germany beginning in 1979 with the BIBB/BAuA Employment Survey.[21]

On a smaller scale, but designed specifically to inform research into skills and employment, a survey series collecting task data was developed in the United Kingdom, starting with the 'Social Change in Economic Life Initiative' in 1986 and 'Employment in Britain' in 1992, and continuing with much additional detail on generic tasks in four 'Skills Surveys' in 1997, 2001, 2006, and 2012. Similar surveys have recently been developed in Spain, Italy, Denmark, and Singapore, while a two-wave longitudinal survey of job requirements data has been developed in the United States.[22] This multinational blossoming of task-based research is being crowned with an internationally harmonized survey, part of the background data collected for PIAAC by the OECD in a large number of countries.[23]

One indicator of occupation-specific skill is, quite simply, membership of each particular occupation. There are thus as many domains and indicators of occupation-specific skills as there are occupations. One might improve on this formulation by again using task data. Just as generic task data allow researchers to construct indices of generic job skills, information about occupation-specific tasks, collected, for example, for the International Standard Classification of Occupations (ISCO), provides data on occupation-specific tasks.[24] More detailed and up-to-date information is sometimes collected by sectoral bodies, useful for purposes of planning training courses, especially when new tasks emerge. By their very nature, however, the tasks in one occupation are quite different from those in another.

The importance of occupation-specific tasks and skills for economic performance is hard to quantify. An alternative, parsimonious, indicator, often more suited for assessing value and importance, is the education and training requirement for gaining a job in the occupation. As discussed above for overall skill, this indicator gauges the value of the skill via the level of education and training input; however, it also identifies the type of knowledge involved (for example, the subject of study), which can have an additional consequence for skill value over and above the training and education requirement level. Vocational knowledge and skill can sometimes be identified in this way.

Skill formation and loss

Neither the supply of skill formation services nor the demand for learning can be readily observed directly, owing to the difficulties of measuring mismatch in this market (to be reviewed in the next section). An unfulfilled demand for learning, for example, can easily go unobserved. Analyses therefore focus on indicators of skill formation services actually rendered.

Measurement of skill acquisition is typically achieved through indicators of formal training and of informal training or learning (see Table 4.3). Data relating to participation in training are widely collected through labour force surveys and other bespoke instruments. A key reliability principle in such studies is to ensure that respondents report comprehensively on multiple forms of training.[25] Also prone to error are indicators of training intensity, such as the length of training episodes or the proportions of employees covered: one should expect to capture these well in bands, rather than in continuous form.

Is training valid as an indicator of skills acquisition? Most training is typically reviewed positively in this respect. According to the European Working Conditions Survey, for example, among those workers across the European Union in 2010 who had received some employer-provided training in the previous year, nine out of ten agreed that the training had improved the way they worked. So it seems that most, but not all, training is perceived to be effective in raising skill. There are, moreover, many studies showing an association between some types of training and subsequent pay and productivity rises.[26] Unfortunately, this reassurance, though necessary, is insufficient to confirm training as an ideal single indicator of skill acquisition. A good deal of learning takes place through participation and practice. Informal learning is the most difficult to capture accurately, because it is embedded in work relationships that may or may not foster such learning, but some of it can be captured in suitable survey items.

Skill loss might in principle be measured directly and is sometimes transparent. In the absence of direct skill measures over time, however, skill loss is typically proxied indirectly and very loosely, primarily through age, with the point of decline specific to occupations. Earnings functions normally capture decline through the quadratic term in age or work experience: a negative coefficient implies that, at some point in a career-long profile, wages decrease. *Skill obsolescence*, when the skills depreciate because the value that can be produced falls, is more commonly indicated by its immediate effects. Examples are loss of employment owing to sectoral decline, strong pressure to update skills in the face of technical obsolescence (common in the IT industry), and devaluation of firm-specific skills through labour mobility.[27]

Changing job skills can be measured retrospectively through comparison of successive representative samples, using the job skills indicators discussed above. They can, however, be supplemented by direct questions about change, posed to employees or employers. Employers are arguably the best informants of how tasks are changing and what may be expected in the near future.[28]

Table 4.3 Skills change indicators

Indicators	Concepts	Advantages	Disadvantages	International comparability	Example(s) of use
Training and education participation; hours (intensity); achievement of new qualifications	Skill acquisition	Objective	Sometimes misses informal training	AES	Whitfield (2000); Zwick (2006); Liu and Batt (2007); Ferster et al. (2008)
Participation in learning; learning requirement of job	Skill acquisition	Salience of contextual learning	Subjects may not be conscious of learning	No	Felstead et al. (2010); MEADOW Consortium (2010)
Age (especially in certain occupations)	Skill loss	Objective	Very loose proxy	Yes	All earnings functions that include quadratic terms in age or work experience
Redundancy and unemployment owing to sector decline; indicators of rapid job skill change	Skill obsolescence	Objective	Captures only sector-specific skills; hard to quantify	Yes	De Grip and van Loo (2002); Tsai et al. (2007)
Indicators from Table 4.2	Change in job skills	See Table 4.2	See Table 4.2	See Table 4.2	Felstead et al. (2007a); A. Green (2011)
Employer reports of changing importance of tasks	Change in job skills, generic and occupation specific	Closely connected to jobs.	Averages over employee groups; short-term perspective	Yes	CEDEFOP Employer Survey http://www.cedefop.europa.eu/EN/about-cedefop/projects/employers-surveys/index.aspx (accessed 16 November 2012)

Mismatch

Indicators for mismatch concepts are described in Table 4.4. Important though these concepts are, the ways of measuring them are at a comparatively immature stage, and there is as yet no consensus about best practice.

Skills under-utilization is especially hard to capture. In principle, if good-quality skills and job skills data were available from the same source in commensurate units, comparisons between the two would offer a way forward. Without that, skills under-utilization has been measured in the only way possible, through the perceptions of job-holders.

Over-education (and its opposite, *under-education*) have received considerably more attention in research, but the indicators vary depending on how the required education for jobs is measured. The best ways, since these come from the most knowledgeable informants, are to use direct measures reported by job-holders, their line managers, or job experts. Their drawback is that internationally commensurate indicators using these methods are rarely available, though the OECD's PIAAC will start to fill this gap.[29] As an alternative, some studies proxy educational requirements with statistical measures of the average or modal educational achievements of the workers in the occupation in which a worker is classified. This 'statistical' method comes, however, at a heavy cost in terms of validity, given that the rapidly expanding, and internationally varied, educational achievements of the workforce implies these averages and modes are continually rising and country specific. Its use for estimating trends and international comparisons is not recommended.

Indicators for *skill gaps* derive from judgements of whether performance is less than fully competent. The primary instruments are the reports of managers about their employees, rather than self-reports; the judgements' reliability depends on the quality and impartiality of the manager. Typically, only around 1 in 15 employees is judged to have skill gaps (though many more are reported to be in need of skills updating).

Skill shortages are also best captured through reports from employers, by collecting details about the recruitment process. The primary issue here is that respondents should be clear about when vacancies might be deemed 'hard to fill', and that a substantive reason for this shortfall must concern skill rather than offputting working conditions.

Worker training barriers (*learning barriers*) can take several forms and are hard to measure. Given the importance of work-based learning, one learning barrier may be unemployment: if you are involuntarily out of work, you are not acquiring work skills and experience. This simple fact underlines the consequences of sharp economic restructuring, such as occurred during the economic crisis of 2008 and subsequent years. In the worst scenarios,

Table 4.4 Mismatch indicators

Indicators	Concepts	Advantages	Disadvantages	International comparability	Example(s) of use
Perceived under-utilization	*Skills under-utilization*	Close to concept	Subjective; reliability not well established	No	Allen, J. and van der Velden (2001); Green and McIntosh (2007)
Difference between highest education levels required and held	Over-education/under-education; education subject mismatch	Close to concept	Looseness of interpretation of 'required'	Via PIAAC	McGuinness (2006); C. Green et al. (2007)
Managers' assessment of employees' competence	Skill gap	Closely relevant to performance	Subjective	No	Strietska-Ilina (2004); Shury et al. (2010)
Hard-to-fill vacancies for skill reasons	Skill shortage	Close to concept	Affected by stage of business cycle	In principle	Strietska-Ilina (2004)
Unemployment and indicators of discrimination, lack of capacity, and self-esteem	Learning barrier	Objective measures possible	Other than unemployment, data scarce, owing to lack of adequate design effort	Via unemployment data	Cully et al. (2000); Wooden et al. (2001); Sussman (2002)
Absence of formal training needs analysis; perceived lack of training information/capacity	Employer training barrier	Related to short-termist management	Loose; misses informal strategies	In principle	Davies et al. (2011)
Benchmarking against other similar countries/regions	Skills deficit	Increasingly possible for more indicators	Benchmarked countries not necessarily similar; concept not agreed	Inherent	Ministry of Education, Youth and Sports (2007); CIPD (2011)

unemployment leaves a 'scar' that affects how workers succeed in the labour market for many years afterwards. Thus the unemployment rate is a loose proxy indicator for learning barriers. The learning barrier of unemployment can be partially ameliorated by lifting barriers to other forms of skill acquisition, such as through training schemes. Institutional learning barriers might arise from employer discrimination based on unjustified stereotypes (concerning, for example, older workers), or through lack of information and support; a disposition learning barrier might derive from low self-esteem. An employed worker encounters a learning barrier if there is little choice of moving to a better-quality job with a decent learning environment.

Evidence of low participation in learning is not in itself, however, a valid indicator of a learning barrier, since non-participation could be a freely made choice manifesting a low demand for learning that reflects workers' needs. The idea of 'situational barriers', arising, for example, from being too busy at work, is also misconceived, merely reflecting a genuine high cost of training. Unfortunately, little effort has been made in empirical research to design indicators that properly capture learning barriers rather than, say, low participation.

A similar caveat applies to *employer training barriers*. Just because an employer provides little training, this does not necessarily mean that there is a training barrier. As described in Chapter 3, lack of training can be termed a barrier when it occurs through poor decision-making, deriving from insufficient information or lack of capacity. The principle is important, but plausible indicators are scarce. One indicator measures whether employers have developed formal strategies to assess training and skills needs; yet even this item is only a loose proxy. Other indicators derive from survey questions that directly identify the reasons for not training. Training barriers are an adjunct of particular management cultures, sometimes associated with 'short-termism', an orientation in investment decisions that is also hard to measure.

Finally, a *skills deficit* can be captured in practice by suitable benchmarking. If the skills equilibrium is thought to be too low in a particular region or country, it should be reflected in lower levels of skill and of training than in comparable regions or countries that are closer to the skills frontier. However, there is no guarantee that the benchmarked country is sufficiently similar, and if so whether that country is itself not experiencing a skills deficit to some extent. Commonly, countries in Europe will compare themselves to the EU average. Measuring skills deficits through benchmarking is thus a very approximate game. Unfortunately, *skills deficit* also remains a loosely used concept in practice: in public discourse, the phrase is used interchangeably with *skill shortage*, or sometimes with *skill gap*. In developmental psychology a 'social skills deficit' is essentially a type of skill gap. It would be better if the term *skills deficit* could start to acquire the status of an ideal scientific concept with agreed meaning and indicators.

Skill measurement as a work in progress

Are the available indicators of skills, job skills, skill changes, and mismatches fit for purpose? A full answer to this question would require that the criteria of validity and reliability are systematically addressed, a thesis in itself when one considers the plurality of concepts involved. In addition, since indicator collection typically requires public funding, considerations of cost are always to the fore.

Yet, this brief overview suggests that there is much to work with at present and in prospect, despite the imperfections. Indicators of skill hold themselves up well when set squarely against the basic PES concept discussed in Chapter 2. The progress that has taken place in recent decades includes the vast extension in the worldwide collection of education and training data, the evolution of testing methods, refinement, and measurement of skill mismatch concepts way beyond the simplistic concepts in past currency, the compilation of detailed occupational skill profiles, and the advance on several fronts of the task-based approach to job skills measurement. Given that it seems unlikely that skills will fade from arenas of public importance, it can be expected that future decades will see ongoing improvements in the availability of suitable indicators. Measurement is worth doing, and these improvements worth having. Whether these developments will lead to better analysis and policy-making in future is another matter.

Part II
The Players

5

Employers and the Evolution of Skilled Work

Why employers matter

Part II is about the behaviour of the two key players in the skill markets: employers and workers. Beginning with the former, the premises of this chapter and the next is that, owing to their implications for skill use, what employers decide upon and do makes a substantial difference to the quality of work life, to learning, and to prosperity in modern economies. However the relationship between workers and their bosses is construed, whether it is seen as harmonious or conflictual, employers' heterogeneous and changing practices matter a great deal for everybody. So we should find a good way of understanding what they do.

The employer is fundamental to the role of skill in modern life, for three strong reasons. First, as an increasing body of evidence shows, how managers deploy workers' skills affects both job quality and economic performance. Second, employers' demand for skill is changing in steady but persistent ways, which need to be understood and well responded to. Third, employers are indispensable actors in the supply of skill formation services, through the provisions they make for work-based learning. Thus employers are at the same time *both* skill demanders and necessary actors for ensuring the future supply of skill. Each of these reasons, on its own, would be enough to suggest a close look; together the case for a thorough investigation of what employers do for skills is compelling. It will be argued that employers are not mere carriers of a competitively imposed imperative for profit maximization, but that their characters, cultures, capacities, and beliefs have a sustained effect on the evolution of skilled work.

The chapter begins with the factors underlying the demand for skill. From the economic perspective the demand depends on its price: using a simple model of how firms behave in a competitive and known environment, it is shown that the demand for high-skilled, relative to low-skilled, labour decreases, the higher is the relative wage. Extensions to this model are then noted, which introduce realistic complications such as imperfect competition without altering the underlying rational actor assumption about employers. Once a world of deep uncertainty and imperfect management is introduced, however, the chapter departs from the conventional model of the rational actor, and the significance of the proposition that 'employers matter' emerges.

These different approaches then allow an examination of how the demand for skill is changing in the modern era. A hundred years ago, even though a minority of more educated workers earned a pay premium, most young people could grow up with, perhaps, only a basic level of education, find a factory job, and pick up most of the necessary technical skills while working. Nowadays such jobs still exist, but, in developed countries, are in the minority. Most jobs are for applicants with at least high-school graduation level. Increasingly higher levels of education are needed in growing sectors of all modern economies, and this is typically taken to reflect a trend towards greater skills demand. To some readers, rising skills demand might appear too obvious an issue to merit extensive treatment. To others, however, the assertion will be contentious, and they will want to see a bank of evidence. They will point to the history of early industrialization in parts of the West, which not untypically saw long trends of workforce deskilling with the loss of handicraft skills: such periods show that there is no necessity for skills demand to rise in capitalist economies. And as late as the 1970s, it was suggested that employees were coming under ever-closer supervisory control, and that this was accompanied by ever-lower skills demand. What can be made in the twenty-first century of this 'deskilling' school of thought? Many modern economies have exhibited a certain polarization of workforce skills even while overall the average demand for skills has increased. How can such a picture be framed? While addressing these questions, the chapter reviews the significance of the evidence linking skills to employers' economic performance.

Employers' demand for skilled labour

Skills and profit

The 'demand for skill' is the amount of skilled labour that an employer would like to employ, given the productive and market environment. For each skill, demand is derived from its essential quality of creating value. It is conventional to assume that an employer's strategy is driven by the aim of maximizing profits or, in the case of public employers supplying non-market services, maximizing the net social value of the outputs provided. Strategies differ greatly according to how they are formed and informed, whether they take a long-term or short-term perspective, and whether they stem from a culture that takes a positive view on the value of skills. While such differences affect employers' decisions, suppose that one were to set aside such complications, for a moment, and imagine a 'perfect' labour market—one where there is an unfettered freedom for well-informed workers to switch from job to job, where employers can hire and fire as their strategy dictates, and where neither workers nor employers are held back by uncertainty over the future.

In this simplified setting, one can predict that high-skilled workers will be substituted for low-skilled workers, but only up to a certain point. Define the 'marginal product' as the extra output from employing an extra worker. Assume, furthermore, that there are eventually diminishing marginal products, as the amounts of either skilled or unskilled labour are raised. Thus, as one raises inputs of high-skilled and lowers low-skilled labour, the ratio of the marginal products of high-skilled and low-skilled labour gradually decreases. Then, an optimum of maximum profits is reached when the ratio of the marginal products exactly matches the ratio of their wages. That this must be so can be proved by contradiction: if the ratio of marginal products were to differ from the wage ratio, it would be possible to raise profits by hiring relatively more, or less, high-skilled labour.

From this deduction a core prediction arises directly—namely, that the demand for high-skilled labour is negatively related to its wage rate. In effect, an increase in the wage ratio of high-skilled to low-skilled labour makes it profitable to hire relatively more low-skilled labour. A diagrammatic representation of this basic economic deduction is shown in the appendix to this chapter.

Skills demand and company strategy

The model just described has an attractive simplicity in that, from only a few assumptions, a verifiable prediction is derived. For the demand for labour, there are established methods for estimating key parameters such as the elasticity of demand (the proportional change in demand from a proportional change in the wage).[1] The theory, essentially a straightforward piece of applied mathematics, is easily extendable to account for more complex realities, and three significant types of extension to the conventional model are to be noted here: the inclusion of other production inputs, theories that respect a time perspective on jobs, and theories that make realistic assumptions about competition in the labour market. There are also other ways in which skills demand needs to be modelled in a more complex and realistic manner, which entail departures from, rather than extensions to, the conventional model; these elaborations see skills demand as an aspect of an organization's strategy. This alternative framework takes account of the uncertain outlook in which business decisions are taken, and the subordinate character of skills decisions within the overall strategy of organizations. Strategies, while externally constrained, are rarely imposed, and are therefore subject to managerial beliefs and norms. Hence, the demand for skill is affected by cultural and strategic choices, as well as by the technologies that determine possible production processes.

While still maintaining the assumption that the employer's objective is the maximization of profits, this section sets out in more detail these extensions and departures from the basic model.

EXTENSIONS TO THE CONVENTIONAL MODEL

Consider first the extensions. The simple model considered only two inputs, high-skilled and low-skilled labour, but both these inputs work with physical capital and other inputs such as land. Managers are simultaneously making decisions about the disposition of these other inputs. While the two-input model abstracts from these other decisions, the relationship between capital and the different qualities of labour affects their marginal products. If new capital equipment, for example, is substitutable for low-skilled labour but highly complementary with high-skilled labour, then investment in new equipment will reshape the trade-off between low-skilled and high-skilled labour. This 'capital-skill complementarity' is one of the core ideas supporting economists' perspectives about changing technology in the modern era.

Incorporating a time perspective is important because most labour is not exchanged on a spot market, like fresh fruit. Employers cannot, except in unusual circumstances, choose each day how many skilled workers to hire. Regulatory restraints would not permit such a practice in most countries; even in the absence of legal inhibitions, it would be prohibitively costly to renew firm-specific skills frequently. Workers are typically hired with an explicit or implicit contract extending over some, usually unspecified, time. Employers, too, see themselves as remaining in business for usually unspecified periods into the future. Planning their demand for skilled labour to achieve long-term objectives is part of the essence of strategic management. The longevity of the jobs that employers create is affected by the adjustment costs of firing and hiring, including recruitment and training costs, by the use of seniority incentives for eliciting work effort and rewarding the acquisition of skills, and by the institutional and wage-bargaining environment. Because firm-specific and transferable skills are often complementary with each other, for high-skill jobs employers tend to engender a longer-term, more stable, workforce, so that it is worthwhile to invest in employees' skills. Because high-skill jobs also sometimes give rise to scale economies in the deployment of weekly work hours, employers are more likely to want their employees to work full time.

Another consequence of a long-term perspective concerns the demand for skilled labour in a time of recession. Since adjustment costs are likely to be greater for skilled labour, employers commonly hoard their skilled workers when business is temporarily slack. In a downturn of the business cycle, therefore, one typically sees a relative fall in the proportion of low-skilled workers, a phenomenon that should not be confused with a secular trend in the use of skilled labour.

Diversions from the assumptions of a perfectly competitive labour market bring further reasons to question the conclusion that skilled labour is deployed until its relative marginal product equals its wage premium. The conclusion has to be adapted where there are either monopoly or monopsony tendencies, or where there are systematic information deficiencies on either side of the labour market. Monopoly tendencies occur when a group or class of employees is able to effect social closure, barring or deterring others from entering a particular occupation. The classic method is to operate an artificial skills barrier: the social construction of skill. In such cases, wages can be maintained above the true marginal product of the skilled labour. The opposite scenario is the monopsonistic exploitation of market power by employers who are able to lower wages without losing all their workers. Through lack of information or mobility, many workers do not quit when wages are lowered; their wages can be forced below marginal product.[2]

Another type of information deficiency refers to the difficulty of monitoring and managing complex work processes where it is necessary to afford employees a degree of autonomy. In this case, the information (about working hard on the job) is asymmetric: the employee knows better than the boss. To ensure compliance, employers may pay 'efficiency wages' (wages above market levels) so that employees have something to lose if they are dismissed for shirking their duties, or to encourage reciprocal effort and commitment.[3] Efficiency wages are just one example of the sub-field 'personnel economics', which uses conventional economics to study work organization, including the ways that human resource practices are aligned with each organization's needs.[4]

DEPARTURES: THE RESOURCE-BASED VIEW
OF THE FIRM AND SKILLS DEMAND

In all the conventional economic models just described, the employer faces a set of external constraints given by technology and the market environment, and, given the profit maximization objective, makes the appropriate decision about resource allocation, including the employment of skilled labour. There is no room for employers to deviate from this decision. Analysts from outside mainstream economics, however, question the plausibility of the conclusion that there is a unique predictable route for employers. An alternative take on the demand for skilled labour arises from the perspectives of management science and organization studies. These schools of thought, though they do not eschew the assumption of profit maximization, allow room for the agency of the employer. In the perspective of strategic management, firms' managers make their choices in the face of 'bounded rationality', with varying sets of norms, expectations, and capabilities.[5]

A compelling suggestive piece of evidence that we should take the agency of management seriously is the finding that there are substantial differences between companies in the adoption of effective management practices.[6] Differences are found among firms in the same industry, across industries, and across countries; typically, a long tail of inferior human resource practices prevails. Moreover, the quality of management, as measured by adoption of best practice, is robustly and strongly correlated with company performance outcomes, including profitability. These findings raise the question, to be considered below, as to why bad practices are not discarded, or selected out as low-profit firms fail to expand or survive.

Over and above managers' varied knowledge and understanding of generalized good practices, however, their skills are significant in building up distinctive 'social architectures', which are hard for other firms to adopt, even those blessed with observant managers. One influential school of strategic management, the resource-based view (RBV) of the firm, focuses on the dynamics of rent-seeking, whereby competing firms attempt to find resources or capacities that give them a persistent edge over rivals. Seeking rents through innovations, whether in products or processes, has been seen as the essence of entrepreneurship since at least the time of Joseph Schumpeter and the Austrian school of economic thought in the early twentieth century. The argument of the RBV school is that, in the current era of heightened competition and global trade, enhanced by the rise of the Internet, it is becoming ever more difficult to maintain a competitive advantage. Across the world, financial, marketing, and other organizational functions have matured and converged towards best practices, so that firms are compelled to seek forms of competitive advantage that cannot so easily be followed by others. One important channel is through human capital.

Strategic human resource management theories have developed this perspective in ways that have important implications for the demand for skilled labour. Thus, successful organizations develop 'core competencies', captured in routines, processes, and relationships that are at once value-creating and hard to imitate by others.[7] The human resources of a company are said to be inimitable, owing to the unique history through which its workers have developed their skills, to the difficulties that outsiders would have replicating success because of the causal ambiguity attached to a firm's upskilling workers, and to social complexity—the fact that skills are often attached to the development of idiosyncratic customer or internal relationships.[8] Human capital is thus linked to the firm's other assets and is embedded in an evolutionary social architecture that cannot change quickly. Since it is also rooted in the lives of the workers themselves, human capital also has reasons to be less mobile than many forms of physical and financial capital. The 'dynamic capability' approach extends the RBV perspective in stressing the importance of the managerial skills that set up the organizational and strategic routines.[9] In a curious echo of Taylor's original paean to scientific management at the beginning of the twentieth century, now for the twenty-first a 'scientific' or 'strategic' approach to talent management is advocated.[10]

The implication of the RBV perspective is that adopting a high-skilled approach to organizing production may yield greater profits in the long term. There is thus an association between having a long-term horizon and opting for production methods that demand high skills. Firms that are able to sustain competitiveness through other means (such as access to scarce natural resources or to a captive market), or that have a short-term strategic horizon, have more reason to opt for low-skilled, low-cost, production strategies. In contrast to the approach of mainstream economics, the demand for skill is thus dependent on more than just the relative cost of skilled labour and technology: it rests also on the chosen management strategy.

An implication of the evolutionary character of a firm's social architecture is that possible development paths are constrained by the existing skills of its workforce. The current management of a company makes strategic choices about how the company is to develop, with appropriate related skills decisions following on. Yet it rarely begins with an empty table. Its strategy is limited by earlier decisions that affect the skills available in the current workforce. Past choices about the path of skills development may be hard to reverse because they establish the norms and expectations of the present.

An interesting example of historical legacy is shown in the association between the demand for skilled labour and choices about product specification, which are constrained by the firm's brand, physical plant, and existing workforce, none of which can be quickly changed except at enormous cost.[11] At the high-spec end of markets, products tend to have more characteristics, to change those characteristics more frequently, and to be able to be customized to the flexible tastes of small consumer groups. Linked to these features, high-spec products and services tend to require more complex technologies in their production. Low-spec products, by contrast, tend to be simpler, both in their generation and in their features. Moreover, low-spec products are, it is observed, more likely to be able to be produced with technologies requiring low skills. At one extreme, low-spec manufactured goods can be made on Fordist assembly lines, with jobs designed to be low skilled so that managers can easily monitor and control the work flows, and reduce the wage bill. By contrast, high-spec products or services need workers who have the skills to work with the usually more complex technologies and who can respond to flexible requirements. Such high-spec production lines would be expected to occupy niches in product and service markets that afford high value added for employers, derived partly from the greater productivity (net of the higher wages) of the employees relative to low-spec lines, and partly from the sustained rents that can be earned where the products or services are hard to imitate.

WORK ORGANIZATION AND SKILLS DEMAND

Managers' choices over internal organization also have implications for skills. Decisions about either the design of jobs or the systems of communication and hierarchy within the firm can affect the use of communication and other generic skills. Within jobs, the level of autonomy is likely to be related to the broad level of skill, for reasons already noted in Chapter 2: the more that workers are asked to have an influence over their own tasks, the more they must be able to judge what is needed to be done and plan their own activities. Typically, worker discretion is found to be correlated with education level as expected, though not especially closely. Some low-paid, low-skilled jobs require non-routine activities over which limited autonomy is granted. An important factor is the extent to which workers are committed to their jobs, prepared to devote discretionary effort, and stick with the job. While autonomy helps to engender more commitment, the reverse is also true: where there is more commitment, employers are more likely to trust their employees with greater discretion.[12]

Designing jobs with more task discretion is one way of involving employees in the company. Another is through increased participation, something that can take many forms. Teamworking is one route, though it is important to distinguish between different types of team, according to how far team members are able to decide matters for themselves rather than just working as a group in a detailed line of command and control. More self-direction in teams is associated with greater workplace skills development.[13] Other forms of participation involve a range of communication channels, both upwards and downwards within the firm. Downward channels keep workers informed of organization-level developments, while upward channels allow suggestions, complaints, and aspirations to be fed through to management. Quality improvement groups, regular meetings with management, and suggestion schemes are just three examples of the routes used. The top end of the participation spectrum involves genuine consultation and incentives linked to organizational performance. Combining several employee involvement channels as part of a bundle of self-reinforcing 'High Involvement Work Practices' (HIWPs) is an especially favoured human resource strategy among many researchers and consultants, even if some remain sceptical.[14] Deciding on these forms of organization (whether piecemeal or combined) implies a demand for interaction skills, including the ability to communicate and listen well, and to be able to persuade and influence others about the value of their suggestions. Since much communication is written (on paper or screen), there arises also an additional need for literacy skills.[15] More broadly, there is substantive evidence that internal organizational changes have in recent decades been associated with a rising demand for skills.[16]

EMPLOYERS' AGENCY AND SKILLS DEMAND

An overarching theme of this chapter is that employers matter. The foregoing overview of conventional and of resource-based theories of the firm, of strategic human resource management, and of theories of skill's relationship with work organization delivers a closer understanding of what this theme signifies about the demand for skilled labour.

In the conventional perspective on the firm, the 'rational actor' assumption about managers places them at the centre of affairs, since it is they who are taking the decisions about product markets, processes, and work organization, and hence about the deployment of different types of skilled labour. It is assumed that the profit maximization objective is sustained through managers observing and learning about the relative efficacy of different practices and organizational forms, and through a competitive mechanism of survival (with those not maximizing profits more likely to face bankruptcy). Yet, given this objective, along with the technological and market environments, the conventional model ultimately allots employers no real choices. They must decide on the 'best' practices and types of work organization, or lose profits. Employers matter, but only in the limited sense that they are at the centre of the game. Their characters, cultures, and individual beliefs do not have an independent effect. The strategies and practices they choose, as also the skills they demand, are endogenous. Any employer, faced with the same circumstances, would choose the same strategy, practices, type of work organization, and skills demand, unless they cede some profits. Loss of profit could occur only if managers are able to subvert shareholders' objectives, or if owners choose to forgo them to pursue philanthropic or other ends, resisting takeovers from more profit-oriented wealth-holders.

In the perspective of strategic human resource management, however, employers matter in a deeper sense. The demand for skilled labour is significantly affected by the agency of employers who, with their managers, may select from a range of strategies for profit maximizing the value of the firm, with different skill implications. The strategies may evolve and be learned over time, but one cannot rely on competition rapidly to diffuse best practice management processes across and between economies; nor can the pace of learning be relied on to ensure companies are close to using best practice. Heterogeneity among employers is thus the norm. Neither evolution through competitive selection nor management learning processes ensure that managers seek out and reach any hypothetical best way. Optimal skill mixes are deeply affected by past trajectories, and cannot simply be deduced by copying the core competencies of successful companies.

Cited reasons for the slow adoption of generalized good practice are low levels of management capabilities and of competitive pressures.[17] These reasons must be combined with others derived from the fields of learning and culture. The incremental character of much learning is significant, whereby managers try out new tactics one by one, such as testing their products on a small scale in an export market. Such incremental learning may not provide a path to learning about the effects of non-incremental changes: small changes that lead to profit reduction induce managers to revert to their original 'equilibrium'. With the search for improvement restricted by a bounded rationality, learning becomes localized and restricted to proven routines.[18] In that circumstance it may be impossible for firms to learn to traverse non-incrementally from one equilibrium to another, even if they would be more successful at the end of the road. Learning from other competitors' human capital deployment may be especially difficult if they have developed idiosyncratic social architectures and complex configurations of human capital within firms that are hard to imitate.

The embeddedness of firms in markets and spatial localities means that learning is likely to be a collective process, with each firm's learning responding to that of its competitors, and hence to a management culture of expectations about the use of skills. Culture and a firm's surrounding institutions come into play as significant features guiding the strategic orientations taken by managers in various settings.[19] Country and regional differences are to be expected, reflecting differential norms, the localization of management learning that hinders the adoption of new practices, and external institutions that affect local constraints and the norms of other agents. Thus, the management and organization of work differs considerably between countries, even for apparently identical jobs. As one illustration of this outcome, a recent study found that vocational training teachers in Norway have significantly greater autonomy than their counterparts doing the same job in England.[20]

When the learning of good practice is inhibited, and when good practice is partly firm specific because of each firm's history and social architecture, the abstract conception of a unique optimal profit-maximizing strategy may not be a useful way of understanding managements' decisions. In a dynamic and uncertain context, each organization's best strategy can be determined only with bounded rationality.

The implication of there being an independent role for strategy is that policies can be conceived that affect choices about skills, whether through voluntarist methods or with partnership institutions or through regulatory constraints such as minimum wages. Where policies are designed to improve strategies, the rationale falls mainly outside the conventional perspective on social intervention, which is premised on redressing market failure, a theme to be taken up in more detail in Chapter 9.

The role of evidence linking skills to performance

In all these theories of skills demand, the connection between skill and value production is central—indeed, the PES concept defines the scope of 'skill' in part through the assumption that there is some positive link. Before asking where the insights of the different approaches take us, it is useful to consider empirical assessments of this assumption. The link with value production is relevant, first, for decision-makers: managers, policy-makers, and individuals contemplating the setting-up of skills programmes want to know which skill indicators are productive, and to what extent. Second, the marginal effect of skills on financial performance (profitability)—the effect of increasing skills inputs by one unit—is of particular interest. Where this link is positive, one may suspect that some companies are under-investing in skills, and such information should be useful to support policy implications and to enlighten management education. Third, the study of the value of skills is at the heart of economics' account of the changing distribution of pay.

What sort of picture does the evidence provide? Much of the empirical support for links between skill measures and performance is indirect, in the form of studies about how skills are associated with pay. The principle is: since businesses are prepared to pay for a skill, it must be delivering better performance. Evidence about the skills premium is described in Chapter 7, because it impinges directly on the analysis of workers. Yet an implication of the theory of the social construction of skill is that the market price of skilled labour can easily differ from the value of its marginal product. Therefore, direct evidence of skills indicators' associations with performance is going to be useful.

A common approach is to look for the effect of skill measures on job performance. Studies typically examine detailed micro-settings. As an illustration, in one recent study the communication skills of gynaecologists are investigated: in this case, female physicians performed better, as measured by patient satisfaction, the difference being accounted for by their superior communication skills.[21] Job performance studies also allow the study of interactions between different skill types.[22] There are countless evaluative micro-studies of the effects of training on measures of job performance in multiple fields of endeavour. Most are positive, though some find no appreciable impact on performance. Good-quality evaluations are important management tools.[23]

Research that links organizations with their employees has studied the effects of employee skills on intermediate organizational goals such as productivity, typically using a production function framework.[24] One US-based study has shown, for example, that an increase by one year in the average length of employees' education is associated with 8.5 per cent greater productivity in manufacturing industry (after allowing for other factors). An Israel-based study focused on the importance of the skills of managers, showing that these were linked to both objective and subjective performance measures of local government authorities. A study in Germany, using a panel of establishments, found that a 1 percentage point rise in the share of employees who received training led to at least a 0.7 per cent rise in average productivity over the subsequent three years. A cross-country organizational study in engineering industries has also established that productivity differences are attributable to skills, and there are further studies in this vein. Nevertheless, the difficulties of measuring both skills and organizational performance have limited the extent of this form of evidence. Indeed, there are few studies of the links between skills and companies' financial performance.[25] One type of study focuses on training in a large company and uses assumptions to link wage gains to company performance: these show a very large range in the estimated rate of return to training, always positive. In another type, using linked establishment–employee data, both training and the average education level of the workforce are found to be positively related to the commercial survival of the establishment (which is treated as a proxy indicator of profitability).

At the aggregate level, employers' performance is gauged by the productivity of the business sector, which is correlated fairly closely with that of the overall economy as measured by GDP per capita. A substantial empirical literature has shown that raising the education level of the population helps to account for GDP per capita, through augmentation of the quality of labour. Additionally, the educational attainment of populations is related to the rate of economic growth. The leading interpretation of this latter finding is that greater skills enable a faster pace of technological innovation in the country.[26]

Cognitive skills, however, have a more impressive effect than education per se. Studies that include measures of the cognitive skills of the population find that educational attainment is only a loose indicator of a nation's skill. Average cognitive skills measures were obtained by collecting and normalizing scores from internationally comparable maths skills tests for children in lower secondary schooling, over a long period. Improvement by one standard deviation in this average skills score raises annual economic growth by around 2 percentage points—a very substantial amount. Education has very little impact on growth if it does not have a substantial association with a better cognitive skills score. The overriding implication of studies that focus on cognitive skills is that policy attention should be directed at the quality of education and on other aspects of the social and family environment that affect cognitive development.[27]

In sum, large associations are found between a number of skills measures and employers' economic performance. These provide criterion validity for the skills indicators and point up the analytical and policy importance of skill. However, these studies are not yet so robust or well developed that they provide systematic and comprehensive guidance to public policy-makers or to businesses in different countries, and there are methodological difficulties in establishing that associations are indicative of causal processes.

How the demand for skill is changing overall

The importance of skill for economic performance and well-being, combined with the theoretical centrality of skill in social and economic theory, motivate an understanding of how and why employers' demand for and use of skills is changing in modern capitalism. In sociology, secular trends and polarizations of job skill modify the class structure, the core variable determining life chances and experiences. In economics, the race between the changing demand for, and supply of, skill is central to accounts of increased inequality in the labour market and in society generally.[28] Policy-makers across the world, steeped in either discipline, realize that they must build their social stratagems upon a foundation of knowledge about how work is changing locally. This section draws on the theories of skills demand described above to summarize some fundamental ideas about how and why the nature of employment is changing and to describe the type of evidence that has been used in their support.

A strong empirical observation impels this discussion: the average level of employers' skills demand has been increasing over recent decades. The evidence is both direct, based on demand indicators, and indirect, drawn from the evolution of wages and what is known about skills supply:

- One direct piece of evidence is the growing share of employment taken up by skilled workers—typically delineated by occupational groups with higher presumed skill content (see Chapter 4). For example, the growth of professional and managerial occupations in all industrialized countries signals robust skills demand growth. A further illustration is given in Figure 8.4. Similarly, studies of skill content as measured by the US *Dictionary of Occupational Titles* show growing skill as the composition of occupations change. However, such studies do not cover changes within occupations and therefore may misrepresent the overall change.[29]

- Direct studies of activities in workplaces find, using decomposition methods, that overall skill requirements have been increasing, both within particular well-defined occupations such as clerical work, and across whole economies. These studies show that restructuring between occupations accounts for only part of the overall change.[30]

- Workplace studies also find that it is the more complex skills domains that have been increasing, relative to simpler skills domains. In Germany, complex analytical and interactive skills have become more important, relative to manual and cognitive routine skills. Across Britain between 1992 and 2006, computing skills, problem-solving skills, high-level communication skills ('influencing' skills), and self-planning skills were increasing the fastest. Literacy and numeracy were also being increasingly required, while the demand for physical skills was largely static.[31]

- Complementing this direct evidence, the fact that ubiquitous substantial rises in the supply of educated labour have been accompanied by a rise in the wages of highly educated labour is indirect evidence of rising demand. It is argued, using the basic economics of supply and demand, that for each wage rate the demand must have been shifted upwards at least as fast as the supply.[32] With assumptions about the substitutability between high-skilled and low-skilled labour, the effect can be quantified. To illustrate, the evidence on the wages and supplies of college-educated and high-school-educated labour has been used to deduce that the relative demand for college-educated labour in the United States rose by around 5 per cent a year over the 1980s.[33] This evidence assumes that supply and demand trump other possible causes of rising wage inequality, such as institutional changes. The timing and location of changes in inequality are not always consistent with a purely technological explanation.[34]

Since these elements of evidence are about averages they do not preclude areas of deskilling. There are recent examples of neo-Taylorist labour processes where skill requirements have been decreasing.[35] Yet, the overall multifaceted empirical evidence points to increasing demand for skills in recent decades. To assess whether this trend is likely to persist, however, one has to think about the factors underlying the changes. If skills demand is, on the whole, increasing, what are the potential causes?

The supply and location of highly/low-educated workers

A rising demand for skilled labour could in part be supply driven via the labour market. A long-term increase in the stock of highly educated labour, perhaps arising from factors that have nothing directly to do with the economy or the workplace, is a potential route to cheapening the cost of skilled labour. This might in turn increase the demand for skilled labour, as the simple economic model predicts. Thus, via the price mechanism supply might in the long run thereby generate greater demand. Yet in general this appears unlikely to have taken place, since, as noted, the relative price of skilled labour has not fallen. Nevertheless, increasing supplies of skilled labour may have dampened rises in skilled worker wages.

An associated development has been the integration of developing countries in the industrialised global economy, which has led to a change in the international division and location of skilled labour. The recent era of globalization is hardly new, but the significant character of modern times is that employers in developing countries—chiefly China and India—have become major players in manufacturing industries, and increasingly too in service sectors. Expanded trade, and the internationalization of production, introduce a large segment of the world's population into the potential labour pool for all those products and services that can be traded, and for all processes that can be outsourced offshore. For many employers operating in the industrialized countries, globalization means a fall in the price of low-skilled labour if they can relocate some production processes to low-wage economies or import the products and services made by low-skilled labour. Either way, the average skill of labour deployed in industrialized countries can be expected to increase.

It is, however, a considerable oversimplification to think of the world as one vast labour market. The cheapening of low-skilled labour is directly relevant only for those firms that can manage offshore production facilities, or source their inputs cheaply from low-wage countries. After two decades of rapid growth in China and India, the trade of the industrialized world with these and other low-wage countries remained only a relatively small proportion of international trade among the rich nations, not least because trade within the industrialized world has also been expanding. The upskilling taking place in industrialized economies has occurred as well in sectors that are quite distant from the global competition. The verdict of labour economists has been that the emergence of China and India as manufacturing nations between the 1970s and 1990s was not in practice a major cause of the changing skill composition in the industrialized economies at that time.[36] The importance of this driver for skill change seems likely to be greatest in a later phase of globalization, from 2000 onwards: with third-world industrial growth continuing and broadening, competitive pressure on first-world labour markets has persisted and is intensifying. Moreover, more recent reappraisals imply that outsourcing and expanded trade have had a significant role, and suggest that these factors may induce technological changes, which then reduce the relative demand for low-skilled labour in the industrialized world.[37] Against this, however, a portion of outsourcing to developing countries is for skilled jobs, taking advantage of the growing education levels in low-wage countries.

Technology

Technological change has also been a major force determining employers' demand for skill. In post-war sociology competing schools of thought have emerged as to how new technologies would affect work and society. The optimistic scenario anticipated a progressive if gradual increase in the use of skill with the spread of modern automated technologies: these were expected to liberate workers from being tied to individual machines, to change the balance of work tasks towards more conceptual activities, and to foster the decentralization of responsibilities. In stark contrast, the neo-Marxian school associated with Harry Braverman's 'Labor and Monopoly Capital' focused on the spread of Taylorism and Fordism through the twentieth century. The essence of Taylorism was the pursuit of a detailed division of labour so as to raise the ability of managers to control labour processes in the interests of employers; Fordist assembly-line processes summoned machinery and automation to the same end. The net result, it was argued, was that most workers had become overspecialized in repetitive activities, entailing a loss of technical skill as well as autonomy. The decline of the craft labourer was seen as the paradigmatic case of this deskilling.

The deskilling school did not weather well the criticisms that it was incorrect to focus exclusively on the concept of control (rather than profit), and that it was unduly centred on the United States in its perspective on modern capitalism, ignoring quite divergent developments in Europe and Japan. It was superseded by the post-Fordist perspective, in which the central proposition was that it was profitable to harness the productive powers of workers in complex production and service sites, and that this necessitated the granting of a limited or 'responsible' autonomy to many workers. Allied to this view, it was recognized that countries had developed segmented workforces with centres of privileged jobs that had prospects for pay and skills enhancement over the course of careers. Thus, an alternative possibility was that employers' demands for skill were becoming more unequal: deskilling strategies, according to this view, would still be pursued for some jobs, while others would have their skill requirements gradually advanced as technologies called for ever more complex tasks.[38]

In modern socio-economic accounts of the association of skills demand with technology, a positive story is told through the notion of the knowledge economy. This concept is intimately related both to globalization and to the imprint of the computer. Global trade and production networks, in this view, have been changing the terms in which economies or societies interact and compete. Whereas in the past economies could grow with more exploitation of natural resources, more investment in plant and equipment, and privileged access to finance, capital now has such freedom to relocate that the only way to obtain a sustained competitive advantage is through a progressively more educated and knowledgeable workforce, a factor of production that is assumed less mobile than physical and financial capital. In this new situation, more higher-educated workers are needed to fill the growing jobs in 'symbolic–analytic services' that entail 'problem-solving, problem-identifying and strategic-brokering activities'.[39]

The same idea is expressed in the economists' concept of 'skill-biased' technological change (SBTC): the hypothesis that the parameters of the production function evolve to enhance the productivity of high-skilled labour relative to that of low-skilled labour; such changes would come about directly where the new technologies are better handled by more skilled workers and indirectly if physical capital is complementary with skilled labour, so that the accumulation of capital itself leads to the same result. New technologies are, in any case, normally embodied in new plant and equipment. The pervasive new technology of the current era, based on the computer, is said to be inherently skill biased (on average); other major innovations derived from the modern supremacy of science and engineering, such as in the bio-technology sectors, have the same character.

Whether increasing the productivity of high-skilled labour leads to an increased demand for it is, however, an open question. There has been a two-century-long debate on whether technology's benefits are universal, reflecting the ambivalent relation to new technologies throughout history. Classical economist David Ricardo was at first on the side of the optimists, holding in the first editions of his *Principles of Political Economy* that new machinery was always beneficial for workers; yet in the third edition (1821) he famously recanted, suggesting that 'the employment of machinery is frequently detrimental to their interests'.[40]

Possible outcomes of skill-biased technological change can be illustrated for the case where the inputs can be varied but the output is assumed fixed. Although artificial, this case serves to show the key importance of the substitutability between high- and low-skilled labour. Suppose that, through new technology, high-skilled labour became much more productive, while both low-skilled labour's productivity and the high-skill/low-skill wage premium are unaltered. If the degree of substitutability is large enough, high-skilled labour would be substituted for low-skilled labour to such an extent that its quantity increases. If the degree of substitutability is low, by contrast, employers would demand less high-skilled labour while still displacing some low-skilled labour through substitution. These two possibilities are shown diagrammatically in the Appendix.

What, then, does empirical research tell us about which of these two cases is most relevant? When comparing college-educated and high-school-educated labour, the consensus of empirical estimates of the 'elasticity of substitution' (the parameter measuring the degree of substitutability) are high enough to imply that the technical changes augmenting the productivity of college-educated workers in recent decades led to a rise in the demand for college-educated labour, relative to the demand for high-school-educated labour.[41] Low-skilled workers have been in effect displaced in large numbers, as the same tasks have been performed more cheaply by skilled workers using the computers that embodied the new technologies. SBTC thereby can explain why the prevailing new technologies of the modern era have led to greater demand for high-skilled labour.

In addition to the aggregate evidence that skills demand has been rising, substantial empirical evidence supports the hypothesis that technological change of the modern era has overall been skill biased:

- Especially large rises in the use of high-skilled labour have concentrated in the same industries across countries. On the assumption that technologies are ubiquitous, this is circumstantial evidence that the skills rises are associated with the technology. Comparing the United States and the United Kingdom over 1970–90, for example, there were especially fast-rising proportions of skilled jobs in Printing and Publishing, Machinery and Electronics, Electrical Equipment, and Transportation in both countries; but the share grew much more slowly in Metal Products and Food industries, again in both countries. The industry rate of skills growth is more generally found to be well correlated across many countries.[42]

- Not only has the industry share or occupation share of skilled labour risen comparably across countries, but the rise is associated with indicators of new technologies, such as R&D spending or computer use—direct evidence of skill-biased technological change.[43]

- Task-based studies of workplaces show correlations across industries and occupations between the levels and changes in computer technology indicators and the levels and growth in the uses of generic skills.[44]

Taken together, there is thus good scientific support for accepting that employer demand for skill has been increasing, and that technology is an important driving force. Deskilling, as a proposition about the average impact of modern technology on skills, or about the general trend of skills in recent history, is not supported. Yet there are some important provisos. The evidence refers to average, not universal, tendencies: there will be areas where technology is changing in ways that lower what is required of skilled workers, or increase the demand for one kind of skill but diminish the demand for another. The romanticized picture of the knowledge economy, with its visions of rising skills for all and of greater equality, should be treated with considerable scepticism.

Computer-driven technological change may be having a partial polarizing effect on employment, reducing the share of workers in intermediate-level jobs relative both to high-skilled and low-skilled jobs. Computers are complementary with high-skilled labour, not only because of the higher levels of technical skill required to work directly with them, but also because the required higher cognitive skills are complementary with high levels of interactive skill needed to find and introduce productive ways of using information technologies. In contrast, computerization substitutes for the labour involved in tasks that can more easily be programmed and automated—likely to be the more routine tasks. Jobs involving such routine tasks are not necessarily the least skilled and by no means the lowest paid, as prior to their automation they could have been quite complex and required a degree of responsibility. For example, one detailed occupation group in strong relative decline was 'rail signal operators and crossing keepers'. Such routine but responsible jobs tend to get displaced by information technologies. In contrast, low-skilled jobs that require non-routine tasks are less easily automated. Care assistants, for example, are among the most rapidly growing occupations in many countries: as populations age, there is more need for them, and robots (thankfully) cannot oblige. Rather than an unadulterated thesis of skill-biased technological change at all levels, therefore, the evidence is more in support of this nuanced version, which says that the productivity-enhancing bias is rendering some of the intermediate-skilled labour relatively less productive. It is in these areas that computerized processes have been introduced most rapidly.

A parallel argument applies to the demand for skill in industrialized countries arising from globalization. The extent to which production processes can be relocated to offshore production facilities depends on the nature of the process. Many routine processes that do not require customer interaction are also activities that could equally well be done in India as in the United States, and even some that do have a customer interface, such as call centre operations, can be offshored. Often it is the less routine activities that are also hard or impossible to relocate: the barber must be where the customer is and everyone is different.

In relative terms, therefore, in a period of intensive automation through computer technologies and when more activities are being relocated to low-wage countries, employment is expected to rise substantially at the top end of the skills spectrum relative to employment in intermediate-level jobs; at the lower end of the skills spectrum there will also be some, albeit lesser, increase in employment relative to those in the middle: an asymmetric polarization in the structure of employment. This has been the experience in the United States and across some European countries in recent decades.[45]

A sometimes-hidden and problematic assumption in this discussion needs to be noted—namely, that technological change is exogenous, a fount of extra knowledge that arrives from some alternative space. While such a story may be tenable from the perspective of most employers over a short enough horizon, in the long term technology can be influenced. In one approach developed from within economics, skill-biased technological change is endogenous, driven by the potential profitability of innovation and invention that takes advantage of a more skilled labour force.[46] Analysis from feminist sociology suggests that technology use and processes of innovation have aspects that are socially constructed and gendered.[47] As noted above, technological change may also be induced through exposure to global competition.

Management practice

Though technological change is an important factor underlying the changing demand for skill, decisions taken by managers about how to organize their production sites are also of significance. To some extent, these decisions are themselves affected by the available technology, but the managerial cultures and strategies that emerge are not predetermined by technological imperatives. There is scope for managerial choice to play a role in determining the route to company growth. Especially relevant is the approach taken by managers to involve their employees in the organization at all levels, as noted above. Secular trends in the approach to employee involvement influence employers' demand for several interaction skills: rises in the uses of communication and influence skills, for example, are associated with an increased use of employee involvement practices, effects that are independent of the technology.[48] Internal organizational changes are a general source of ongoing changing demand for skills.

Aggregate indicators of change in managers' practices are scarce because there has been a failure to collect the relevant data; but the prevalence of organizational change is hardly in doubt. Survey series and subjective reports suggest modest expansions in the uses of high-involvement work practices, notably in forms of communication between management and non-managerial workers.[49] The trends in job design, however, have been mixed. While across Europe as a whole there has been muted change in indicators of task discretion, during the 1990s there was a sharp decline in Britain across all sectors. In the United States, by contrast, there is evidence of an increase over the long interval from 1977 to 2002, though at what stage this increase took place is unknown.[50] Sometimes the term 'deskilling' is taken to refer to diminishing worker control, rather than to falling skill; with that meaning, there are regions and cases in support.

Industrial demand

Changing product demand is an additional source of change in the demand for skilled labour as tastes change, incomes grow, and populations age. With these, the industrial and sectoral composition of the economy evolves; projections of future industrial demand are part of the raw material for forecasts of changing skills demand.[51]

Anticipation of the industrial composition of the economy is a widespread tool for policy-makers but is especially pertinent where there exists a national industrial strategy. Largely eschewed in recent decades in liberal market economies like the United States and Britain, industrial policy is the parent of skills policy in East Asian economies. The remarkable transitions from underdevelopment to mass production and thence to high-value-added production systems Singapore, South Korea, Taiwan, and Hong Kong were fostered through an awareness of their implications for skills demand, and through substantial institutional transformations in vocational education and training to meet the growing needs. It was largely because of their success at foreseeing linkages with the demand side that these governments were able to match their economic miracles with equally radical structural transformations in their skill formation systems.[52]

Thinking about the future

This chapter has described factors underpinning employer skills demand and the evidence for, and reasons behind, increased demand. Taken overall, the evidence is strong that skills demand has been increasing throughout the industrialized world in the modern era. Changing technology as embodied in the computer and in the products of corporate science has been a key driver, supplemented and induced by global relocations of supply, by industrial demand shifts, and by some slow evolutions in management practices, especially with respect to work organization. Within the framework of strategic managerial decision-making under conditions of deep uncertainty, it has emerged that employers are significant independent actors in the determination of skilled work.

Recent forecasts continue to project rising skills demands overall (see Chapter 10), but whether these are accurate rests on especially uncertain scenarios for the determining factors. Uncertainty over globalization, not least the onset of climate change, potential food shortages with the expanding world population, and rising energy prices is problematic enough. Technological and managerial directions are equally hard to predict. One scenario suggests that a process of ongoing change and deepening (broadening deployment), rather than acceleration, is likely to characterize the next phase of development of digital technologies, and that there will be an increasing recognition among managers of the role of people in the generation of value.[53] The most likely skills scenario for the medium term is that employers will continue to demand higher-level skills in coming years. The expansion will be fuelled in part by an increasingly educated workforce, which will dampen rises, and perhaps induce falls, in the costs of graduate labour. Technology and new capital will continue to complement high-skilled labour, organizations will continue to innovate, and hence sustain the need for high-level communication and technical skills; while industrial demand will give rise to new skills such as those associated with the growing number of 'green' jobs in economies responding to climate change. With rising education levels and the global spread of industrialization, technologies, and forms of management, skilled work will no longer be confined to the traditional belt of northern nations.

Scenario projections, however, are uncertain and alternatives are plausible. Technology may not continue to be upskilling. There are also counteracting tendencies: consumer demand in ageing and unequal societies, for example, is likely to shift towards service industries that are not traditional users of high-skilled work. With such uncertainties, sophisticated tactics and methods for forecasting skills demands may need to be deployed widely by policy-makers.

Appendix. The basic economic model of skills demand

Shown in Figure 5A.1 is a standard diagram that captures the essence of the basic economic theory of demand for skilled labour. This appendix may be skipped by economics readers.

The curve shows the trade-off between two types of labour, high skilled (H) and low skilled (L), that are being used to produce a valued output. Along the curve, called an 'isoquant', it is assumed that a given quantity of the output is being delivered, but that one can do so with more or less skilled labour. If the firm reduces low-skilled labour by one unit, it must increase its use of high-skilled labour by the ratio MP_L/MP_H in order to keep to the same output, where MP_L is the marginal product of low-skilled labour and MP_H is the marginal product of high-skilled labour. Thus the steepness or slope of the isoquant is $-MP_L/MP_H$ (the negative sign recognizes that the isoquant is downward sloping).

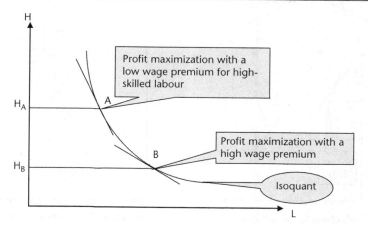

Figure 5A.1. An isoquant for high-skilled and low-skilled labour

The elasticity of substitution between high-skilled and low-skilled labour is a key parameter, because it helps to determine what happens to demand if one type of labour becomes more productive. The elasticity of substitution is defined as the proportional change in the ratio of the inputs of high-skilled and low-skilled labour, divided by the proportional change in the slope of the isoquant. The more sharply the isoquant is convex curved (i.e. the greater the proportional change in its slope), the lower is the elasticity of substitution.

Algebraically, the elasticity of substitution is:

$$\frac{\text{The proportionate change in the ratio of inputs}}{\text{The proportionate change in the slope of the isoquant}} = \frac{dH/dL}{H/L} \div \frac{dMP_H/dMP_L}{MP_H/MP_L}$$

Consider now the simple case of an employer whose aim is to maximize profits while producing a given output. The employer will choose the mix of high-skilled and low-skilled labour to produce that output at least cost. With the optimum choice it should not be possible to switch between the two types of labour and save money. Note now that the cost saved from using one unit less of low-skilled labour is indicated by its wage rate, W_L. At the optimum this must equal the extra cost of the high-skilled labour, equal to W_H times the ratio MP_L/MP_H, where W_H is the unit cost of the high-skilled labour:

$$W_L = W_H \, MP_L \big/ MP_H$$

It follows that the wage premium for high-skilled labour, W_H/W_L, equals the ratio of the marginal products, MP_H/MP_L. This profit-maximizing condition is just a logical deduction from the assumption of profit maximization: if it did not hold, it would be possible to lower costs by changing the proportions of

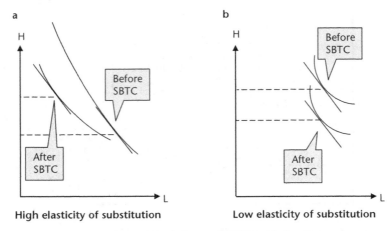

Figure 5A.2. Skill-biased technological change (SBTC) with fixed output

high-skilled and low-skilled labour. The wage premium is shown by a straight line in the diagram, depicting the constant cost trade-off between high-skilled and low-skilled labour. Point A shows a possible optimum, with high-skilled labour demand H_A, where the straight line is a tangent to the isoquant: in other words, the wage premium is equal to the slope of the isoquant at this point.

The relationship between the demand for skilled labour and the relative wage is also illustrated on Figure 5A.1. Point B shows another optimum, where the wage premium for skilled labour is relatively higher than before; the consequence is that the demand for skilled labour, H_B, is lower. In other words, the demand for skilled labour falls when its relative wage rises. The elasticity of demand for skilled labour is an important parameter because of its implications for the distribution of wages as supplies and demands interact. Estimates show that the elasticity of demand for labour increases with the skill level.[54]

Possible outcomes of skill-biased technological change are shown in Figure 5A.2, again for the case where the inputs can be varied but the output is assumed fixed. In both parts of this figure a technological change is assumed that causes high-skilled labour to become more productive, while low-skilled labour's productivity is unaltered; this is illustrated by the isoquant shifting downwards and becoming flatter. With the relative wage rate unchanged, Figure 5A.2a illustrates an outcome where high-skilled labour is substituted for low-skilled labour to such an extent that the demand for high-skilled labour has increased. A key feature that generates this outcome is the assumed high substitutability between high-skilled and low-skilled labour, shown by the relatively straight isoquants. If the elasticity of substitution were low, by contrast, as illustrated in Figure 5A.2b with more sharply curved isoquants, employers would lower their demand for both high-skilled and low-skilled labour.

6

Employers and Skill Formation

The importance of work for skill formation

If skills are so important for employers, and if they have accordingly been demanding ever higher skills from their workers, their fate lies in their own hands: they are, at the same time, actors who can augment the skills supply that they themselves will deploy. Though prior education and training are needed—sometimes for relevant knowledge and attitudes, always for enhancing the facility for acquiring further skills—the formation of skills through work, through training, and through everyday activities is extremely important. Done well, skills acquisition at work is effective and hard or impossible to substitute through other channels.

The efficacy of skill formation at the workplace is shown in the relatively recent development of understanding about the value of 'situated learning'— that is, through learning in communities of practice.[1] The theory of 'learning organizations' promotes the virtues of job rotation, inter-divisional teams, delegation of responsibilities, short hierarchies, and high levels of communication within and between levels. These characteristics contribute towards the creation of firms' dynamic capabilities.[2] Linking these ideas with a broader political economy approach, the 'Working as Learning Framework', shows not only the importance of informal learning processes, but also that these processes are quite heterogeneous across workplaces, and vary a great deal in their efficiency. Some organizations develop 'expansive', others 'restrictive', learning environments; the course they take depends on a complex web of associations with the wider productive system of power relationships and institutions in which organizations operate.[3] Thus, it is not merely the amount of work experience that counts: the extent of training, its utilization, and the quality of the learning environment are crucial. The implication for policy-makers is that, much as one might try to perfect a country's education system, it will still be an inadequate skill system if the workplace is neglected.

The significance of skill formation at work is not easy to demonstrate with quantitative evidence that would allocate the precise extent to which each skill is obtained through work as opposed to elsewhere. Most skills are acquired through sequenced interactive processes at multiple sites, including home, school, college, and workplace. Nevertheless, several pieces of evidence are indicative of the importance of the workplace:

- In a representative survey of workers in thirty-four countries across Europe, as many as two-thirds (67 per cent) reported in 2010 that their jobs required them to 'keep learning new things'. In the United States in the same year, the proportion was 87 per cent. Such high proportions are common findings from surveys. The prevalence of a learning requirement is normally greater in more skilled occupations, but it also differs across countries, even in similar occupations. The full European range is from 50 per cent in Lithuania to 91 per cent in Sweden.[4] Variations in the nature of the work environment appear to make a large difference to whether learning is required to take place.

- When employees are asked where they acquired particular skills, the knowledge they gained from education is likely to be understated. Nevertheless, the workplace typically assumes major importance. In respect of computing, a skill that is widely taught in schools and colleges, workers in a recent survey pointed largely to their jobs as the source of their computing skills: 50 per cent cited formal training at work, followed by help from colleagues (48 per cent), practice at work (46 per cent), practice at home (41 per cent), and watching others at work (32 per cent). Full-time education came way down at 15 per cent.[5]

- A gauge of the importance that employers themselves attach to skill formation is the amount they spend on it. The full amount of resources is hard to capture, but one lower-bound indicator is the amount devoted to formal continuing vocational training—that is, training for those with work contracts as opposed to traineeships or apprenticeships. In 2005 across all enterprises in the European Union's fifteen older member states, a third of all employees took part, each participant having an average 27 hours of training during the year, at a cost amounting to approximately 1.6 per cent of labour cost.[6]

- Formal education and training typically provide only a limited, explanation for pay. In earnings regressions, variations in education and training are the most important set of variables, but they typically account for much less than half the variation in pay. Length of work experience also contributes but to a varying extent. This heterogeneity and the large residual of unexplained pay leaves space for hypothesizing that variations in the character of workplaces, including their learning environments, will be important in affecting both skills and pay.

A theoretical framework for skill formation by employers

A framework is, therefore, needed for understanding the decisions that employers make about fostering skills formation at their workplaces. As we shall see, both conventional economic theory and the managerial perspective show that there are fundamental problems behind these decisions, implying that some employers will fail to provide for as much skill formation as could be desirable for their own or for the social benefit. Given the importance of the employer as provider of skill formation services, a role for social actors in potentially addressing the undersupply of employer-based skill formation is apparent. Also considered are the roles of collective associations of employers, sometimes alongside trade unions, in addressing some of these problems.

A conventional account

From a mainstream economic perspective, the analysis of training decisions is relatively straightforward. Suppose that the investment is gauged by a metric of training days, and consider the benefits and the costs of training. The benefits to an employer of its employees acquiring more skills are those underlying the demand for skills, discussed in the previous chapter. The better-trained worker will have a higher marginal productivity and hence the future profit gain is this extra productivity net of any increase in the wage paid. The marginal benefit of an additional training day is the net future gain discounted to the present. It is a reasonable presumption that, beyond a certain point, the marginal benefit falls as the number of days rises.

Costs arise from the forgone production of trainees and company trainers, and any fees to external trainers. The organization and delivery of training entail fixed costs, such as for curriculum design, and variable costs, such as for teaching and assessment. The marginal cost, which is the additional cost of one more training day, is likely to increase beyond a certain point, since it becomes progressively more costly to spare workers from production as they do more training.

With marginal benefits falling and marginal costs rising, there will be a point of intersection at which the marginal benefits equal the marginal costs. The profit-maximizing employer will decide on the number of training days at this intersection—another deduction that can be proved by contradiction. If, for example, marginal benefits were greater than marginal costs, profits could be raised by increasing the number of training days—and vice versa. An exception to the rule happens only in cases where the marginal benefit is less than the marginal cost whatever the level of training: in such cases no training will take place.

This analysis becomes insightful when one asks: what is the effect of changing benefits and costs? Within this simple framework, anything that raises the marginal benefits of training at each level would raise the amount of training at the intersection point. One example is that benefits could be greater for higher-level occupations, since job-holders are more likely to be faced with the necessity of acquiring new skills. In a very wide range of studies, it is universally found that jobs in higher-level occupations carry greater exposure to ongoing training. Another example looks at industries: employers' training benefits are predicted and found to be greatest in those sectors where technological change is known to be high.

On the other hand, anything that lowers the employers' marginal cost would also raise the amount of training decided upon. A prime example is the positive relationship between training and size of establishment, another widespread finding. Smaller employers cannot access training at the same price as larger employers, not least because the costs of withdrawing employees from the work station are raised by the difficulty of temporary replacement when the numbers of workers are low.[7]

The analysis becomes more sophisticated when one looks at costs and benefits in realistic settings that managers face. Since future productivity gains and business conditions are uncertain, managers' attitudes towards the future—their horizons and their expectations—are central in determining their decisions on skill formation. A 'short-termist' managerial approach, for example, is characterized by a tendency heavily to discount future benefits; a 'pessimist' approach derives from unrealistically low expectations of the future benefits of learning. A shift from pessimistic to more optimistic expectations, or from short-termism to having a longer-term horizon, is represented by an outward shift in the marginal benefit curve, in which case the firm is likely to decide to devote more to learning.[8]

An important source of uncertainty about future productivity is whether the trained employee will remain with the employer. The main determinants of the likelihood of someone staying are the wages to be paid, compared with the wages offered by competitors. Another aspect is whether the workplace is unionized. Trade unions provide a collective voice for workers' issues and needs to be represented before managers. Workers who might otherwise have no choice other than to leave for another employer might stay if their needs can be 'voiced' and responded to. Similarly, if local unions bargain up the wages of trained workers, this also reduces the probability of workers' quitting. As is widely found, unionized workforces are more stable. This allows a longer time horizon for the benefits of training to be realized—most, though not all, studies find that unionized workplaces undertake more training than non-union workplaces.[9] Yet, whatever the environment, there remains an element of chance, driven by each worker's personal circumstances. It is the potential for the employee to quit that provides, from the economics perspective, the fundamental constraint on employers' decisions to provide training and learning.

The complication addressed by neoclassical economist Becker in Human Capital, his exposition of training theory, is that workplaces have both characteristics in common and idiosyncratic features. Thus some skills are 'general': they can generate higher value wherever they are applied. One example might be word-processing skills. Another might be the craft skills generated through apprenticeship in a general trade such as carpentry. In such cases, with a freely competitive labour market, workers can bid up their wages to the going rate. The marginal benefit to employers, therefore, is driven down to zero, so in a competitive world they would not supply this training opportunity unless the marginal cost is also reduced to zero; for this to happen the trainees/apprentices must meet the whole cost, which would involve them paying fees and taking reduced wages below what they could earn elsewhere as untrained workers. The employee, then, bears the cost of the investment and receives all the rewards. Other skills are 'firm-specific', raising workers' productivity in the place where they are acquired but not elsewhere. This situation is exemplified by the skills for handling proprietary machinery not used by any other company, or in 'knowing your way round' the organization you work for. In such cases the training costs and benefits are likely to be shared between worker and employer.[10]

As subsequent writers have shown, however, Becker's analysis oversimplifies matters. Most skills are transferable among employers to some extent, but not 'general'. This fact implies that workers are unable to gain the full wage increase warranted by their increased skills, thus giving the employer an incentive to invest.[11] Where wages are compressed by trade union or social intervention, this also reduces the incentive for workers to invest and provides one for the employer.[12] Training that both engenders new skills and acts as a signal to employees of the good intentions of the employer, and which thereby garner employees' affective commitment to the firm, also acquires the character of reduced transferability. In some cases mobility is restricted by asymmetric information: if outside employers are less able to judge the potential of workers whom they have not trained, the consequence can be 'adverse selection', whereby trained workers who quit are seen on average to be less productive than those who stay—this discourages quitting. Taken altogether, these conditions of partial transferability and/or wage compression obtain in most circumstances.

Therefore, it is normally employers who pay for transferable skills acquisition, with the direct costs and the wages of trainees summing to more than the value of what they are producing while being trained. Even in the intensive context of the German dual system, where the costs of apprenticeships over three years are substantial, the incentive logic is driven by compressed wages and limits on mobility, rather than by an emphasis on training for firm-specific skills.[13] Of course, employees may also bear part of the costs through accepting lower wages than they could get if they did not undertake training. Yet they may not be in a position to make informed decisions about skill acquisition (see next chapter). Studies of decision-making among younger employees suggest that identity may be more important than rational calculation in determining the skills decisions that youths take in their transitions to work.[14] In situations where employees contribute less than optimal resources to skill acquisition, employers have a further incentive to make up the gap.

Despite the employer paying for the acquisition of transferable skills, from the perspective of the whole industry or economy there will normally be too little learning going on. The possibility that their employees may quit reduces the amount of skill formation that employers decides upon, because some of the benefits will go to the other employers who hire the trained workers but do not have to pay the full value of their enhanced skills. Employers will want to limit their investment below the amount that would be warranted by the overall benefits and costs of the learning to the industry. The economy loses out in this way, and this market failure can be redressed only by some form of social intervention, including levies, subsidies, occupational licences, or standards-driven regulations.

The managerial approach

While this analysis of support for different types of training, given its transferability and the consequent potential of the worker to quit, has preoccupied the economic theory of training in recent decades, it has led to a restricted understanding of what employers do and how their attitudes and cultures can affect what sort of learning environment they foster. The typical approach of economics directs attention mainly to the results of optimizing the training decision; in so far as it looks at the tactics of affecting the marginal benefit and marginal cost curves, it focuses only on the implications of the degree of transferability and its interaction with labour market structure. In neglecting to look inside the 'black box' of the learning process, economics thus professes an idealist view of the decision processes that employers undertake, which conditions their view of the social interventions that might follow.

By contrast, the managerial approach examines the ways that the marginal benefits can be improved through management policies to generate a learning environment for workers.[15] Evidence shows that training and learning opportunities are enhanced when various combinations of other high-involvement working practices are also adopted by management; when they are adopted, the quality of the training is likely to be greater.[16] In affording degrees of autonomy to their workers, firms are offering learning opportunities; in organizing work through teams, especially in semi-autonomous or autonomous teams, employees learn while they are working. The marginal cost of an hour spent learning is lowered if it can be done while producing something, a procedure that is often achievable through proper work design. The marginal benefit is raised if more or better skills are acquired, and if opportunities are given to utilize new skills. Firms that organize work in this way become 'learning organizations'. Equally, decisions about training are affected by the different beliefs about the efficacy of learning new skills, and about their impacts on the future productivity of the organization.[17] As we have seen, these beliefs are affected by the optimism of managers, underpinning which is their capability for correctly modelling the advantages and costs of learning activities.

Training advocates unsurprisingly hypothesize that some groups of managers have insufficient appreciation of the benefits of learning and therefore underestimate the net value of skills acquisition, and so both learning and the utilization of skills are too low for the good of their organizations.[18] This undervaluation of workplace learning and associated practices is used to account for the piecemeal adoption of high-productivity HRM systems, including High Involvement Work Practices, despite their superior performance delivery.[19] Undertaking too little training can also be seen as consistent with loss aversion behaviour in Prospect Theory and with the hypothesis of short-termism.[20] The opposite case is also possible—some employers might be too optimistic about training for their own good, incurring too high costs—though no cases have been identified where reductions in training are associated with better performance.

The influence of managerial cultures and norms on skill formation is nowhere more evident than in the very large and persistent differences across countries in the amount of training that employers decide to support. In 1999, for example, enterprises in Denmark spent 3.0 per cent of labour costs on training compared with 1.6 per cent in Belgium and as little as 0.9 per cent in Greece; similar stark contrasts occur within the same industries and size classes. These enterprise cultural differences are, in turn, prime drivers of the European cross-country variation in access to training.[21]

Collective skill formation

Consumers tend to be wary when employers get together, but when employers cooperate informally or formally over learning there are several potential arguments in favour. Formal inter-firm training collaboration has only a sporadic presence in many countries, being reported at various points in the United States, the United Kingdom, Japan, Italy, and Australia. Collective skill formation takes its most formal aspect in the corporatist countries of northern Europe. Informal alliances in clusters and value chains are more widespread.

The informal relationships that arise in everyday trading and problem-solving activities, sometimes within distinct industrial and regional clusters, or within value chains, are also an important source of collective learning. Individual learning and the collective learning of organizations occur through active participation in these relationships within occupational communities of practice, or through collective participation by firms in activities that glean new ideas. The skills acquired in these ways are unlikely to be certified yet may be an especially important accompaniment of incremental innovations and economic growth.[22]

Formal employer training collectives can secure economies of scale in core processes, including both technical and design functions. Such economies may be especially relevant for small and medium-sized enterprises that do not on their own have the resources to devise curricula, set standards, promote courses, and hire the expensive equipment needed for substantive initial training of young workers. For the provision of training services, collectives can also negotiate directly with external providers to secure better value. Collectives devoted to training may also be able to deliver a more holistic, strategic approach to training, coupled with a long-term perspective, than individual companies can find for themselves.[23]

At a more complex level characteristic of the corporatist organization of labour markets, employers' chambers and collectives have additional functions:

- They act as socializing institutions that can internalize the externalities of transferable training through incentives and sanctions of members, thereby maintaining a supply of skilled workers. In this social intervention they are, it is argued, more efficient than national government, since associations can maintain their close links with, and be more responsive to, employers. They can also negotiate directly with external providers. In these functions employers' collectives are supported by the circulation of information that helps to secure the transparency and, over time, the trust needed to persuade private employers of the value to be gained from their ongoing membership; at the same time they enable the exaction of sanctions (such as the withdrawal of services) from firms that do not cooperate. Training young workers through apprenticeships can thus be maintained as an obligation of membership. The resilience of this system of mutual gains, with all employers in an industry benefiting from having a greater stock of trained workers, is the essence of the 'dual' system found in Germany and similar corporatist countries.

- In these functions, collective employers' associations are reinforced if they are also involved in bargaining, or at least consultation, with trade unions. For a union's presence to make itself felt in influencing skills formation, the bargaining need not concern whether or not the unions' members have access to training. Such bargaining is a rare phenomenon. Rather, unions in corporatist systems have an especially important role in the monitoring and development of training standards. The importance of quality control cascades from unions' primary function, the negotiation of wages and conditions. For private employers to participate fully they need the incentive of low costs, so that apprentices' low productivity can be borne without threatening costs too much. So an essential cog in the dual system is an assured supply of committed and able students, willing to work for lower wages than they could obtain elsewhere. The *quid pro quo* of the lower wage for young workers is access to good-quality training, which may be better guaranteed by their unions than by employers who could have the incentive to 'cheat' by lowering training quality. Unions' attentions, in this respect, focus on both training depth and its breadth, ensuring the inclusion of transferable skills development. Such guarantees can be delivered, both through participation in collective training design and through helping to sanction non-cooperative employers.

- The information-circulation function of employers' associations is also a part of their education function, in which employers learn, through participation in group training institutions, about both the productivity of training and the pay-offs of the cooperation in which they are engaged.[24]

Despite these advantages, attempts to corral employers into an association often fail, owing to the heterogeneity among employers' interests, the impossibility of compulsion, and the limited extent to which employers can be sanctioned for non-cooperation. Moreover, the persistence of existing associations is not guaranteed, since employers have incentives to reduce their cooperation, or even withdraw, if they come to perceive insufficient economies of scale, a fall in the benefits of cooperation, or few opportunities for learning. Their stability is potentially threatened by changes in related institutions (such as the strength of trade unions and the governance of banks), and by cleavages among the interests of employers, notably between small and large companies, and by the rise of neo-liberal ideology with its emphasis on individualism.[25] Although such possibilities fuel periodic concern for the stability of the training function of employers' associations, its persistence in the face of such threats affords some testimony to the considerable benefits of collective organization.[26]

The consequences of employers' dual functions

Work organizations not only create goods and services; they are also major potential sources of learning. Moreover, much of the learning they provide can *only* be acquired at work. The peculiar position of employers, as both the demanders of skilled labour and the necessary suppliers of skill formation services, combined with the demonstrated high importance of skill as a determinant of economic and wider performance, means that employers are crucial agents whose decisions and behaviours drive the generation and utilization of skill in the economy. Where there has been an increasing demand for skilled labour, it is likely that a substantive (though not necessarily increasing) volume of workplace learning has taken place, more than enough to counteract skill losses through ageing, quits, and retirements. As has been noted, a large volume of employer-provided training takes place in some countries, but the amount is highly variable.

This chapter has delved into the two sets of issues that the employers' peculiar position gives rise to. On the one hand, the fact that employers cannot compel their employees to remain with them diminishes their incentive to support skill formation. Nevertheless, the rigidities of markets and institutional constraints, together with strategies to enhance employee commitment, have been shown to yield some ways around this fundamental dilemma. On the other hand, the potential for some managers to opt for relatively low levels of skills demand is paralleled by a pessimistic attitude to skill formation. From the perspective of the private interests of the companies' shareholders, the managerial perspective implies that some managers will plan for too low a level of skill, given their circumstances. They do this partly because they do not have the capacity, given the history of relationships and skills in the company, to introduce high-involvement working practices that would entail redesigning jobs, granting workers more autonomy, and inducing commitment from employees. Their strategies can be developed only with bounded rationality about their current and future circumstances. Marginal changes in the direction of a better work organization may not lead to reinforcement, so some employers can become entrenched in a low skills trap. A low demand for skilled labour, therefore, adds to the potential for training to be set at low levels. Ambitions in the two articulated markets are merged for better or for worse.

From the perspective of society, it would be better if employers that use and generate skills at low levels could be incentivized or otherwise persuaded to raise both. The managerial perspective suggests that many of these could achieve greater profit outcomes over time as a result. Labour market imperfections also mean that, even if all employers were able to arrive at privately optimal decisions, there remains a systemic market failure: some of the gains from skill acquisition through learning opportunities with the employer are claimed by other employers who take on those employees who leave.

To both these sets of issues, collective organization of employers offers a potential partial resolution. Collectives enable externalities to be internalized, and offer the platforms and networks for trust-building and for learning about the benefits of high-skill strategies. Yet they require agreements to be negotiated and sanctioned, and work best when supported by trades unions. Whether governments can play a substitute social role, through incentives, subsidies, and regulations, depends in part on the relative efficiency of government in comparison with private organizations. Arguments surrounding the rationales for social interventions will be taken up in Chapter 9.

7

Skilled Workers for Skilled Work

Sources of skills

This chapter examines the motives and behaviours of the other main actors in the markets for skilled labour and skill formation services, the workers themselves. The skills being their own, workers are *ipso facto* at the centre of the analysis. If skilled work is to become a pervasive experience in modern societies, workers must be able, available, and willing to do it.

As young people arrive at adult working life, they will have acquired their skills from multiple institutions—families, schools, colleges, and through early work experiences—and different skill domains are variously associated with each site. From families and schools people gain both cognitive skills and attitudes, while colleges and universities vary across the academic–vocational spectrum. Yet the qualities that these institutions help to instil are not just skills for work. Indeed, the aims of education are contested, and the dilemmas surrounding work attitudes as skills are mirrored in potential contradictions in schools and universities between economistic and educational values, between conformity and creativity, or between protest and compliance.

The modern era has witnessed profound changes in these institutions, some with skills implications. Rising divorce rates and associated family instability, for example, might be thought to be a threat to the supplies of future skilled workers. Yet any such negative trends have been more than matched by the ubiquitous expansion of education at all levels, including pre-school institutions. Academic achievements are increasing almost everywhere, in countries rich and poor, while each generation spends more time in school than the previous one, traversing longer periods of 'emerging adulthood', on the way to a hopefully more settled adult identity. Competitive pressures of globalization on nation states have transformed the discourse on education policy, making it an aspect of economic policy, and raising the stakes; education has furthermore become the natural travelling companion of a long-term, if sporadic, rise in the politics of democracy and equal opportunity.

If adult populations are now more educated, what influences them to apply their skills in paid work, and what determines that they have a demand for learning so that they can do more skilled work in the future? The chapter sets out a socio-economic framework for addressing each of these questions about how people come to supply skilled labour power—their potential and willingness to do skilled work—to the market. The issue involves several related fields of enquiry, and both of the articulated markets for skills and skill formation services set out in Chapter 3. In advanced capitalist society people decide for themselves but are oriented by institutions and by socio-economic relationships that affect their perceived opportunities, their preferences, and their capacity to make life course investments. Social class, family, school, gender, ethnicity, labour market institutions, and the macroeconomic environment all condition the demand for learning. Even in a post-traditional society, where workers confronting uncertainty develop 'reflexivity', freedoms are serially bounded. The constraints are cumulative, in that the kind of work and learning opportunities that people can strive for are limited by those they have previously taken up: the tracks off the road not travelled are seldom reached.

Skill and labour supply

The motive underpinning the supply of skilled labour is to earn a living and if possible to experience the satisfactions of skilled work. There are substantive choices to be made about when to start a life of paid work, when to interrupt it or retire, and about how many hours to work each week. The quantity of available skilled labour from any population will depend upon these choices.

Going to work means giving up whatever one could be doing otherwise during work time. The decision to participate in the labour market therefore focuses on the trade-off between the value of working and the value of other possible activities, be they domestic, leisure, or educational. The same trade-off characterizes the marginal decision—whether or not to take on an extra hour's work. Historically the significant twentieth-century developments affecting this trade-off included the cleaning, domestic, and textile technologies that have displaced routine domestic labour, the changing family norms that structure the costs of not working, and the rise of service jobs. All these factors have fundamentally altered the balance between paid work and other activities, especially for women: in most countries, men's hours of work declined over the long term through the twentieth century, while in all industrialized countries women increased their share in the paid labour force.

Also potentially important, however, are the increasing educational levels achieved by both men and women. The rise in education not only increases the stock of skills in the population, but also affects the proportion of the population that participate in the labour market, and their weekly hours. For each person the propensity to supply labour is affected by the 'skills premium'—the monetary and non-monetary rewards of high-skilled work relative to those of low-skilled work—attached to the jobs he or she can perform competently.

The theoretical effect is ambivalent. More education raises the potential wage rate, the chief variable of interest in many economics studies of labour supply dating back to the beginnings of neoclassical economics in the 1870s.[1] Pay has a theoretically indeterminate effect on labour force participation and on hours of work. On the one hand, a higher wage makes it more worthwhile to do paid work (or, in other words, more costly to stay away from it)—termed the 'substitution effect'. On the other hand, a higher wage also increases income, enabling a worker to 'buy' more non-work time if desired—this is termed the 'income effect'. If the substitution effect is greater than the income effect, a rise in wages increases participation and hours, and vice versa. It is an empirical issue, and one can expect the overall impact to be positive for some workers, negative for others, and for many to be low and insignificant if the two effects roughly cancel each other out. Two findings from a large research literature can illustrate this heterogeneity. For male New York taxi-drivers, the long-run hours–wage elasticity in the 1990s and 2000s is estimated to have been -0.2 (meaning that a 10 per cent rise in pay leads them to cut their hours of work by 2 per cent); by contrast, among married women in the 1990s in Hungary, a transitional economy, the participation elasticity is found to be +1.8 (a wage rise of 10 per cent leads to an 18 per cent rise in the participation rate).[2] In short, the indirect impact of skill on labour supply, via wages, is theoretically indeterminate and empirically varies from case to case.

Yet being more skilled can also have a direct impact on participation, other than through any effect that skill has on the potential wage rate. If skilled work is more fulfilling, other things being equal, this changes the balance between work and other activities. Relatively speaking, work becomes more attractive for those who can gain skilled work. Other things are not always equal, of course. Many jobs have simultaneously high skill and effort demands.[3] Other correlates of skill make skilled work even more attractive. Skilled workers are typically afforded more personal discretion in the organization of their jobs, and where this happens it moderates the pressures of hard work.[4]

What, then, does the evidence tell us about the overall effect of skill on labour supply? Undoubtedly the labour market participation rate of those with better education is higher than for the less educated, and the effect is found to be quite substantial. To take two practical illustrations: in a study of Italian women in their twenties and thirties in 1993, it was found that highly educated women postponed fertility and were very much more likely to participate in the labour market; a more recent Australian study found that women with at least a university degree are 17 percentage points more likely to participate in the labour force than those with Year 11 qualifications.[5] In short, having a more skilled population increases the supply of skilled labour, not only because the share of skills in the population is higher but also because the contribution of that population to paid work rises. This increased contribution arises because of the fulfilment of participating in more skilled work, and an ambivalent effect of higher wages.

This empirical relationship between skill and participation underpins the idea that strategies to raise the employment rate in industrialized countries should incorporate policies to improve both population skills and the opportunity to do skilled work. To address the financial consequences of increased longevity, for example, persuading increasingly well-educated workers to retire later may be easier if work becomes a more attractive and fulfilling option.

Framing workers' demand for skill formation services (the 'demand for learning')

While workers are suppliers in the market for skilled labour, they are situated on the demand side in the market for skill formation services. How and why do people come to try to acquire more skills? There is an evident benefit for people to learn the skills that can give them access to skilled work, which is attractive both for its pay premium and for its offer of greater fulfilment; this incentive underpins the demand for learning. There are also costs. Sometimes there circulates the idea of effortless superiority: the view that certain people have, through their genetic inheritance, such high and exquisite faculties that they can do what they do with little prior exertion. Yet almost always effortless skilled performance is an illusion: it becomes part of the display that the performance is laced with ease and needs no perspiration, concealing the great devotion that has gone into learning, practice, and preparation. Learning comes free of effort for no one, not even for the greatest geniuses of artistic, sporting, and intellectual endeavour. The personal costs are the most valued alternative activities that could have been undertaken instead, and may also include course fees and expenses. A substantial, if variable, amount of work-related learning takes place at work, in which case the time cost is not borne by the employee. Yet there may be a cost in lower wages and greater effort from choosing an employer that offers good learning opportunities. In the case of apprenticeships within the German dual system, for example, it has been computed that workers' share of the costs is as much as 72 per cent. Similarly, a worker's choice of a firm with 'high performance work practices' including enhanced learning opportunities must be set against the greater work intensity.[6]

This section discusses how workers balance the incentives and costs of learning. It argues that people's decisions and behaviours are driven by a complex process that entails not just benefits and costs, but an interdependent system of beliefs, resources, and dispositions surrounding learning, which is not yet fully understood in social science.

The simple model of benefits and costs

At first sight the process used by people to plan their demand for learning appears to be simple: a balancing of the benefits of skill acquisition—the access to skilled work and its skills premium—against the costs. Against the objection that some courses are embarked upon, not for economic rewards, but for their wider benefits (for example, the satisfaction from learning to make and appreciate music), the values of such alternative preferences can be added into the assessment. Since most of the benefits come in the future, learning is like any investment. Sometimes, using the language of investment, studies refer to the skills premium incorrectly as the rate of return from a skills investment. This is misleading, since to calculate a rate of return it is necessary to estimate and include, not only the benefits for every year in the coming life span, but also the costs.

According to the life-cycle model of education and training that is central for mainstream economics, people are thought continually to plan their learning of work skills, using the benefit–cost framework. The value of the benefits is the sum of the benefits expected each year over the remaining life span. Typically, it is assumed that people discount future benefits: the discount is given by their 'time preference', which describes how they value the present compared with the future, with a lower 'time preference' meaning that people care more about their long-term prospects. The reason for valuing the future less than the present is typically taken to be either myopia (an assumption that sits rather uncomfortably in a rational-actor framework) or risk that is presumed to increase with a longer horizon.

The marginal benefit (the increment to the value of the benefits from an extra unit input of learning), though positive, is assumed to fall as the intensity of learning is increased. The marginal cost of learning is assumed to rise along the same axis. Therefore two outcomes are possible. One is that there will be some positive optimal amount of learning where the marginal benefit intersects with the marginal cost, thus giving the individual's optimal amount of learning. A second possible outcome arises when the marginal cost exceeds the marginal benefits at all positive levels; in that situation, the optimal amount of learning is none. This process is the individual's equivalent to the employer's optimization of training described in the previous chapter, with the difference that individuals plan their own lives and are not obliged to stay working for the same employer in future.

This 'rational investment' model of learning leads to certain predictions:

- the costs of learning relative to the benefits are central:[7]
  - Anything that lowers the marginal cost of learning, while not altering the benefits, will raise investment in learning. Education subsidies that compensate parents for losses in children's earnings, for example, stimulate school attendance: a remarkable Mexican government programme begun in 1998 demonstrated the efficacy of such subsidies. As a second example, the transportation costs of reaching a place of learning significantly affect whether people judge the learning to be worthwhile.
  - For the same costs, enrolments and learning are likely to be higher where the expected benefits are greater. For example, learning will on average diminish with age, because the time span in which the benefits can be reaped decreases. Studies in Canada and elsewhere support this prediction. There is also direct evidence that choices follow the skills premium: for example, enrolments in higher education in the Netherlands have been found to be correlated with future earnings expectations; in Britain, students choose subjects to get good jobs as well as for intrinsic reasons of interest.
- Those with a high future discount rate will plan on less learning because for them the same future premiums will have lower marginal (discounted) benefits. Yet formal evidence is scarce. One way of measuring a person's discount rate is through smoking behaviour, the idea being that smoking indicates a relatively low valuation of the future, especially for those growing up in an era when the health risks were widely known. A study in Austria reported, for example, that smoking at 16 was associated with nearly half a year's less schooling, even after controlling for other relevant factors.

Thus the basic rational investment model has a plausible track record of explanation in these areas; it affords a rationale for studying the skills premium. The model shows the importance of studying the financial incentive structures surrounding learning, and implies that subsidies may have some success in affecting learning decisions. Indeed, it would be unwise to suppose that learners are immune to incentives.

Yet the fact that incentives have *some* effect does not justify resting on the laurels of individual rationality: incentives and costs explain only part of the differences in learning behaviour among individuals between and across societies. The apparent simplicity of the comparison between current costs and future benefits belies the complexity of how people form a demand for learning.

The complexity lies, on the one hand, in the uncertainty that surrounds the investment, and, on the other hand, in the relationships among people's beliefs, resources, preferences, and experiences, which together govern the choices that individuals make.

The uncertainty surrounding learning

It could be tempting to trivialize the uncertainty surrounding learning decisions, merely assigning each one a risk of failure (or of partial success). With some experience and advice, prospective applicants might acquire an unbiased assessment of the risk, and in a competitive learning market premia would emerge to compensate for greater risk. On average, a more risky learning strategy would then be predicted to receive a greater average return (after allowing for the probability of failure), in order to compensate learners who will predominantly be averse to risk. This framework could be a way of thinking about short-horizon, low-cost decisions, such as whether or not to go on a half-day training course.

Yet, even leaving aside the fact that markets for training and learning are far from perfectly competitive, the risk-adjusted benefit–cost perspective does not capture the character of the uncertainty that people face when deciding about acquiring skills. In most cases, learning decisions are looking at a long horizon, with multiple elements of uncertainty, where the information and capacity to assess subjective probabilities of success and failure are circumscribed and structurally affected by social context. These decisions are set in front of the linearity of the life course that each person treads. Many learning decisions are entwined with major life course transitions such as from youth through to adulthood, which can be prolonged, delayed, or accelerated, but only within bounds.[8] Generally, such transitions involve high-stakes decisions, where financial futures are being selected and personal identities forged through chosen occupations. Life course transition decisions are also irreversible: no one can turn back the clock to when they were younger, and only in the most flexible skill systems can one revisit and rectify education or job choices that have misfired.

This profound uncertainty for learners is composed of two elements, which may be termed 'learning uncertainty' and 'value uncertainty'. With the former, there is uncertainty over the extent to which a course of learning will generate the desired personal qualities. Low self-efficacy, which may differ according to gender and social class, can lead people to be unsure about whether they are capable of succeeding. Insufficient knowledge about the learning environment adds to the problem. The varied and contradictory roles of schools and colleges, preparing students for multiple roles in life, pile on the uncertainty about what kind of skills one is likely to acquire.

Value uncertainty concerns the value of the skills acquired. One might be confident enough in succeeding on a particular university course, but could still hesitate if the economic environment renders the value of the skills acquired highly risky. Approximate backward-looking estimates of the skills premium achieved from previous investment can be a guide, but these may be only loose forecasts of the future skills premium, which depends on how employers' demands, technology, and the economy evolve over a long horizon. Even where the rewards are judged to be sufficient *on average* to make it worth the sacrifices, any one individual may face considerable uncertainty about landing a job that utilizes and rewards the acquired skills.

The macroeconomic environment affects value uncertainty, employment insecurity being at its worst in low points of the business cycle. The uncertainty during high periods of unemployment tends to be channelled towards young people who are 'outsiders' in the labour market, disrupting school-to-work transitions. A person's life outside work also intrudes, placing spatial or domestic constraints on the ability to make use of the learned skills. There is also the potential uncertainty about the identities to be acquired when pursuing life transitions. Finding what one wants to become is possibly the greatest challenge that young people face. The uncertainty surrounding identity selection is reduced and managed by the norms that people are exposed to in their family and class origins.

Part of value uncertainty lies in the conceptual ambivalence about skills discussed in Chapter 2: work attitudes and productive dispositions are skills, but their values are inherently hard to assess when the prospective skills are to be embedded in conflictual and changing employment relationships. In some circumstances one might conceive of a deliberative approach to learning attitudes—such as the decision to follow an anger-management course. In other circumstances, processes of cultural learning will be structural, even if contested, rather than individually purposive. In Bowles and Gintis's sociological account of the evolution of education, the inter-generational transmission of cultural traits is conceived as an 'oblique' process in which students choose which skills to adopt and learn, driven by a circumscribed knowledge of the skills' labour market values as passed on by parents and teachers.[9]

Decision-making

This deep, multidimensional, uncertainty is one reason why the demand for skill acquisition should not be construed merely as a rational investment problem setting benefits against costs, and with calculable risks. Another reason is that beliefs about, and dispositions towards, the benefits and costs of learning need to be studied in their social context—these are endogenous variables shaped by the life course for which skill acquisition decisions are being made.

To establish an adequate framework, it is necessary to study, not only the incentives, but the full process through which people derive their demand to learn new skills. Researchers have to examine multiple interlocking factors: how people form their beliefs and perspectives on the future, their capacity to take decisions and to be forward-looking and to cope with uncertainty, the influence of social institutions including their family backgrounds, and the ways in which economic opportunities and barriers dislodge and distort the agency behind these decisions. Rather than the unidirectional simple structure of the cost–benefit model, with learning outcomes following from individuals' preferences and their rational beliefs about the opportunities they face, skill formation decisions in a deeply uncertain world may be pictured as a multi-causal framework with feedbacks, as shown in Figure 7.1.

At the centre of the diagram are three sets of factors that interact to form the demand for learning. The first set comprises beliefs about the benefits, costs, and constraints of skill formation. People form beliefs about the chances of each course of action achieving meaningful ends. Those beliefs may be influenced by (possibly biased) perceptions of past investments by others, by their

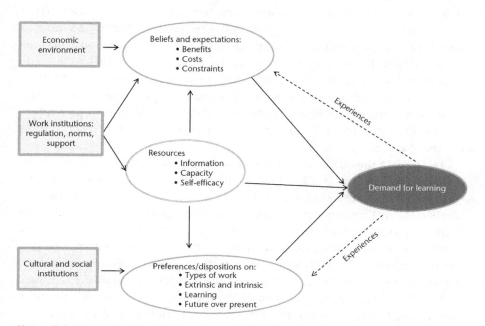

Figure 7.1. Framework for the formation of the demand for learning

own previous experiences of learning, and/or by their perspectives on economic and technological futures, and by their knowledge of the costs of participation. Facing deep uncertainty about learning, they cannot formulate unbiased probability distributions. They may, rather, deploy a bounded rationality, or sometimes also a heuristic, a rule of thumb, that makes use of available slices of information (such as, what parents or friends have done). Once this context is recognized, the door is open to psychological as well as economic explanations of attitudes, and to the possibilities of persuasion.

The extent of the bounded rationality—including how thoroughly past events are properly assessed—depends in part on the second set of factors that affect the demand for learning, people's resources (personal, family, and social) for deciding.[10] These resources include the available information about what life might be like during and after the course of learning. For training in a particular occupation, it could be an impression of future earnings; more generally, it may be a model of what a particular occupation involves. Resources also comprise people's capacities to process the information, to think outside the confines of close personal experiences, to assess and be strategic about future consequences, and to evaluate their own previous experiences of learning. Also included here is self-efficacy: the extent to which people expect that a course of learning will be effective for them and whether they feel in control of their learning and its consequences.[11]

The third set of factors comprises people's attitudes towards work and skills—preferences among, or dispositions towards, available actions. These include preferences over types of work and between the extrinsic and intrinsic aspects of work, dispositions towards learning for itself, aspirations and preference for the future over the present. To a large extent, preferences and dispositions are erected on a foundation of human needs, including the need for meaningful work. Some studies combine preferences and dispositions with personal resources. Including self-efficacy along with preferences and dispositions gives the concept of 'motivation'—the propensity to drive towards particular goals.[12]

The study of the effects of all three factors, as they combine to generate the demand for learning, is a key part of the research agenda. Studies are also considering the ways that each set of factors is itself influenced, and the feedback from learning experiences. The starting point for any causal chain is the economic environment in which skills are learned and utilized. The environment affects both the way in which things are learned and the prospective values of the skills when used in the workplace. Common contemporary factors are the pressures of competitiveness intensified by international competition, macroeconomic instability (notably the contemporary economic crisis), technological and organizational change, and ageing of the workforce. At the micro-level are the opportunities afforded by the local economy and the current workplace, and the constraints of a person's domestic circumstances. Any or all such factors contribute to a person's beliefs about the opportunities for skill formation, in so far as they impinge upon the costs, benefits, and personal constraints.

These beliefs are adapted and modified in the presence of a range of work-related institutions, also shown on the left side of the figure. Skill formation and wage-setting institutions, with the support sometimes of governments, can alter costs and benefits, whether through subsidies and levies, or through facilitating efficient provision. Workplace institutions—notably trade unions—may also affect behavioural norms and beliefs about the benefits of skill formation, while providing bargaining power and economic or social support, which contribute to personal resources.[13] The beliefs are also influenced by the resources that people have, in particular by the information that they have obtained or are provided with. For example, their beliefs about the economic value of training for a particular occupation will be influenced by the information they have about the wage premia experienced by previous participants in this training.

Also included is the role of cultural and social institutions (family, class, gender, and ethnicity) in directly affecting the preferences and dispositions that people form over work and skill. Social institutions also alter the resources with which families can be strategic about learning decisions, with evidence of significant class variation in the capacity to negotiate forward-looking education decisions.[14]

Research shows, too, the importance of feedback loops from previous experiences of learning, both on people's preferences or dispositions and on their beliefs about the opportunities they face.[15] The significance of feedback loops is that they lead to positive or negative reinforcements, one bad experience of learning, for example, leading to an avoidance of further attempts, and vice versa. One recent qualitative study demonstrated both negative and positive reinforcements: the former from bad experiences of school, the latter from good experiences in adult basic skills courses. Motivation, which can be the key driver behind the status transitions to be discussed below, also evolves from social experiences, sometimes through critical moments.

The causal sequences depicted by the arrows in Figure 7.1 take place against real time as people follow their trajectories through the life course.[16] The speed of feedback loops can be important, and, in the face of uncertainty, a common reaction is to opt for flexibility, so as not to narrow down future possibilities. This tactic often speaks in favour of academic, rather than vocational, options during education. Flexibility is also manifested, however, in the wait-and-see approach, in which learning courses are postponed; yet the scope for delay is limited as one grows older, especially when the institutional skill system is inflexible. For major transitions, prevarication means keeping identities fluid for an extended period and can undermine motivation. And then, to add more to the complication, history is not standing still: not only skill systems, but also the economic environment, change through periods comparable to the horizons over which people must contemplate their skill formation decisions.

The framework in Figure 7.1 provides a way of thinking about, researching, and intervening in the demand for learning in an uncertain world; ongoing research in different national and cultural settings can be expected to enrich knowledge about the relationships highlighted. Yet the framework is not a full theory in itself, since it is as yet too general to yield system-wide analyses and predictions that can be assessed against observations drawn from empirical research. The manner and strength of the relationships and feedbacks remain to be specified. One is, therefore, dealing here with a decidedly incomplete domain of social science, which could, if better developed, help researchers and policy-makers to understand and intervene more satisfactorily in the changing paths that people navigate through skill systems.

'Bounded agency' in the demand for learning

Set behind the relationships depicted in Figure 7.1 is an ancient controversy over the role of individuals in making their own independent decisions. How far does their demand for learning reflect what they want as individual agents rather than the effects of structural forces or of impersonal constraints on rational behaviour?

The concept of 'bounded agency' nicely sums up the complexities inherent in the framework.[17] The proposition is that individuals' environments and their previous experiences of learning affect, but do not uniquely determine, both their resources and their perceptions about the opportunities they have. Moreover, even though preferences are also socially influenced, agents are assumed to be individuals with independent minds and dispositions, again within social bounds. Provided that they have some personal resources, the choices of these individuals matter. The result is considerable variation in attitudes and choices. 'Bounded agency' directs attention to the strength and range of the social bounds, which can vary across countrie,s with different institutions governing skill formation; and helps to account for individuals' varying perceptions of success and failure in skill formation. Where it is perceived that opportunities for choice are prevalent, failure is the more easily attributable to the individual than to the rules of the system.

Bounded agency in skill formation is one formulation lying between the extremes of structural determination and agency. In the former, social class, gender, and ethnic identity in various ways are seen to constrain beliefs about opportunities to one or just a few channels for each socio-economic type. These structural forces restrict resources to the extent that individuals are seen as not having the capacity or information to make decisions for themselves, and to dominate and determine preferences with overwhelming force, leaving no room for individual variation within socio-economic groups. From this perspective, whether or not individuals appear to make their own choices, in reality they are not genuinely free agents. The primary evidence for this structural approach has always been the dramatic variations across social class, gender, and ethnicity in levels and channels of skill formation. However, contemporary sociology notes the relevance of reflexivity in several areas of social life, learning included, and, without advocating a 'free agent' model, takes the view that there are genuine possibilities in modern life for 'agentic' behaviour, in which people vary and take partial control of their careers.[18]

The opposite extreme—namely, that the individual is sovereign and that the outcomes must be understood as reflecting their heterogeneous attitudes to skill formation—might be seen as another special case of Figure 7.1. In this instance, the influence of cultural and social institutions is seen as minor and long term; feedbacks from experience to dispositions and motivations are downplayed or ignored. As well as removing those arrows, the extreme agency approach views the set of decision-making resources as unconstrained, and the beliefs about opportunities as expressible in quantitative and unbiased terms. One is effectively back in the world where the theory of the demand for learning is a simple benefit–cost analysis.

Three themes: skills premia, youth transitions, and learning barriers

This section highlights three themes surrounding workers' supply of labour and demand for learning: the quest to estimate and interpret the skills premium, youth transitions from education to work, and learning barriers. These themes both reflect expanding areas of research knowledge and are relevant for understanding and rationalizing forms of social intervention.

The skills premium

Skills create values and, as long as those values are associated with work rewards, there will be a positive relationship between skills and rewards. The skills premium is a factor in the analysis of both the supply of skilled labour and the demand for learning. The monetary rewards from skilled work also constitute the raw material for the distribution of income. What, then, is known about the skills premium in practice?

Most of the evidence about the skills premium concerns the education–pay association, which is found to be substantial and durable. The link varies according to the level, type, location, and time of education. This variability, together with the growth of available data sets and the ease of the computing era, has led the education–pay association to become one of the most extensively studied of all economic relationships. In its most conventional form, studies relate workers' wages to their schooling, measured in terms of either years of education or levels of attainment, using regression techniques that control for years of work experience. Surveys with samples ranging from just a few hundreds of persons to millions are used. That there is *some* substantive association between pay and education is an extremely robust and enduring finding from across the globe. If you knew nothing of a person's occupation but were allowed just two questions in order to help you guess the person's income, you could hardly do better than enquire about the level of educational attainment and where the workplace is located (that is, which country). A smaller number of studies show, in addition, that more educated workers on average enjoy, *inter alia*, more meaningful work, better working conditions, higher-status jobs, a better work–life balance, and better health for themselves and their families.[19]

Trends over time in the skills premium—as captured by the education–pay association—have tended to vary, and often the changes are explicable in broad supply and demand terms. A typical example is that of Portugal, where the skills premium rose in the 1980s and early 1990s, a development attributed to the rising demand for skilled labour outpacing the rise in education. In contrast, the skills premium fell in France between 1962 and 1985, before stabilizing for the next decade.[20] In Britain the premium for attainment of higher education was stable or increasing for the quarter of a century from 1980, but since the millennium evidence is emerging of an increased dispersion in this premium between the more and less successful graduates.[21]

Yet there remain several questions and incomplete agreements as to the significance of the relationship between education and pay. One set of questions surround whether the relationship is uncovering a causal relationship that predicts the effect of raising education on pay. A serious concern is that unseen variables could be related to both pay and the level of education. If 'ability' led people to stay longer in school, and independently raised their productivity and pay at work, the estimated association between education and pay would be overstating the causal impact of education on pay. Researchers have had to devise strategies to circumvent this problem. Although it is rarely possible to conduct experiments, they have used 'instrumental variables' that mimic experimental situations—external policy-driven changes such as increases in education that are driven by legislation. Alternatively, they have used samples of twins, since, especially in the case of identical twins, it is possible to net out the influences of both family back-ground and most genetic differences. Sometimes, separate tests of cognitive abilities in early life are available that can be used to control for ability when estimating the effects of education that took place later. These varying methods sometimes raise or lower the basic association between education and pay, but do not eliminate the effect of education overall. The causal overall effect of education on work rewards is on average substantial.[22]

A second set of questions concerns the interpretation of the education–pay relationship. In the conventional approach, the interpretation is at once linear, simple, and profound: education inculcates skills that make people more productive, which enables them to obtain better jobs with higher wages, or to be more successful entrepreneurs. An alternative viewpoint is that education provides, not new skills, but a signal of a person's ability. Here 'ability' is used as a shorthand for a set of qualities that facilitate better performance both at school and at work. Only those with high ability choose to stay on at school because they can achieve given levels of skill with greater ease than those with lower ability. If employers find it hard directly to observe young people's abilities, they use job applicants' performance in school as a signal of their future productivity in the workplace. Often what employers look for is not so much the knowledge gained in school as the facility to learn quickly in the job. This alternative interpretation has an aura of qualified plausibility when not taken in the extreme form: education does provide a signal as well as skills. Yet employers can find out about their employees' performance in many other ways, including prior work experience and achievements, monitoring, and sophisticated recruitment practices. No robust formal evidence has been uncovered to support the view that educa-tion's primary economic function is to yield a signal for employers.[23]

Although the skills premium has mainly been construed as an education premium, some of the value of education lies in the access it gives to jobs that afford more opportunities to learn through work. Part of this advantage is manifested through a greater access to training, and a smaller literature has examined the premium for participating in training. Such a premium would be expected to vary between labour markets with different forms of regulation, depending on whether training is formally recognized in pay negotiations. Several studies have reported a positive association between training and wages, but, as with the education–pay literature, encounter the problem of establishing that participation in training causes higher wages. The 'instru-mental variable' technique is again brought into play, in order to allow for the fact that those workers who participate in training will be rather different from those who do not. Studies that do make this allowance have tended to find that the effect of training on wages is considerably reduced.[24]

Direct measures of skills are also found to yield pay and employment advantages.[25] The incentive is therefore to acquire certain skills, whether through education or through other means. Direct measures of literacy, numeracy, and combinations of cognitive skills, both at the basic level and across the spectrum, have been found to have a premium, even after controlling for prior educational achievements, and so to affect the distribution of income. The interpretation is that there are some valued skills that are not well captured by educational attainments, while nevertheless there are other skills that have not been separately well measured and remain best captured by education. In effect, this evidence confirms the common knowledge that educational attainment is a loose but valid indicator of skill. For example, in a study of US high-school students, it was found that educational attainment had the usual impact on pay a decade later, but that pay was further augmented by both maths ability and leadership skill. With one exclusive measure of leadership skill, pay rose by as much as a third.

It is worth stressing, however, that the notion of a skills premium, with its labour market connotations, does not cover all the personal advantages of education and learning through the life course. There are wider personal benefits from outside the economic domain: those with higher education attainments gain better health for themselves and for family members, and are more efficient in their consumer activities; their children achieve higher levels of educational and cognitive development. These advantages contribute in no small part to the private argument for choosing more education. Mention should be made also of the several external effects of education—for example, on crime, trust, social cohesion, and civic contributions—which should be incorporated into the calculations of governments (see Chapter 9).[26]

Education to Work Transitions

Life course transitions—relatively abrupt changes from one status to another and embedded in characteristic trajectories—typically involve changes in skills. The education to work transition, in particular, involves a period of major and concentrated skill acquisition, the like of which will not normally be repeated in later life, even among those fortunate enough to gain employment in a strong learning organization. It also entails the assumption of an identity, which may not fit with that assumed before transition. Such transition choices are normally hugely consequential. While the skills premium is the incentive for acquiring skills, it is very far from being the only factor involved when it comes to understanding such transitions. Also central are the resources (social, economic, and psychological) that are required for navigating those transitions, and the macroeconomic, cultural, and political environment.

The education to work transition is intimately linked with other life transitions such as leaving the family home and family formation. It may be only one stage in the life course, yet its evolution in the modern era is an important part of the ongoing reconstruction and enhancement of social and economic inequality. It is a prime example of a zone in need of a multidisciplinary perspective, one that uses a broad concept of skill as advocated in Chapter 2, and that incorporates the formation of incentives, resources, beliefs, and their interactions.[27]

The education to work transition is the occasion for the first intensive learning of work skills that are not picked up in school, often but not always incorporating a period of vocational training, either at work or in colleges. There are a number of standard transition patterns, characteristic pathways from schools (which may or may not be differentiated by type) to jobs with differential quality and prospects. Striking aspects of this transition in recent years are its postponement, its fragmentation and consequent call on personal resources, and its increasingly problematic nature.

That this transition occurs at a later age than for previous generations is a consequence of the expansion of education worldwide. With this trend there also emerges a gap between the end of adolescence and the completion of the education-to-work transition. Psychologists have construed the import of this decoupling as the making of a new developmental stage, 'emerging adulthood', with characteristic psychological states that are quite different from those of adolescence and of mature adulthood. At this new stage there is considerable individual heterogeneity, and young adults increasingly take 'rational' decisions in accordance with their own aims. Sociology, by contrast, stresses the continuing importance of structural factors, not only determining the constraints young adults face, but also conditioning their aspirations and expectations. Labour market institutions, class, and gender mould the pathways followed through this stage of life.[28]

The transition from education to work has also become more drawn out, with periods of overlapping work and education. With boundaries blurred, the point of transition is harder to pin down and prolongs the zone of uncertainty. Traditional ties between the achievement of stable employment and other evolving transitions such as leaving home and family formation are loosened, their orders reversed and interchanged. Another trend is for increased differentiation and complexity in transition patterns—a destandardization of routes. In one recent study of two successive British cohorts making the transition into work, the first in the 1970s and the second in the 1980s/90s, it was found that the commonest route was straight from school into work at age 16; this route was becoming less frequent, and there emerged in the later cohort a greater diversity of trajectories. In Catalonia another study has concluded, by contrast, that the Mediterranean welfare regime built upon

the family has still maintained a certain clarity, with only four main trajectories covering the large majority of youth.[29]

With expanding education and this greater differentiation of trajectories,
young people are thought to take more of an active part in determining their
own futures than in previous generations—a process of 'individuation'—and
it is maintained that to do so they have had to become more 'reflexive': in
previous eras most would have had their futures mapped out for them by
structural regularities—the chains of social class. While the requirement to
choose is welcome if it allows individuals more opportunity to break away
from traditional patterns of disadvantage, it is also more challenging, emphasizing the utility of coping strategies. If the additional burden is greatest for
those with insufficient resources, capacity, or self-knowledge, more diverse
opportunities can reinforce unequal outcomes rather than undermine them.
The extent to which 'individuation' has occurred is an ongoing discussion,
with important consequences for both theory and policy. Different institutional regimes are thought to provide a variable scope for young people to
navigate their ways through their diverse trajectories.[30]

Underpinning the evolution of these transitions have been a number of
social and economic trends, including the postponement of marriage and of
child-bearing and the increasing affluence and longevity of older generations.[31] In economic terms, the demand for the labour of younger workers
has declined, relative to that of other adults, in many countries. This relative
decline may, it is speculated, be associated with younger workers' lack of
experience, set against the increasing demand for skilled labour whose origins
were discussed in the previous chapter, though this explanation is unproven.
The decline is manifested mainly in rising youth unemployment relative to
that of adults, and, to a much smaller extent, in a decline in relative pay. The
trend is found broadly across the developed world, yet there are differences:
countries with liberal market economies tend to show more of a relative
decline in youth pay than in employment, while the highly developed
apprenticeship system in Germany and the established school–employer
hiring networks in Japan have helped to insulate the prospects of young
people in these two countries from relative decline.

This trend, which predominated in the period before 2008, was then over-
laid with the onset of the Great Recession. Young people are quintessential
outsiders in labour markets: they have to queue for stable jobs, which are
scarce when employers are not hiring, and they risk being the first to be made
redundant in recessions. Across the developed economies in the OECD, while
the overall unemployment rate jumped from 5.8 per cent in 2007 to 8.5 per
cent by 2010 in the aftermath of the recession, the youth unemployment rate
(for those aged 15–24) soared from 12.0 per cent to 16.7 per cent. The

prospects for youth were especially severe in some countries (such as Spain, from 18.2 per cent to 41.6 per cent).[32]

The consequence is that education to work transitions have become increasingly problematic. Young people have to navigate their way through increasingly diverse pathways, each with uncertain outcomes. As well as their successes, immediate experiences include periods of unemployment, under-employment in part-time work, temporary work, or work for which they are over-educated, all of which limit learning opportunities in early years of adulthood. Such experiences can then close down future trajectories—one's current choices are path dependent. Nevertheless, when expectations of earlier transitions are unfulfilled, there arises a tendency for some reversibility—going back to education, to live with the family, to being single, or all three.

The emergence of these trends, exacerbated by the recession, highlights the need for flexibility in youth transitions systems: institutions that allow options to be kept open, and mistakes to be remedied. The crisis of youth unemployment in the current era—characterized by the metaphor of the 'lost generation'—has become the close focus of policy-makers in many countries. Well-devised policies may be aimed at providing employment opportunities, learning opportunities, and enhanced guidance through the diverse trajectories, in order to make up for the disruptive effects of the recession on normal transitions. However, the effectiveness of compensatory education and employment policies should not be mis-sold, since proper elimination of the disruptions awaits a resolution of the macroeconomic crisis.

Sub-optimality and learning barriers

In contrast to the troubled education to work transition that primarily disadvantages young adults, the 'learning barrier' is a concern that can be encountered at any stage of the life course. Learning barriers, which form the third theme to be considered here, are often poorly understood, owing to a combination of loose conceptualization and the scarcity of satisfactory indicators for this concept that was noted in Chapter 4. This is unfortunate, given that they form one of the areas in which governments are keen to intervene.

To give substance and meaning to the concept of learning barrier, it is first necessary to allow credence to the notion that there is some 'best' or 'optimal' course of learning that should be undertaken in a person's interests if only the circumstances were right and the individual well enough informed. Some might flinch at this pretension: if individuals are faced with deep uncertainty and are unable to compute what amount or type of learning to undertake with a precise calculus, how could anyone say what is optimal, and does it make sense even to conceive of there being an optimal amount of learning? Nevertheless, doubters might also wish to consider whether they could really support the sometimes-expressed view that no amount of learning is enough, and that learning should always be intensified no matter what. Conversely, for many individuals, one can easily defend the view that some learning is better than none. It must follow that, for them, there is some positive but finite amount of learning that is best, even if that level cannot be calculated precisely. At any rate, without such a notion the concept of a learning barrier has no foothold.

A learning barrier is said to occur when learning is less than this optimal amount. There is no universal rule for determining what the optimal amount of learning is, but it is possible to adopt a pragmatic benchmarking principle: one can propose that the optimal amount of learning from the individual's perspective would be the amount chosen by similar people who had all the (individual and collective) resources necessary for thinking strategically about their learning desires and opportunities, including a full awareness of the implications of their various preferences, and who were not constrained in their access to learning opportunities other than by its market cost.

Learning barriers may be classified as extrinsic or intrinsic. Extrinsic barriers derive from constraints in the markets and other systems that impinge on the demand for learning. For example, suppose that a certain course of learning requires access to the capital market, so that learners can meet their living costs and service their debts with future enhanced earnings. Credit is often rationed by suppliers, however, for a variety of reasons, such as moral hazard (where individuals could increase the risk of debt default through their own behaviour), or where the risks are perceived by lenders as especially great. A learning course might also interlink with and be held back by other markets that are deficient, such as a lack of child-care facilities in particular localities. To take a third extrinsic example, someone might want to take a job with a firm that has a good learning environment but be unable to do so owing to location constraints. For any of these external reasons, the demand for learning opportunities is lower than its best level.

Intrinsic barriers describe reasons why individuals may opt for low levels of learning, quite apart from the external constraints they face. Lacking resources, for example, individuals may lack confidence in their ability to learn, perhaps resulting from poor schooling experiences. Spatial factors may limit their horizons.[33] Or, to take yet another example, it might simply be the case that there is insufficient information available about the value of the learning, leading people to err on the side of caution.

Barriers to learning are a widespread focus of policy attention, where it is thought that learning levels are deficient because individuals do not demand enough learning. Policies to try to lower barriers can be readily justified—for example, the provision of state-backed credit, or subsidies for child care—as aides to individuals' skill formation. Other policies can be directed towards the improvement of information, advice, and guidance services, or towards projects and institutions that engage with individuals lacking self-efficacy in respect of their learning abilities. In some countries trade unions influence and broker workers' demand for learning, sometimes with state support, often for those with relatively low initial skills—examples are Britain and Singapore. Where there is, in addition, a presumption that each individual's learning has benefits for others (that cannot be marketized), that is, where there are positive externalities, attempts to remove such barriers are doubly warranted.

Retreating to the middle range

Even though workers and learners may not always get what they want, in skill systems that are driven by employers and governments and by the large abstract forces of technology and competition, it remains important to see their desires about learning and doing skilled work in a coherent framework. This chapter has aimed at showing some key evidence; and at presenting a manageable framework of the economic and social interactions in which findings about the demand for learning and the supply of labour can be located.

A striking empirical finding about workers' labour supply is that this is enhanced where workers have greater skills. One can take this as contributory testimony, if it were needed, for the assumption that doing skilled work meets a basic human need, though the effect may also be due to the effect that more-skilled labour is better paid. The analysis and evidence about workers' demand for learning is, by contrast, more complex and in some respects embryonic. This is a quintessentially multidisciplinary field, where social, economic, and psychological factors combine; and, because learning takes place in the sequences of a life course, the field calls for an inherently dynamic formulation, in which individuals' prior biographies matter, and where current decisions foreclose or open future choice sets. The import of these dynamics is encapsulated in the deep uncertainty surrounding skill acquisition investments. The chapter has elaborated a framework that incorporates the interactions, contexts, and feedbacks that are absent from the simple cost–benefit model of learning.

Yet the framework is nowhere near being a theory that can account for all patterns of learning, and it is wise to shun grand narratives, and to favour 'middle-range' theories and studies that bring evidence to bear on parts of the framework. The chapter highlights three areas relevant for policy-makers. Understanding the skills premium is an ongoing project, in which findings vary across locations and time. A useful approach as studies develop is for a renewed focus on the intrinsic benefits of doing skilled work alongside the rewards of its higher pay. Understanding transitions—especially that from education to work—has become a sub-field of study, even though the amount of empirical evidence is quite limited. Considering its importance as a crucial life stage for intensive learning of work skills, one might think that governments the world over would consider putting more effort into finding out what young people believe, expect, and want as they pass through this stage of life.

Finally, the chapter has aimed to clarify the concept of 'learning barrier', this being a common potential zone of conflation with other concepts. Making this clarification is important, because learning barriers are one of the areas where governments like to intervene with subsidies and other means of persuasion, if only because it usually avoids direct engagement with private employers who defend their sphere of influence from outsiders. A learning barrier is characterized, not by an individual's low amount of learning per se, but by the demand for learning being below its optimal level; the latter may be imprecisely determined, but one can conceive it in principle and find proxy indicators in practice through benchmarking.

Faulty transitions, low skills premia, and learning barriers are far from the only considerations and problems that may be inhibiting the acquisition and use of skills in modern economies. To gain a more comprehensive understanding, it is necessary to consider the systemic functioning of skills and learning markets, to which the book now turns in Part III.

Part III
Systems and Interventions

8

Skill Matching Processes, Problems, and Outcomes

In examining the behaviours of the actors who demand and supply skilled labour, and who provide, seek, and organize opportunities for skill formation, Part II has emphasized the social as well as the economic character of skill. Part III focuses on the outcomes as actors engage with each other. Across the globe, employers and employees are brought together in markets, with an allocation and distribution of skilled work and skill formation services the outcome. Yet there are many varieties of capitalism, and as many ways for behaviours to interact. To investigate the determination of skills and skilled work—and to frame an understanding of how far the supply of skill and the deployment of skilled work are both economically successful and desirable from the standpoint of equity—Part III examines these processes of coming together.

This chapter begins with an examination of the general processes through which supplies and demands are matched, and a classification of common issues and problems that arise in many countries. It continues with an empirical picture of skills and skilled work in the modern world, aiming to highlight both the successes and the problems.

Prices or quantities?

The matching in skills markets is both a classic economic process of resource allocation and a socio-political process. As an economic process, the main province of this chapter, the central matching problems are the allocation, prior to deployment, of skilled labour, and the allocation of skill formation services. As a socio-political process, the institutions that develop the knowledge, culture, and identity of nations are articulated with labour market institutions that operate in the supra-national context of the global capitalist economy.

The significance of the potential contradiction between these processes is that one should not expect to construct a perfect arrangement, an ideal match between the economy and the culture of a nation. Nor, in most people's eyes, would such an outcome be seen as desirable, if it meant that the purposes of an education and training system were entirely subordinated to capitalist economic imperatives. Universities, colleges, and schools form parts of a broader cultural system, and to subsume them within the economic realm would be offensive, alienating, and command little support. In practice, education systems steer between objectives, and policy-makers stress commonalities between economy and society. Yet international competition and fiscal pressures on state funds for education can turn up the pressure to conform to market principles, subvert broader educational aims, and occasion heightened conflict surrounding the nature of education and lifelong learning.[1]

How, then, does skills matching come about? Two contrasting principles can govern the economic process: price signalling and planning; in parallel lies the duality of individual and collective forms of negotiation and organization of skills. In all capitalist economies (hence almost everywhere on earth), the relative price of skilled labour plays some role, even if its importance as an allocative mechanism varies. According to the market principle, wages adjust organically when there is an imbalance in the supply and demand for skilled labour. Wages rise in response to a scarcity, as employers try to attract employees with the recognized skills. Workers respond by switching between employers and away from other activities. If a skill is in surplus, reverse processes occur: the associated skilled wage falls and workers quit or are laid off. Changes in the wages of skilled labour also modify the prospective returns to learning new skills, so affecting over time the stock of skills available in the population. In the training market, current or prospective workers adjust their demands for learning, and providers (including employers) alter their costs and their courses.

With the supplies of, and demands for, skilled labour and skill formation services all responding to prices, there is an ever-present tendency for imbalances to be reduced. Adjustment processes are not seamless, since there are costs in the transitions. Workers spend periods searching for their best jobs, either in unmatched employment or in unemployment; and they take time to find the right courses of learning. Firms devote resources to devising new training and learning practices and to recruiting employees with the appropriate skills and demands for learning. Yet, if markets are thick enough with participants, the skills mismatches that characterize these transitional search periods are each short lived. In this free labour market nirvana, an equilibrium is always being approached, yet there remains a permanent low-level noise of temporarily mismatched workers occasioned by the continuum of technological and environmental shocks to markets.

This idealized picture is complicated only slightly by the fact that some skills are learned far more effectively at work than in the classroom. Employees and employers must therefore contract (implicitly or explicitly) for learning to take place; where some of the skills are organization specific, the benefits and costs of learning must be shared. Yet, as long as such contractual cooperation is feasible, the same process of skill acquisition and adjustment towards equilibrium in response to price signals is enabled.

The contrasting principle for the matching of skilled work and of skill formation is that skill formation should be coordinated collectively. Broad-based skills training, with emphases on knowledge acquisition, supports this system by reducing the need for new training in response to all changes in the workplace. When a skill becomes scarce, training is planned by groups of employers and employees and their representatives. If the skill is industry-wide, it can be organized through sectoral cooperation among firms. Social partners take decisions about the quality of skill formation, covering intensity of learning, curricula, forms of learning, assessment, and certification. If it is necessary for employees to bear some costs in acquiring new skills (to make it profitable for employers), a premium is negotiated in a collective bargaining system in which the wages of skilled labour and of trainees are regulated.[2] Where the skill is national, it can be planned through a mobilization of university and college providers.[3] In this organized labour market nirvana, freedom of labour movement still holds. Most workers are successfully matched to their jobs, but the permanent noise of temporarily mismatched workers exists here too. Temporary imbalances are fuelled by the lagged responses of the collective skills planning processes.

While in the abstract these two principles are in apparent opposition, the differences become less stark when the institutional requirements and the wider economic environment are added into the picture. To support price-signalling processes, there should be an infrastructure of high-quality information advice and guidance services and transparent economic intelligence for firms in order to facilitate decision-taking about the acquisition and future use of skills. An environment that is sufficiently stable for individuals and firms to make reasonably precise and unbiased judgements about future trends is needed. A regulatory coating must also be added to ensure the maintenance of competition: workers must have sufficient choices of employers and of skills providers. And an egalitarian top coat of learning support is required to maintain an equitable and socially efficient distribution of primary income. These are challenging requirements. Even in a 'liberal market economy'—the United States being the archetype—the skilled labour market is built upon a substantial institutional pyramid, including extensive information services about training, a good deal of occupational licensing, and some basic wage and health regulations.

Equally, with a coordinated skill formation system, the setting is, notwithstanding all the planning by social partners, a market economy. Anticipating future skill needs in a market economy, so that collective agents can plan education and training provision, is also a major challenge; and the negotiation of skill premia has costs and is subject to the risk of interest group capture. There is juridical freedom of employment, and public university systems enjoy only a qualified and tense autonomy from economic imperatives.

The wider environment, with its modifying effects on the two allocation principles, will be woven in the next chapter into a review of archetypal skill systems, constellations of institutions that are thought to form coherent wholes. Before so proceeding, however, the focus will be on the outcomes for skills, skilled work, and skill formation. These outcomes reflect the varied forces affecting agents' behaviours that have been discussed in Part II, but also depend on the processes of matching.

If either markets or planners can bring about an allocation of skilled work and of skills acquisition so as to diminish gaps between skills supply and demand, all the while steadily broadening the opportunities for skilled work, what could go wrong? Regrettably, there are many pitfalls. On the one hand, there can be failures in the aforementioned institutional and political supports needed for the ideal adjustment mechanisms to work. On the other hand, as previous chapters have discussed, employers and employees do not and cannot normally behave as implied in a rational-actor framework. The long-term and uncertain environment for skill decisions, the symbiotic link between work and skill acquisition, the variable capacities of managers who control the deployment of skilled work and of learning opportunities, externalities in training, individuals' learning barriers, inherent tendencies to inequality in learning opportunities, and the contradictions of an education and training policy driven by the logics of two contradictory processes, all combine to raise a catalogue of socio-economic issues for modern market-based skill systems.

The intention of this chapter is, first, to delineate the types of problems that can occur in the matching processes. This is not to dwell on the negative side for its own sake, but rather to facilitate some thought about what could be improved. Policy-makers need to address and try to resolve the problems that arise in their zones of influence. The second aim is empirically to illustrate outcomes of the skill-matching process as manifested in trends in skills, skilled work, and skills mismatches. Here, both the positive and the negative sides of the story are portrayed.

Classes of skills problems

Some of the more prominent issues, which have already been introduced in Part II, are private and social inefficiency, including the possibility of a low-skills equilibrium, persistent skills mismatches, skills inequalities including segmentation, and skills poverty.

Actors' behaviour may be privately inefficient

In the light of the deep uncertainty, and the importance of capacity and cultural determination in their skill decisions, informed rational responses to skills incentives are precluded for many employers. Individuals, meanwhile, may face multiple barriers to learning. Thus policy-makers cannot (and do not) always assume that actors' decisions are the best ones in respect of their own interests. In the worst situations, underachievement becomes endemic. Informed social advice and persuasion could be expected to improve decision-making.

Privately rational behaviour may be socially inefficient

A separate problem is that some organizational decisions about employee learning may be coloured by the risk of employees quitting, while individuals wanting to learn may be precluded because they are denied credit, perhaps owing to the moral hazard that deters lenders. Hence investments that would be socially efficient may not be undertaken, without social interventions beneficially to modify private incentives.

Multiple equilibria

Because employers' and workers' behaviours are each conditioned on expectations about how other agents act, there may be more than one attainable, persistent, equilibrium. A skilled labour market can then settle into a 'low-skills equilibrium', where both the supply and the demand are at relatively low levels. Even though a 'high-skills equilibrium' is preferable for both employers and employees, incremental movements in that direction may be resisted rather than reinforced. For example, employees might be reluctant to train if they expect that employers will not utilize their increased skills. Thus, substantive variation in skills between regions or nations with distinct labour markets can persist if each region or nation settles into its own distinct equilibrium. A system that gravitates towards a low-skills equilibrium condemns its actors to settle collectively for lost potential and offers them no escape; its symptom is the skills deficit.

Persistent skills mismatches

Skilled labour markets are frequently perturbed by the arrival of new technologies or forms of work organization, by changing market pressures, and by demographic movements, especially the arrival and maturity of new waves of well-educated young people. Adjustment to these new circumstances depends on the effectiveness of price-signalling and planning processes: whether relative wages change, thereby providing robust signals and inducing adjustments in supply and demand, or, alternatively, actors are able collectively to organize the needed changes in a timely manner. Both these conditions are questionable. Movements in the relative wages of skilled labour are slow, given the institutional constraints, and the long-term implicit contracts of many skilled employees. Deep uncertainties limit the sensitivity of supply and demand to wage signals; organizational and economic foresight on skills is far from perfect. Hence, skill mismatches arise, and may persist. A residue of skills mismatches is inevitable, even in well-adjusting economies; in less-well-adjusting labour markets there will be inefficiencies arising from skills mis-allocations, with too many firms and workers unable to meet their needs, or matches that take too long to wither away through search processes. Over and above such excessive short-term mismatches there is the potential for growing long-term mismatches given the long-term horizon for skills investments.

If people find themselves in jobs where their educational achievements are not needed and where their skills are under-utilized, they are likely to become disillusioned and dissatisfied; they have to settle also for lower wages than they expected. For employers, skill gaps or skill shortages will be experienced as lower productivity.[4]

Skills inequality and skills poverty

It is a widely held moral principle that everyone in a society should have equal access to a decent education. Indeed, for some writers it is taken to be a basic human right. The egalitarian principle is, however, typically flouted, since elites are able to marshal greater resources for educating their own children than their governments can for the general population of children. Inequalities in schooling become cumulative, in that tertiary education builds upon school achievements, which themselves are built upon variations in both natural abilities and social background.

Access to training in workplaces additionally compounds the inequality, since training opportunities widely favour those who have received a better education. This latter bias occurs for two reasons: because it gets easier to learn as one becomes more educated, and because the jobs filled by more educated workers require ongoing skills acquisition and accordingly provide better learning opportunities. The cumulative outcome is potentially a deep inequality in the skills of the adult population and in access to lifelong learning. The extent of the inequality varies, depending on the character of the learning institutions (including workplaces) in a society. Cumulative disadvantage can be counterbalanced if training is planned to counter prior educational shortfalls.

An extreme manifestation of skills inequality is skills poverty, where a lack of basic skills entraps workers in unemployment, non-employment, or precarious low-skilled jobs with obstructed routes to learning and a diet of unrewarding work that lacks any meaning and sense of fulfilment. Adam Smith bewailed the inevitability of such work if there was to be economic growth, and later Karl Marx feared that alienating work was endemic wherever there were capitalist relations of production. In the twenty-first century, low-skilled work is by no means universal but, together with the precariousness of employment, remains the reality for substantial minorities. The social problem of skills poverty may be heightened by the fragmentation and low levels of organization of the groups in skills poverty, thereby precluding alternative routes to economic security.

Segmentation

Skills inequality is reinforced by compartmentalization of labour markets into near-distinct segments, with transitions between them limited. Such mobility restrictions underpin wage differentials between labour market segments. Most fundamental are the segmentations of nation and region, where language barriers and constraints on migration limit mobility. International mobility is further hampered by insufficient transferability of skill certificates, which may occur for reasons of non-compatibility between cultures, or artificially as a protection for native trades. Also important are the segmentations that arise from gender and ethnic segregation of workforces and from the development of 'internal labour markets' (whereby those in jobs are implicitly promised long-term career structures), excluding those on the outside who have no jobs or access only to insecure temporary jobs.[5] These divisions are exacerbated when there is insufficient flexibility for individuals' career paths, so that segmentations that appear in youth risk becoming sealed in.

These classes of problems for the determination of skills and skilled work do not occur *solely* as a result of malfunctioning principles of adjustment in the two markets. Outcomes are connected also to broader institutions and practices. Most prominently, macroeconomic policies and institutions strongly affect unemployment, which in turn has a scarring impact on skills development. Those who lose their jobs through plant closures can be permanently affected.[6] Young workers who emerge from school or college at a time of recession, and find no work to go to or only jobs that under-utilize their skills, are denied opportunities for work-based learning. Bad luck in the timing of this transition is known to have long-lasting detrimental effects.[7] The consequences may be especially telling for the post-2008 cohort of young adults entering the labour market. Skills outcomes are also influenced by employment relations institutions and policies, which condition the pace of wage adjustments, the links between skill and pay, and the determination of companies' human resource practices. Managers' beliefs and attitudes about skills use and acquisition will reflect the extent to which they are able to sustain a long-term orientation. These attitudes are sometimes argued to be associated with dominant forms of financial institutions in the country, including the types of corporate governance.[8]

A tableau of skills outcomes and problems

The combination of adjustment processes and varied broader forces play out in myriad actions—or inactions—across the globe to give a dynamic and complex pattern of skilled work. The aim of this section is to present a sketch of the outcomes for the three core concepts whose meaning, analytical place, and measurement were discussed in Chapters 2–4—namely, skill, skills match, and skill formation. In looking at the skills trends that reflect the forces impinging on employers and workers' behaviours in the modern world, positive outcomes are highlighted as well as some of the common types of problems just discussed, including inequality and skills mismatches.

Skill and job skill

First, is it possible to say how the level of skills has been changing over recent decades? The level of skill in any population is only very imperfectly gauged by its educational attainments. Nevertheless, without better and more comprehensive indicators for a person's skill, the amount of education experienced is a good start. Educational attainment has increased rapidly over the last half century, sometimes just matching, sometimes far exceeding, progress in the material sphere. A question that frequently arises is whether expanded education attainment equates to increased educational achievement. Resolution of this question is hampered by changing certification standards and by

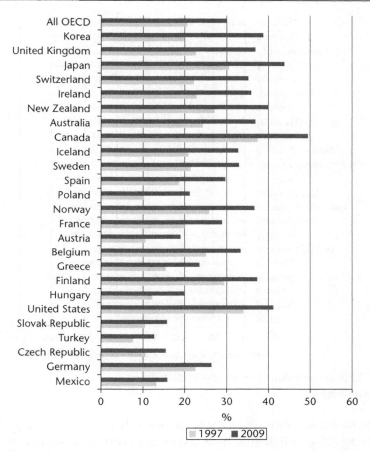

Figure 8.1. Tertiary educational attainment of 25–64-year-olds, 1997 and 2009
Data source: Table 8A.1.

altering population compositions over time, complexities that not infrequently occasion misuses of statistics in public debate with potential consequences for educational decision-making.[9]

Recent changes in educational attainments are striking. Figure 8.1 shows
that between 1997 and 2009 the proportion of the 25–64 age population with
tertiary education behind them increased in every OECD country we know
about, ranging from the modest rise of 2.6 percentage points in Mexico to the
remarkable rise of 19 percentage points in the Republic of Korea. Taking all
OECD countries as a group, the share of tertiary educated workers rose by 9
percentage points, while the share of persons with less than upper secondary
education declined by 10 percentage points (Table 8A.1).

Commentators with a predilection for superlatives about the modern pace
of change in society could happily dwell on these statistics: educational

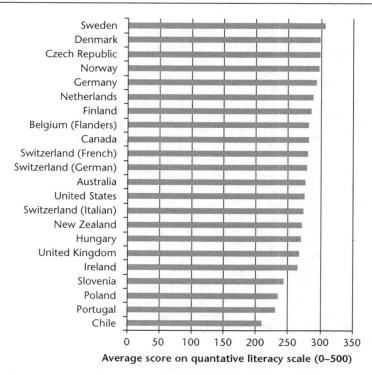

Figure 8.2. Numeracy skills in the early–mid-1990s
Data source: Table 8A.2.

attainment is much more dynamic than most other forms of social change. It is reasonable to conclude that there has been an expansion and deepening of knowledge among much broader sections of populations than was the case in earlier generations. Across a broad sweep of countries, the increases in education attainment have also been accompanied by steady reductions in the inequality of education attainment.[10] Among the 15-year-old population, skills inequality varies considerably between countries, being associated with low levels of school selectivity and least in the Nordic region.[11]

Other than through the indicator of education, it is difficult to state with any confidence what has happened over time to the skills of adult populations. The most notable exercise to date has been the International Adult Literacy Survey, which in the early 1990s mapped a limited range of generic skills across many countries. The highest average score on the quantitative literacy scale (range 0 to 500) was 306 for Sweden. The study exposed substantial differences between countries, as shown in Figure 8.2, yet the differences among the populations of each country were very much larger. A simple measure of this dispersion is the difference between the test scores of the

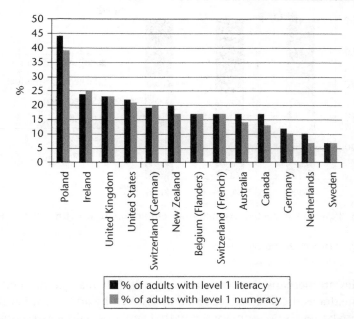

Figure 8.3. Skills poverty: low-level literacy and numeracy skills in the early–mid-1990s

Note: Scores are divided into 5 levels. For explanation of the levels, see OECD (2000). Level 1 literacy is described as indicating 'persons with very poor skills, where the individual may, for example, be unable to determine the correct amount of medicine to give a child from information printed on the package' (OECD 2000: p. xi).

Source: OECD, Human Resources Development Canada and Statistics Canada (1997), also reproduced in Moser (1999).

95th and 5th percentiles. By this indicator (shown in Table 8A.2), the dispersion is relatively low in the corporatist countries, such as Germany (149) and Denmark (147), where skills supplies and demands are organized and directed, and much greater in the liberal market economies of the United Kingdom (220) and the United States (238).

In some countries this inequality in skills has been manifested by significant levels of skills poverty. Thus paradoxically, alongside rising education, many governments have found themselves confronted by the depressing fact that a substantial minority of their adult populations lacked basic skills in literacy and numeracy. In some cases this problem has been associated with migration and consequent language difficulties, but more often lack of literacy indicates a failure of the school system compounding a legacy of social inequality. Figure 8.3 shows the variability of this problem across countries. In Poland, Ireland, the United Kingdom, and the United States more than 20 per cent of adults had only 'Level 1' literacy and numeracy levels. The potential consequences of basic skills deficiencies for social exclusion in modern developed

127

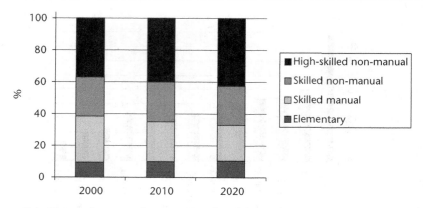

Figure 8.4. Past and expected occupational employment structure in the European Union

Data source: CEDEFOP (2010b: 59).

economies are perhaps too obvious to mention. It may be debated exactly where one draws the line between skill levels. Yet, by any token Level 1 skills are minimal; there is no room for doubt that very low skills was a serious social problem in the 1990s.

Have rising educational achievements since the early 1990s led to increases in adults' skills, and have policy programmes that address basic skill deficiencies succeeded in alleviating skills poverty? For a few countries (United States, Canada, and Switzerland), the Adult Literacy and Life Skills Survey allowed a look at trends between 1994 and 2003, focusing on items that were common to the two. Somewhat depressingly, although there were some rises in proficiency at the bottom end of the scale, there were also some falls at the top end, with the result that the mean scores changed very little over the decade.[12] A fuller picture is due in 2013 from the OECD's Programme for the International Assessment of Adult Competencies (PIAAC).

The level of job skill has also been increasing on a broad scale (as already discussed in Chapter 5). Figure 8.4 gives one picture for the European Union: the share of jobs in high-skilled non-manual occupations rose by 3.1 percentage points over the 2000s decade, from 36.7 per cent to 39.8 per cent, and is expected by forecasters to continue to advance at a steady, if slightly reduced, pace. This story is balanced by a decline in skilled manual occupations, while the share of those in elementary occupations remains steady—a picture that is consistent with the asymmetric polarization of the occupational structure.

Yet the changing occupational structure understates the rising use of skill because there are many changes *within* these occupations that entail greater use of skill. Figure 8.5 shows what happened in Great Britain over the course of the decade from 1997 to 2006. There was a rising use of several generic skills,

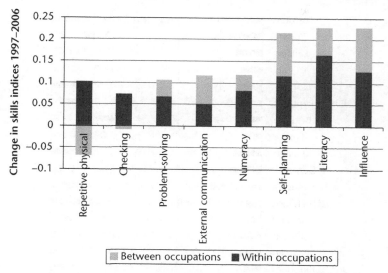

Figure 8.5 Changes in the use of generic skills in Great Britain, 1997–2006

Note: Each skills index averages the importance of several tasks, and ranges from 0 (all tasks not at all important/not applicable) to 3 (all tasks essential). 'Within occupations' covers changes that would have taken place if the occupation structure (shares of employment) had remained the same over the period; 'Between occupations' covers the changes that are attributable to changes in the occupation structure.

Data source: F. Green (2012).

most notably 'influence skills' (a combination of high-level communication skills, literacy, and self-planning skills); in most cases the majority of these rises were associated, not with the changing occupational structure, but with changes taking place within occupations. While such data are not available in most countries, it would be surprising if similar increases were not taking place on a broad canvass.

Skill match and mismatch

Aside from the problem of skills poverty and inequality, and of the persistence in shares of low-skill jobs, there arise further social problems from skills mismatch.

First, the broad skills requirements of jobs may not be increasing fast enough. One need only compare the pace of change in Figure 8.1 with that in Figure 8.4 to contemplate a possible disjuncture at the tertiary level— namely, that the rate of change of the stock of people with tertiary education has recently been much greater than the rate of increase of jobs in high-skilled non-manual occupations (the traditional destination for tertiary-educated workers). More generally, the matching of people to jobs is imperfect when

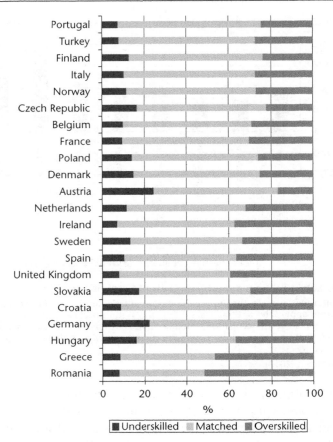

Figure 8.6. Subjective skill matching in Europe, 2010

Note: Selected countries, ordered by share of subjectively skills-matched workers.

Data source: Table 8A.3, for 34 countries in Europe.

workers have a limited choice of jobs, most especially when unemployment is high. Thus, workers find themselves in jobs where their skills are under-utilized.

Though it is hard to measure objectively how far skills are being under-utilized, surveys can ascertain workers' own perceptions. According to the European Working Conditions Survey, across Europe around one in three workers reported in 2010 that he or she had under-utilized skills. The proportion ranged greatly from 17.0 per cent in Austria to 51.7 per cent in Romania (see Figure 8.6). Although one cannot accept individuals' self-assessments of competence at face value, they appear to reflect a rather negative and variable view of the matching efficiency of labour markets; there is no sign, however, that this assessment is deteriorating.

Alternatively, one can examine over-education—whether a person's educational qualifications exceed those required for getting the job—a concept related, though loosely, to skill under-utilization.[13] Studies of over-education, when calculated in a satisfactory way (using job-holders' or job analysts' assessments of education requirements), have hitherto rarely been available on a comparable cross-national basis. A harmonized survey in 2001 showed higher rates of over-education in Germany, Israel, and the United Kingdom than in Bulgaria, Italy, and Norway. Separate studies have been carried out in a number of individual countries, indicating that over-education is prevalent in upwards of 20 per cent of the population, the figure varying according to how it is measured.

Such findings on their own allow no conclusions about whether there is a socially inefficient level of short-term mismatch. Where there are data on a consistent basis over time, however, an increase in over-education (not accompanied by a decline in the efficacy of job-search institutions) is an indication that there is a problem of long-term mismatch. Data for Germany and Great Britain indicate that the prevalence of over-education has been growing in both countries (see Figure 8.7); with the rapidly rising participation in tertiary education in many countries, it could be expected that this trend is valid for more than just these two countries. The problem that this trend poses is that over-education is associated, not only with lower wages for the employees who find themselves in this state, but also with a degree of job dissatisfaction.

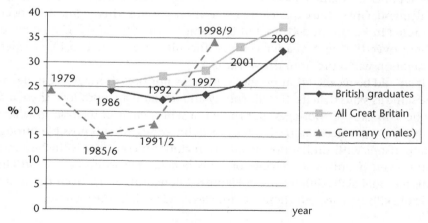

Figure 8.7. Trends in over-education in Great Britain and Germany

Note: Great Britain: % of employees aged 25–60 whose education level exceeds that required to get the job; Germany: % of males aged 25–65 working full-time who report that their job could be performed by someone with a lower qualification.

Sources: Author's analysis, using the UK Skills Survey series, described in Felstead et al. (2007a); Rohrbach-Schmidt and Tiemann (2011).

A sign of imperfect sorting is when skills under-utilization may coexist in the same labour market with the converse phenomena of skill gaps and skill shortages. Employers report skills gaps where they perceive employees to be lacking the skills needed to do their jobs well. This type of skills mismatch is likely to be relatively uncommon, since it is easily remedied if even limited flexibility is present: a prevalence of less-than-competent employees, often the product of a misjudged hiring, can be met with additional training or dismissal, or minimized through improved recruitment tactics. In one recent survey, just 7 per cent of employees were reported by employers to have skill gaps in 2009.[14]

A more common concern is the extent of recruitment difficulties associated with a lack of skills in applicants (skill shortage vacancies), owing to their negative impact on productivity. Skill shortages tend to vary with the state of the business cycle, simply because less hiring takes place during the downside of the cycle. For example, among Australian companies advertising for recruits among Technicians and Trades occupations, 51 per cent were filled within four weeks during 2008; in 2009 during the Great Recession the figure had risen to 67 per cent.[15] In both Australia and New Zealand recruitment difficulties are systematically linked to immigration policy: lists of occupations are maintained where companies find difficulty recruiting. Those experienced and qualified for these areas of work have access to these countries through skilled migration programmes.

At the aggregate level, concern about skill shortages derives from forecasts of the supplies of highly educated workers falling short of the projected growth of demand. Given the expansion of education systems, this aggregate concern is muted in European debates, but is salient for the case of the United States, where over the next quarter century the highly educated 'baby-boomers' generation will retire from the workforce.[16]

It should be recalled that neither skills gaps nor skill shortage vacancies are the same as skills deficits. If skills supply and demand are both low, there may be no skill gaps or shortages, but there is a skills deficit in relation to what is possible. As pointed out in Chapter 4, benchmarking what is possible through comparisons with similar organizations, regions, or countries is the best indicator, even if only a loose one, of skills deficits. For example, the striking international skills differences in Figure 8.2 constitute hints from the supply side of skills deficits, but these are not classified as skills mismatches.

Skill formation

Rising skills reflect levels of participation in learning through education and training that are high enough to exceed skill losses and obsolescence in society. In fact, not only is it high enough; in most cases, enrolments and

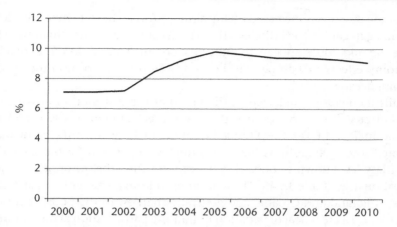

Figure 8.8. Participation in lifelong learning in the European Union

Note: Persons aged 25–64 who received education or training in the four weeks preceding the survey as a percentage of the total population of the same age; covers 25 countries.

Data source: European Labour Force Survey, downloaded from Eurostat <http://epp.eurostat.ec.europa.eu/portal/page/portal/education/data/main_tables> (accessed 17 November 2012).

achievements in education continue to rise. Across the OECD countries, between 1995 and 2009 the enrolment rate of 15–19-year-olds in education rose from 74 per cent to 83 per cent, that of 20–29-year-olds from 19 per cent to 27 per cent.[17]

Learning continues when at work in adult life, with substantial resources being devoted annually by employers—some 1.6 per cent of labour costs in the European Union—and a great deal of commitment and time by employees. With job skills increasing, and at the same time the increased education levels of the workforce, one might foresee workplace learning intensifying. Trends in work-related training, however, are only partially consistent with this expectation. Figure 8.8 shows that participation in European Union countries rose from just over 7 per cent in the mid-1990s to as much as 10 per cent in 2005. Such a rise has typically been regarded as reflecting the impact of the spreading knowledge economy. After 2005, however, training participation dropped back to around 9 per cent by the end of the decade. A mixed trend has also been observed in Australia: training participation over twelve months rose steadily from 30 per cent of the workforce in 1993 to 48 per cent in 2005, but the length of training courses plummeted by 29 per cent between 1997 and 2005.[18]

It is noteworthy from Figure 8.8 that there is no visible effect of the Great Recession on training participation in Europe. While a short-termist orientation has led some managers to reduce training opportunities as a way of weathering hard times, others have taken a long-term viewpoint and maintained their training effort, often underpinned by industry and market needs, and some have even increased their training efforts. The net effect is undetectable in aggregate.[19] Nevertheless, the pattern of training participation, which since the mid-2000s appears to indicate a potential saturation in knowledge-economy effects in Europe, will be of special interest to monitor over the coming decade.

Skills inequality is reflected in the fact that the distribution of training is concentrated. In every country there are large differences associated with education level. Over the European Union lifelong learning participation among those aged 25 to 64 has varied from 57.9 per cent for those educated to tertiary level down to only 17.5 per cent for those below upper-secondary education (see Table 8A.4). The education-training gradient is particularly acute in Poland and Croatia, and generally sharpest in the poorer countries. There is also a great deal of variation in training participation across countries, ranging from 73.4 per cent in Sweden (with other Nordic countries not far behind) to 7.4 per cent in Romania. These inequalities reflect not only the cumulative dispersed trajectories of learning noted above, but also a strong segmentation, in which supplies and demands for skills acquisition settle down to quite different levels in distinct national labour markets between which mobility is low. The differences in participation are mirrored by large variations in the amount of resources that employers devote to training (already noted in Chapter 6 as indicative of the role of managerial culture). In 2005 employers in Sweden, for example, spent on average 2.1 per cent of their (already high) labour costs in training; in Latvia the figure was only 0.8 per cent.

Within countries, training access is differentiated not only according to prior education, but also according to the status of the employment contract, with temporary agency workers and others on temporary work contracts experiencing less training than apparently similar workers with open-ended ('permanent') contracts; ethnicity also plays a role, with non-white employees having fewer training opportunities.[20] Both these differences reinforce, rather than ameliorate, disadvantage in the labour market. Gender differences, however, are less one-sided, with women having worse access than men to training at work in Sweden, but better in the United States, and with the balance of access swinging also in favour of women in Great Britain.[21]

Among those in every country who receive little or no training, there will be some who have experienced learning barriers. Non-employment, which has risen sharply as a result of the Great Recession, is one loose indicator of a learning barrier. Other indicators rely on responses to certain items on surveys, but, as noted in Chapter 4, the data are scarce. In one recent survey, only 15 per cent of workers receiving no training in the previous year from their employer reported that this was either because their employer was unwilling to provide it or because of family commitments.[22] However, this figure does not include workers held back by a learning barrier for other reasons, or from lack of employment.

An optimism downgrade

As skills supplies and demands are brought together in diverse loosely connected labour markets, and as the supplies and demands for skill acquisition are also confronted, a wide range of outcomes for skilled work is conceivable. Having classified some of the issues that can arise, this chapter has set out some illustrative evidence about the distributions and evolutions of skill and skill acquisition in the present conjuncture.

Some of this evidence amounts to an optimistic picture, full of hope for future economic and social development. The broad-based, substantial, and ongoing expansion of education attainments may come to be regarded by social and economic historians as one of the decisive transformations of this era, though one reason for caution is that there is as yet no separate evidence of a concomitant mass transformation in people's skills. The differences between countries in these transformations and the variations within countries give some reason to believe that lagging countries and groups could achieve similar gains. Less dramatically, yet still significantly, the reach of the knowledge economy into many spheres has slowly been raising opportunities for experiencing skilled work. How to develop jobs in ways that broaden the use of skills is one of the key issues meriting attention from labour policy-makers.

Yet other outcomes are far less encouraging, including endemic problems that need addressing, especially for policy-makers who conceive that improving countries' skill systems could be a way to achieve both economic prosperity and social objectives. The evidence has revealed substantial skills inequalities within and between countries, the dispersion being greater in liberal market economies that have less regulated labour markets. Some countries have been home to large populations with low levels of basic skills. Training and learning in the workplace vary a great deal between groups and across countries. The upward trend in over-education has been affording a growing disappointment for those workers unable to get the jobs they might have expected when they set off to get educated. Moreover, one cannot be confident that the skill level of jobs will continue to rise; if anything, the knowledge economy's expansion of training opportunities may have come to a halt.

The complex, varied, and dynamic nature of the skills market calls for regular observance and monitoring, if policy-makers and analysts want to understand and make a difference in this area of life. Since skill systems for non-college jobs are often bounded at sub-national levels, such monitoring needs to be at local and regional levels, as well as at national and supra-national levels; it should also be regular, since no account remains accurate for long. Some of the methods and tools used for observation and analysis are discussed in Chapter 10. In addition to supporting such problem-monitoring, what, if anything, is the role of nation states in addressing these problems? There remains a widely held optimism that governments and other social agencies can and should make a difference in respect of the skills of their populations. To investigate whether and how far such optimism is warranted is the objective of the next chapter.

Appendix

Table 8A.1. Educational attainment: % of 25–64-year-olds by level, OECD

Country	Education	1997	2009
Australia	Below upper secondary	46.7	29.0
	Upper secondary and post-secondary non-tertiary	29.0	34.1
	Tertiary education	24.3	36.9
Austria	Below upper secondary	26.4	18.1
	Upper secondary and post-secondary non-tertiary	63.0	62.8
	Tertiary education	10.6	19.0
Belgium	Below upper secondary	45.0	29.4
	Upper secondary and post-secondary non-tertiary	29.9	37.2
	Tertiary education	25.1	33.4
Canada	Below upper secondary	22.3	12.4
	Upper secondary and post-secondary non-tertiary	40.3	38.1
	Tertiary education	37.4	49.5
Chile	Below upper secondary	n.a.	31.0
	Upper secondary and post-secondary non-tertiary	n.a.	44.7
	Tertiary education	n.a.	24.4
Czech Republic	Below upper secondary	15.0	8.6
	Upper secondary and post-secondary non-tertiary	74.3	75.9
	Tertiary education	10.6	15.5
Denmark	Below upper secondary	n.a.	23.7
	Upper secondary and post-secondary non-tertiary	n.a.	42.0
	Tertiary education	n.a.	34.3
Estonia	Below upper secondary	n.a.	11.1
	Upper secondary and post-secondary non-tertiary	n.a.	53.0
	Tertiary education	n.a.	36.0
Finland	Below upper secondary	31.7	18.0
	Upper secondary and post-secondary non-tertiary	38.9	44.7
	Tertiary education	29.4	37.3
France	Below upper secondary	40.5	30.0
	Upper secondary and post-secondary non-tertiary	39.5	41.1
	Tertiary education	20.0	28.9

Germany	Below upper secondary	16.8	14.5
	Upper secondary and post-secondary non-tertiary	60.6	59.1
	Tertiary education	22.6	26.4
Greece	Below upper secondary	55.9	38.8
	Upper secondary and post-secondary non-tertiary	28.6	37.7
	Tertiary education	15.5	23.5
Hungary	Below upper secondary	37.0	19.4
	Upper secondary and post-secondary non-tertiary	50.8	60.7
	Tertiary education	12.2	19.9
Iceland	Below upper secondary	43.9	34.1
	Upper secondary and post-secondary non-tertiary	35.3	33.1
	Tertiary education	20.9	32.8
Ireland	Below upper secondary	50.4	28.5
	Upper secondary and post-secondary non-tertiary	26.8	35.7
	Tertiary education	22.8	35.9
Israel	Below upper secondary	n.a.	18.2
	Upper secondary and post-secondary non-tertiary	n.a.	36.9
	Tertiary education	n.a.	44.9
Italy	Below upper secondary	n.a.	45.7
	Upper secondary and post-secondary non-tertiary	n.a.	39.8
	Tertiary education	n.a.	14.5
Japan	Below upper secondary	20.3	n.a.
	Upper secondary and post-secondary non-tertiary	49.1	56.2
	Tertiary education	30.5	43.8
Korea	Below upper secondary	37.9	20.1
	Upper secondary and post-secondary non-tertiary	42.3	41.2
	Tertiary education	19.8	38.8
Luxembourg	Below upper secondary	n.a.	22.7
	Upper secondary and post-secondary non-tertiary	n.a.	42.5
	Tertiary education	n.a.	34.8
Mexico	Below upper secondary	72.2	64.8
	Upper secondary and post-secondary non-tertiary	14.5	19.3
	Tertiary education	13.2	15.9
Netherlands	Below upper secondary	n.a.	26.6
	Upper secondary and post-secondary non-tertiary	n.a.	40.6
	Tertiary education	n.a.	32.8
New Zealand	Below upper secondary	39.6	27.8
	Upper secondary and post-secondary non-tertiary	33.4	32.2
	Tertiary education	27.1	40.0
Norway	Below upper secondary	17.0	19.3
	Upper secondary and post-secondary non-tertiary	57.2	44.0
	Tertiary education	25.8	36.7
Poland	Below upper secondary	23.0	12.0
	Upper secondary and post-secondary non-tertiary	66.8	66.8
	Tertiary education	10.2	21.2
Portugal	Below upper secondary	n.a.	70.1
	Upper secondary and post-secondary non-tertiary	n.a.	15.2
	Tertiary education	n.a.	14.7
Slovak Republic	Below upper secondary	21.4	9.1
	Upper secondary and post-secondary non-tertiary	68.1	75.2
	Tertiary education	10.5	15.8
Slovenia	Below upper secondary	n.a.	16.7
	Upper secondary and post-secondary non-tertiary	n.a.	60.0
	Tertiary education	n.a.	23.3

(*continued*)

Table 8A.1. Continued

Country	Education	1997	2009
Spain	Below upper secondary	68.8	48.2
	Upper secondary and post-secondary non-tertiary	12.6	22.1
	Tertiary education	18.6	29.7
Sweden	Below upper secondary	25.1	14.2
	Upper secondary and post-secondary non-tertiary	53.5	52.7
	Tertiary education	21.4	33.0
Switzerland	Below upper secondary	16.4	13.1
	Upper secondary and post-secondary non-tertiary	61.4	51.7
	Tertiary education	22.2	35.2
Turkey	Below upper secondary	79.0	68.9
	Upper secondary and post-secondary non-tertiary	13.4	18.3
	Tertiary education	7.6	12.7
United Kingdom	Below upper secondary	40.9	26.3
	Upper secondary and post-secondary non-tertiary	36.5	36.8
	Tertiary education	22.6	36.9
United States	Below upper secondary	14.1	11.4
	Upper secondary and post-secondary non-tertiary	51.8	47.4
	Tertiary education	34.1	41.2
OECD average	**Below upper secondary**	36.3	26.7
	Upper secondary and post-secondary non-tertiary	43.1	44.1
	Tertiary education	20.6	30.0

Note: n.a. = not available.
Source: OECD (2011).

Table 8A.2. Quantitative literacy scores in the early 1990s

Country	Mean	95th to 5th percentile range
Australia	276	210
Belgium (Flanders)	282	211
Canada	281	220
Chile	209	228
Czech Republic	298	183
Denmark	298	147
Finland	286	160
Germany	293	149
Hungary	270	294
Ireland	265	214
Netherlands	288	158
New Zealand	271	206
Norway	297	158
Poland	235	237
Portugal	231	223
Slovenia	243	234
Sweden	306	165
Switzerland (French)	280	211
Switzerland (German)	279	211
Switzerland (Italian)	274	195
United Kingdom	267	220
United States	275	238

Source: OECD (2000: 136, table 2.1).

Table 8A.3. Subjective skill matching across European countries, 2010 (%)

Country	Underskilled	Matched	Overskilled
Albania	11.0	48.2	40.9
Austria	24.5	58.5	17.0
Belgium	9.8	61.2	29.0
Bulgaria	7.5	64.3	28.2
Croatia	8.7	50.9	40.4
Cyprus	9.1	46.8	44.1
Czech Republic	16.5	61.4	22.1
Denmark	15.1	59.6	25.3
Estonia	21.8	52.6	25.6
Finland	13.0	63.4	23.6
France	9.7	59.9	30.4
FYROM	6.5	62.0	31.5
Germany	22.5	50.7	26.8
Greece	8.4	44.6	46.9
Hungary	16.1	47.0	36.9
Ireland	7.2	55.3	37.6
Italy	10.3	62.1	27.6
Kosovo	13.4	63.4	23.2
Latvia	13.7	47.2	39.1
Lithuania	18.7	60.5	20.8
Luxembourg	15.7	54.1	30.2
Malta	12.1	55.3	32.6
Montenegro	6.4	51.3	42.3
Netherlands	11.7	56.3	32.0
Norway	11.5	61.6	26.9
Poland	14.0	59.6	26.4
Portugal	7.5	67.8	24.8
Romania	8.0	40.4	51.7
Slovakia	17.6	52.4	30.1
Slovenia	12.3	47.7	40.0
Spain	10.2	53.2	36.7
Sweden	13.1	53.2	33.7
Turkey	8.0	64.5	27.4
United Kingdom	7.9	52.5	39.6
Total, all Europe[a]	12.5	56.1	31.4

[a] Weighted by population size. Excludes Switzerland.

Notes: Figures are percentages of those in employment.
Underskilled represents agreement with 'I need further training to cope well with my duties'. Matched represents agreement with 'My present skills correspond well with my duties'. Overskilled represents agreement with 'I have the skills to cope with more demanding duties'.

Data source: Author's analysis, using the 5th European Working Conditions Survey 2010 <http://www.eurofound.europa.eu/surveys/ewcs/2010/index.htm> (accessed 17 November 2012).

Table 8A.4. Lifelong learning participation by education attainment and training costs, across Europe (%)

Country	Pre-primary, primary, and lower secondary education	Upper secondary and post-secondary non-tertiary education	Tertiary education	All	Share of training costs of total labour costs in enterprises
European Union (27 countries)	**17.5**	**34.7**	**57.9**	**34.9**	**1.6**
Austria	19.1	41.9	68.1	41.9	1.4
Belgium	19.8	38.4	63.3	40.5	1.6
Bulgaria	15.1	39.2	52.7	36.4	1.1
Croatia	3.9	21.1	54.9	21.2	n.a.
Cyprus	16.0	39.5	64.7	40.6	1.3
Czech Republic	14.8	36.6	62.4	37.6	1.9
Denmark	29.9	41.3	62.8	44.5	2.7
Estonia	19.7	35.9	60.6	42.1	1.6
Finland	35.2	51.8	72.9	55.0	1.5
France	19.1	34.1	57.1	35.1	2.3
Germany	19.9	45.4	63.2	45.4	1.3
Greece	4.0	15.2	31.8	14.5	0.6
Hungary	2.6	8.6	19.4	9.0	1.9
Italy	8.2	30.2	51.4	22.2	1.2
Latvia	11.0	27.2	58.5	32.7	0.8
Lithuania	8.8	24.9	61.9	33.9	1.2
Luxembourg	n.a.	n.a.	n.a.	n.a.	2.0
Malta	22.5	42.7	75.5	33.7	1.8
Netherlands	25.4	42.0	65.5	44.6	2.0
Norway	37.8	51.9	72.3	54.6	1.3
Poland	4.7	15.8	54.4	21.8	1.3
Portugal	15.9	45.6	63.9	26.4	1.1
Romania	1.3	7.0	20.6	7.4	1.1
Slovakia	14.2	40.8	61.8	44.0	1.8
Slovenia	12.7	39.0	67.6	40.6	2.0
Spain	17.0	35.5	51.1	30.9	1.2
Sweden	55.9	72.4	89.9	73.4	2.1
Switzerland	16.8	46.1	70.2	49.0	n.a.
Turkey	7.3	24.5	43.1	14.1	n.a.
United Kingdom	33.4	52.5	62.6	49.3	1.3

Note: Columns 1–4: annual participation rate in lifelong learning among population aged 25–64. Column 5: participation in lifelong learning among population aged 25–64; training costs include both direct costs and indirect costs of participating employees.
n.a. = not available.

Data sources: Columns 1–4: Adult Education Survey, 2006 <http://epp.eurostat.ec.europa.eu/portal/page/portal/education/data/database> (accessed 17 November 2012); Column 5: Official Statistics of Finland (OSF): CVTS, Continuing vocational training survey [e-publication]. ISSN = 1798–0003. Participation in course-format training 2005, 7. Main results from EU member states and Norway: Helsinki: Statistics Finland [referred: 28.4.2011]. Access method: <http://www.tilastokeskus.fi/til/cvts/2005/02/cvts_2005_02_2009-05-08_tau_008_en.html> (accessed 17 November 2012).

9

Skill Systems and the Role of the State

The need for a normative framework for skills interventions

The aim of this chapter is to devise a framework for how to think about an approach to skills by policy-makers, one that will inform combinations of education, training, and employment policies, and aspects of regional and industrial policies. Until this point, attention has focused on employers and workers as the principal actors; yet governments and their agencies—regional, national, and sometimes supra-national—are the co-starring third actors, and not always just in the minor parts. Around the world, governments have been striving to devise skills strategies, often with little discussion of whether, why, and how far it is their business to be involved. The framework here is intended to be normative (providing rationales and principles for determining actions) rather than explanatory (using political science to fathom what governments do). It is also focused on those principles, rather than on sets of policies that should be nationally specific.

To keep the problem tractable, it shall be considered from the perspective of an essentially democratic government (elected regularly and not corrupt) that, while committed to the maintenance of capitalist markets and employment relations, aims to raise economic growth, to promote equal opportunities for learning, and to mitigate capitalism's tendencies towards large inequalities in outcomes including poverty. It shall be a decent conversation. Second, the scope is to be further restricted by treating government as a quasi-autonomous actor. Little cognisance will be taken at this point of the way that conflicting and powerful interest groups, and international pressures, shape national political cultures and the forms of governments. Notwithstanding these restrictions, there remain still a variety of government types and a challenging problem to deliberate.

The initial question for this framework to address is: why should government be involved at all with skilled work or the generation of skills? It is useful to go back to first principles to see whether governments can improve outcomes. The first part of this chapter focuses on the normative analysis of the state, assessing the rationales and criteria for social intervention in skill formation and deployment. A critique is developed of the conventional approach that derives criteria solely from the principle of market failure. In the second part, attention turns to how what a government actually does is situated in the context of a set of skills-related institutions, termed a 'skill system'.

The chapter then closes, not with a specific list of policies, but with a set of guidelines—principles to be adhered to in the design of skills policies. Social intervention policies stem from a consideration of the balance of the imperatives of market failure with the imperfections of government agencies, from the possible identification of strategic capacity deficiencies among some employers or of learning barriers among some workers, and from the social demand to mitigate inequalities. It emerges that there is no universally recommended strategy, and that policies need to be tailored to fit the context of each country's institutions.

Reasons to be involved

Education

To begin with the easy part, both the cultural and the economic roles of education are widely accepted as intrinsic to modern societies and consistent with the state being the dominant provider of education at primary and secondary levels. Human capital theory underpins the provision of free universal education up to secondary level and partial support for tertiary education. The external benefits of education—that is, the benefits that other people enjoy from living and working in a more educated society—are high, and there are plentiful empirical studies in support of education's wider effects, such as on crime reduction, improved health, and democratic participation, many of which are external to the person educated.[1] There is also an overwhelming egalitarian rationale for state-provided education: without state assistance children's education depends on their parents' attitudes, perceptions, and resources; life chances become irredeemably defined by class and social background. While every country has its private schools, these are for elites or for minorities with special needs; they are often state subsidized, and are contested. Discourse on education policy must address the level and type of education, and the contradictions between economic and cultural imperatives, but rarely extends to questioning whether the state should be fully involved.

The argument is less straightforward for higher education. Given the fact that only part of the population get to go to university, the high private returns available to graduates, and an expectation that the externalities springing from this level of education are rather less in magnitude than for school education, efficiency and equity considerations typically favour shared state/private funding for college attendance.[2]

Training

The issue of social intervention in training is decidedly more complex. A self-evident form of state involvement in skills use and acquisition is the government's own human resource management as an employer. In discharging its functions, whether they be extensive or minimal, it needs trained workers: nurses and doctors, if it wants to have a health service, soldiers for an army, teachers for its schools, and civil servants for its own departments. Typically, public-sector employees in all countries are, on average, doing higher-skilled work than the rest of the population as a whole, and will tend to participate more frequently in training.[3] Of necessity, much of this training has to be provided in the context of the work itself and could not be contracted out to private providers. Sometimes governments may be content that their trained employees transfer to the private sector, this being an indirect form of subsidy.

Yet, beyond its own sphere, the rationale from conventional economics for governments to get involved in private-sector training is equivocal—favourable in theory, but dubious in practice. While the original simplified model of Becker left no theoretical space for intervention, the new human capital theory models (outlined in Chapter 6) incorporating imperfect labour markets or asymmetric information acquired both an explanatory and a normative function. They account for why employers often pay for transferable training; they also normally imply that, under reasonable assumptions, the level of training would be less than socially optimal, paving the way for social intervention. Where the social net benefits exceed the private net benefits, government should intervene, whether through subsidies, levy systems, regulation, subsidized loans, or the provision of information. Most commonly cited is the 'externality' associated with job mobility, whereby future employers benefit from the training paid for by an employee's current employer: this occurs whenever the increased productivity arising from training exceeds the extra pay that a new employer is obliged to concede. The new human capital theory models formed the explicit conceptual basis for state intervention in workplace training in a wide range of circumstances. Where a government saw that there was a training deficit in its domain, in comparison with other countries, this could be put down to the other countries better resolving the associated externalities; the solution would be to support training to match that achieved elsewhere.

Nevertheless, the backing for this conventional reasoning—from theory rather than observation—is fragile. There is little independent evidence of market failure, other than through the training outcome itself; it seems a shaky foundation on which to build one's policies.[4] Human capital theorists have begun to express scepticism that the arguments from principle can be supported in practice.[5] This is not to discredit the new models, but rather to question the magnitude of their implications, and set them against the known problems of government intervention. It is rightly argued that subsidies impinge most on employers at the margin—those who are on the borderline of training decisions. Intra-marginal employers (those who were training intensively anyway) will not alter their behaviour and will simply pocket any subsidies. This 'deadweight loss' is both a transfer of wealth (which may or may not be desirable) and a bureaucratic cost; these minuses have to be set against the positive benefit from behavioural changes by employers near the margin. So the question is, how large are the benefits of intervention? The conventional response is to seek empirical estimates of the private and social costs and benefits of training in a bid to compute the difference between net social benefits and net private benefits. A sufficient condition to warrant intervention to promote training would be if the social net benefits exceeded the private net benefits. However, this evidence is missing, and so the practical case for involvement has lacked support.

The equity case for training intervention is also questioned by human capital theory wherever it is found that training returns tend to be low for those at the lower ends of the spectrum, especially for vocational training programmes.[6] This evidence is incomplete, contested, and spatially variable, yet suggests that there may be more efficient redistribution mechanisms than spending money on government training programmes for low-paid workers.

The new human capital theory, therefore, has tended to breed a renewed scepticism about the wisdom of governments becoming involved in subsidizing, or organizing training for, employed workers, returning the position full circle to something like it was in the 1980s, when Becker's anti-interventionist perfect competition model reigned supreme within conventional economics. This is likely to remain the position within conventional economics unless and until substantive quantitative evidence of market failure is produced. This non-interventionist attitude is compounded in liberal market economies by the rise of neo-liberal ideologies, which in certain guises object to all forms of intervention even where human capital theory suggests they may be economically efficient.[7]

Human capital theory's recipe for skills intervention among the employed can be quite simple: don't do it! Only for the unemployed (poignant victims of market failure) is there a potential case for government-subsidized training— to ease the process of restructuring or to help retrenched workers to become employable.

A critique of human capital theory's negative conclusions on training interventions

There are several ways in which the position of human capital theory about training interventions can be criticized, drawing on literature from outside the economics mainstream. Most fundamentally, as already discussed in Chapters 5 and 6, human capital theory, because of its methodological individualism, fails adequately to recognize that skills and skilled work are socially determined. Second, human capital theory's neglect of the demand side of the labour market is a mistake, especially in an era of rapidly changing education systems. Third, human capital theory uses a too-simplistic conception of the politics of skill formation, whereas a more realistic situating of the nation state within the global economy is required. Let us take each of these points of criticism in turn.

Skills are socially determined

Human capital theory is premised on the assumption that individuals are forward-looking agents, maximizing their utility, with 'adequate' foresight about future returns from training investments. The socially determined character of skill, by contrast, is shown both in the demand for and development of workers' skills by employers and in the acquisition of skills by individuals.

In conventional economic models—including those that incorporate imperfect markets and asymmetric information—the employer faces a set of external constraints given by technology and the market environment and, given the profit maximization objective, makes the appropriate decision about resource allocation, including the employment and development of skilled labour. There is no room for employers to take different decisions, unless their objectives were to depart from maximizing their profits. It is assumed that employers know the private pay-off for training better than anyone else.

The alternative schools of thought described in Chapter 5 do not eschew the assumption of profit maximization, but they allow room for the agency of employers. In the perspective of strategic management, firms' managers have choices over internal organization, the design of jobs, and levels of participation—the various ingredients of 'high involvement working practices'. Managers make their choices in the face of bounded rationality, with varying sets of norms, expectations, and capabilities. Thus the demand for skill is affected by the agency of management. Culture, the constellation of skill-formation institutions, and related institutional envelopes all come into play as significant features guiding the profit-maximizing approach taken by particular groups of managers in various settings.[8] Country and regional differences are to be expected, reflecting differential norms, the localization of management learning that hinders the adoption of new practices from further afield, and external institutions that affect local constraints and the norms of other agents. Thus, the management and organization of work differ considerably between countries, even for apparently identical jobs.[9] Equally, the employers' supplies of good opportunities for learning and skill acquisition are highly variable, and related to culturally and historically determined attitudes, since rational calculation with known risks is precluded. Across countries, opportunities for training vary by a factor of more than three; within countries there is yet more heterogeneity.

In addition, therefore, to the equivocal conventional arguments about intervention, once the agency of management is recognized there is a further potential case for a policy of promoting learning and the greater use of skills. The case in favour of social intervention hinges on whether the agents promoting it can develop a more strategic perspective on the acquisition and use of skills than is available to employers. Sectoral agencies, for example, may have access to knowledge of industry best practices and better foresight capabilities than many individual companies. Compared with central government, both sectoral and regional agencies should be able to develop closer relationships with employers than central governments. Interventions to generate better conditions for inter-firm and inter-sectoral learning can be supported with this rationale.

Once the case for promoting learning and the greater use of skills is made, however, such a policy is not easy to implement. There is always a reluctance to accept advice or other more intrusive interventions if they impinge too far upon the autonomy of capital. It should if possible be tailored appropriately for different groups of managers and sectors, with decisive incentives, changed norms, and persuasive tactics for poorly managed firms. Inevitably, incentive-based policies will involve some deadweight loss transfers to firms that are already providing a good learning environment. Any social intervention needs at a minimum to acquire credibility. Yet to say that there is a political difficulty in effecting any policy does not detract from the potential social validity of the policy; rather, it calls for creative and flexible policies suitable for each political context.

A similar argument applies to individuals. In human capital theory the individual's acquisition of skill is erected upon a cost–benefit analysis, in which rational individuals balance costs and benefits, the latter being discounted from the future back to the present. Yet such an individualistic procedure hides the social nature of skill acquisition, which derives, first, from a consideration of the nature of the uncertainty that individuals face when they take learning decisions, and, second, from the complexity of the social processes through which decisions are made and courses followed. Skill formation decisions in a deeply uncertain world should be conceived as a multi-causal structure involving beliefs and expectations, resources (capacity, information, and self-efficacy), and individuals' preferences or dispositions, with feedbacks deriving from the experiences of learning. This framework, described in Chapter 7, allows for several points of social intervention that both include and extend beyond the conventional perspective of market externalities, such as interventions to break cycles of cumulative disadvantage, the provision of adequate resources for young people to navigate the transition from education to work, and policies to minimize barriers to learning through the life course. Examples of barriers include credit constraints, lack of child-care arrangements, low personal confidence, or lack of awareness of training opportunities. Each of these examples has straightforward policy responses: state-supported loans, subsidies for confidence-building assistance, and information-spreading activities. The point of the critique of human capital theory is that the justification for such policies comes from this wider perspective that accounts for social determination.

Neglect of the demand side and of mismatch

In the marketplace, skilled workers confront a range of jobs—usually long-term contractual arrangements—with varying skills demands. While the individualism of conventional economics based on human capital theory confines social interventions in skills within narrow bounds, equally problematic is the theory's normal presumption that labour markets are sufficiently flexible and thick, such that the large majority of workers find themselves matched with jobs that utilize the particular skills they have. The latter conclusion has led human capital theory to downplay and sometimes ignore altogether the demand side of the economy. There is, for example, a class of conventional economists in this tradition who will simply have no truck with the concept of over-education. They are joined by ministers of education and training who shun over-education's unpleasant overtones.

The issue should be neither ignored nor exaggerated. Over-education and under-utilization of skill have significant negative associations with pay and the well-being of workers. The state of over-education is individually persistent for long or indefinite periods; it is becoming more prevalent in industrialized countries (see the previous chapter). There are thus risks involved in any strategy that simply aims at raising the supply of educated workers, in the absence of an appreciation of the state of the economy and hence of the

147

demand for more educated workers. Yet over-education is not the same as being overskilled, and the rise in over-education does not necessarily imply an increase in the proportions who are overskilled. Education also has other purposes than the economic, and many would advocate a perfectly valid strategy to expand the level and quality of education for social and other ends. Chapter 11 includes a discussion of whether governments should worry about over-education.

If human capital theory's assumption of flexible and thick labour markets is dropped, there emerge two major areas that should form part of the focus of national skill strategies. First, governments can improve their understanding of the demand for skill and address the problem of leveraging that demand side, within the confines of the sources of intervention that are possible in each national context.[10] A demand-side policy is likely to be easier for governments that also contemplate proactive industrial policy. Second, alongside policies to improve the supply of skills, governments should also focus on the skills-matching processes: the information, advice, and guidance services that they provide—often a Cinderella service of minor prestige rather than a central tool of skills strategy. In a deeply uncertain environment, individuals cannot easily access information about employment prospects of heterogeneous courses and subjects studied, and it behoves any state committed to equal opportunities to ensure that good advice, contacts, and guidance are abundant and not skewed in the direction of elites.

The nation state and skill

A third critique of human capital theory relates to its relevance for national skills strategies in an internationalized economy. Conventional economic models pay relatively little attention to the politics of skill and of economic growth: they do not have a way of characterizing skills policy in the context of a nation state in a global economy. From a conventional economic perspective, there is no normative reason to favour the location of skills and skilled work in one country, rather than another, any more than there is a reason to oppose free trade.

An alternative approach to the nation state rooted in political economy recognizes that, in a global economy, the government, its citizens, and its home-oriented employers have interests in locating skilled activities within its borders. With few exceptions, the state's legal or cultural/historical character signifies low cross-border mobility, and the majority of workers do not normally have the choice of relocating abroad to improve their skill acquisition and utilization opportunities. Governments need in part to legitimize their reigns by delivering national economic growth and development, and to fill their coffers with the resulting tax revenues. Similarly, governments claim to deliver equal opportunities for skill development within their domains, for reasons of within-nation equity, social justice, and efficiency, given the high social costs of exclusion. Thus governments should pursue national skill strategies in their own interests, where these are thought to deliver the promised economic and social benefits. Since these benefits are for the long term, a classic contradiction is posed for democratic governments that face regular elections and a chance of losing power: the future pay-off might not be rewarded with current votes. Therefore, a national skills strategy needs to be credible with the electorate and to enjoy cross-party support.

National productivist skill strategies might not seem rational from an international perspective. Indeed, a national objective to become more skilled is sometimes portrayed as a 'skills race'. If education were merely a positional good, such that the growth and competitiveness it gave rise to in one country were at the expense of growth and competitiveness in another, one might be worried that nations were over-investing in human capital. Such normative and distributional factors are especially relevant in the consideration of immigration policy, which has come to be used in some countries as a partial substitute for skills policy. If national governments incentivize skilled labour migration, they can help address skill shortages and skill deficits over a relatively shorter period than it takes to educate and train young non-immigrant workers. Policies that link immigration to occupation or education level, or to an invitation from an employer, come into this category, as do policies to retain international students after they have graduated by allowing them to accept work.[11]

Skill-oriented immigration policies might be justified from a nationalist normative standpoint but are questionable from a supra-national perspective. Where the host country gains from skilled-worker migration, the source country, whose citizens will normally have contributed to the education and training of emigrants, loses. Commonly the host is richer than the source nation, in which cases transfers are not defensible on distributional grounds. Should the fear of losing skilled labour through this 'brain drain' be substantial, it could be a deterrent to education and training, in a manner analogous to employers' disincentive to train arising from the risk of their employees quitting. On the other hand, source countries might benefit if there is substantial income repatriation from emigrants, or where emigrants return after some years with new skills acquired abroad. Subsidies for return migration, and regulation to enable it from host countries, can be justified through this perspective. In many cases evidence is lacking, however, about whether these potential benefits are enough to balance the more obvious disadvantages to a nation of losing its skilled labour.

The role of the state in promoting skilled work and skill formation: a restatement

Let us take stock of the argument so far. All schools of thought support the state's involvement with funding and providing education, even if there are differences about private provision of higher education. Serious controversy arises, however, in the domain of training.

Conventional economics delineates principles for considering whether social intervention to promote workplace learning is desirable, but the case rests on empirical judgements made in the face of insufficient evidence about market failures. Such judgements unsurprisingly vary. Many analysts come to a default position that militates against intervention, until a proper estimate of the magnitude of market failure is produced. The only commonly granted exception is training for the unemployed, this being a self-evident market failure and a palpable arena for redistribution. Other neoclassical economists and those outside the realm of conventional economics face the same limited evidence but come to a different judgement, preferring an interventionist conclusion premised on the assumption of pervasive market failures.

In this book, however, the discussion and case for intervention has been taken a step beyond the conventional economist's theoretical perspective through a critique of its individualism. Given the importance of the agency of managers, an additional driving principle with respect to employers, beyond the redress of market failures, is the idea of promoting workplace learning where there is evidence that employer ambition has been lacking. In some industries, regional and sectoral agencies that are close to employers can claim to have better knowledge of future economic trends, a better appreciation of the evidence about good managerial practices surrounding skills, and a more long-term perspective than is possessed by the tail of poorly managed firms. Where this is argued to be the case, interventions to try to improve management knowledge, capabilities, and practices are potentially warranted, depending on the costs of implementation. This criterion does not apply to private and tacit knowledge about each firm's circumstances. Similarly in respect of individuals, governments have good reason to assist them in the navigation of learning paths where people face deep uncertainty about skills decisions, and lack adequate resources, and where attitudes and dispositions can be a bitter consequence of circumstances and previous bad experiences.

The political economic perspective on the nation state also provides a nationalist rationale beyond the conventional for social intervention in skills—though from a global perspective the normative argument is compromised by equity objectives. To attain legitimacy through growth and to underpin its own resources in the long run, a forward-thinking national government will try to locate its home territory as the locus of skilled work and to raise the skill levels of the domestic workforce above those of workforces in alternative locations, to the benefit of the citizens who vote for it.

Skill systems and forms of state involvement

The framework so far outlined gives criteria for social interventions in skills use and skill formation services, but it remains too abstract. The generality belies the fact that governments operate among constellations of institutions and interest groups who must be induced to consent and sometimes collaborate. The extent to which any policies can be implemented depends in part on the feasibility and costs of securing compliance. Thus each government must take account of the 'skill system' in which it is embedded. For example, a well-functioning apprenticeship system requires that young people are ready to commit to this form of learning, and that employers are individually and collectively prepared to take up apprentices in sufficient numbers, providing good-quality training and induction into occupational knowledge and relationships. The aim of this section is to define and describe the concept of a skill system in general, and some prominent models of national and subnational skill systems.

A skill system is a set of institutions for the production of skills and mechanisms for the articulation of the demand for and supplies of skilled labour, where the phrase 'institutions' encompasses not just legal/political entities but also rules, customs, norms, and beliefs.[12] One might think of the skill system, in relation to the framework described in Figure 3.1, as the ghost behind the circuits described, animating the movements of value and the behaviour of the actors. Formally a skills system comprises:

- all skills formation institutions and their accompanying regulatory frameworks, including providers and employers;
- all the institutions and regulatory systems, controlled either by government or by the other social partners (unions and works councils, chambers of commerce, professional and industry associations, and peak-level representatives), which affect the determination and matching of the supply of skilled work with the demand.

Some institutions influence the supply and nature of education and training provision and available qualifications. Some affect the incentives and opportunities for individuals to access education and training provision. Some directly intervene in the process of matching job-seekers with jobs. Others affect the level and nature of the demand for skilled labour. Even institutions whose primary relationship is with neither skills demand nor skill formation should be regarded as part of the skill system if they have a clear indirect relationship. For example, where countries develop trade and industrial policies to enhance the competitiveness of the national economy, such policies are also considered to be part of the skill system if they have implications for the demand for skilled labour.

Honouring a set of institutions with the title 'system' reflects an ambition to go beyond description, a conception that the constituent parts hang together in some way, complementing each other's functions. The systemic character is partly architectural, just as the different bits of any education system must be vertically and horizontally articulated. Yet skill systems theories also aim to identify where there is coherence between the incentives, rules, and norms of behaviour of interacting groups. The systemic character of the institutions is meant to extend, not only to their mechanical, regulatory, and fiscal functions but also to their cultural functions, affecting managerial practices and the dispositions of workers. Total coherence among all elements is, however, an impossible ideal; typically, analysts identify a few key axes along which consistency and coherence can be demonstrated.

The expectation that coherent institutions are likely to be stable has led analysts to develop the concepts of a 'high-skills equilibrium' and a 'low-skills equilibrium'. In the former, the incentives that employers face induce them to be ambitious in their use of high level of skills, and to invest further in and reward their workforce's skills; while employees perceive through experience that there are genuine opportunities and returns through committing to learning, and to high-skilled work. Thus, the demand and supply of high-skilled labour are both high, as also are the provision and demand for learning. The opposite incentives and motives are reinforced in the low-skills equilibrium. In both cases the coherence of beliefs, incentives, motives, and opportunities is used to account for the persistence of institutions. The case of a low-skill equilibrium exemplifies the difficulty that governments may encounter when introducing piecemeal skills policy innovations that are not coherent with the rest of the system.[13]

The attractiveness of the concept of the skills equilibrium, high or low, as an explanation for persistence goes away when it is realized that systems change and there is a concern to understand their evolution. With the alternative concept of the 'skills ecosystem', this scientific metaphor draws attention also to the inter-related character of policies, incentives, and institutions, but also incorporates innovation and adaptation of the skill system. It accommodates a dynamic perspective, substituting the term 'sustainability' for equilibrium.[14] For example, one hypothesis is that skills ecosystems can become unsustainable if there is an imbalance between the level of skills being formed and the extent of their deployment, resulting either in overload for skilled workers or the opposite, under-employment. The concept has been applied most fruit-fully at the sub-national level to explain the dynamics of industrial clusters of employers using and generating high-skilled labour—among which Silicon Valley in California is the paradigm. A 'high-skill ecosystem', it is hypothe-sized, is likely to develop among firms where there is a high degree of inter-connectedness (through commerce, cooperation, and worker mobility), a supportive environment (including infrastructure and enabling regulation), and a plentiful supply of highly educated workers; cumulative reinforcement suggests also the need for a robust catalyst to start the ball rolling. One approach to policy, then, is for governments to aim to foster the development of high-skill ecosystems in regions within their national boundaries. Yet this approach to skill systems remains relatively undeveloped, and there could be a risk that policies aimed at generating high-skill systems at a sub-national level are not inclusive, with many regions and much of the population left out.

To frame the proposed coherence at a national level, skills systems may be seen as belonging to broader institutional 'regimes' of capitalism.[15] A substan-tial literature advances the idea that heterogeneous national regimes induce differentiated behaviour and forms of conflict between capital and labour, as a result of which divergences in economic and social outcomes between coun-tries persist—even in a world that is increasingly integrated by financial, trade, and production relations. A distinctive institutional characteristic, according to 'production regime' theory, is the extent to which employer strategies involve coordination of labour and product markets. This perspective throws the spotlight upon the institutions that foster this coordination and may involve the government in varying degrees; it suggests that both the level and the degree of firm- or industry-specificity of intermediate skills in a country is distinctly related to the level of coordination that has evolved. Coordination is placed at the heart of this theory because it is assumed, following the conventional economics perspective, that the core function of the institutions involved is to overcome the training externalities associated with labour turnover, and to substitute within each industry a cooperative solution to the problem. In this production regime approach, the aim is to identify the origins and effects on skills of this cooperative behaviour brought about through the strategic orientation of employers.

By contrast, according to 'employment regime' theories, just as decisive as employer coordination is the extent of inclusiveness in institutions for the regulation of employment relations. Coherence is sought between the norms governing distribution in and outside work. In this conception—which also draws upon the social policy characterization of distinct welfare state regimes—key features affecting the level and distribution of skilled work are the strength and degree of centralization of organized labour, together with the level of state involvement. Enquiry centres on the origins and effects of inclusive forms of negotiation across the class divide.

The coherence of regimes should not be exaggerated. In reality one is often confronted by a complex mix of skills institutions that constitute more of a list than an organic totality. Nevertheless, using regime theories the holistic focus has been developed and sharpened by a typology of stylized models that pick out certain constellations of institutions common to groups of countries and that delineate some of the complementarities. Four main systems have been proposed, each associated with a 'variety' or 'regime' of capitalism: two types of Coordinated Market Economy (CME), the Liberal Market Economy (LME), and the Developmental Economy (DE). Some writers use alternative designations for the same or similar groups of nations. While a further group may also sometimes be included, covering southern European countries, most countries do not fall neatly into any cluster.

Coordinated Market Economy (CME) skill systems

Coordinated Market Economies are characterized by the centralization of bargaining, and greater regulation of pay systems. They may, however, be divided into two types, with differing implications for skill formation: social partner-led skill systems, and state-led social partnership skill systems.

SOCIAL PARTNER-LED SKILL SYSTEMS

Social partner-led systems, found in German-speaking countries and other countries proximate to them, favour institutional coordination in the supply of and demand for skills formation services, particularly through the labour market institutions organized by the social partners.

The compulsory schooling and initial training systems are distinguished by the maintenance of selective institutions at the compulsory level, and by the prevalence of apprenticeships at the post-compulsory level for most students not bound for university. Typically school matriculation requirements involve achievement in a range of subjects, including the core subjects of mathematics, and national and foreign languages. Apprenticeship programmes are naturally specialized along occupational lines, but through social partner control maintain curriculum breadth and provide an effective introduction into an occupational community and identity.

The control of education tends to be devolved largely to the regional level, particularly in countries with federal systems. Schools have rather less budgetary and managerial autonomy than those in market-oriented systems. School diversity exists by virtue of the differentiation of schools by ability level, but school choice is quite constrained.

The regulation and funding of the 'dual systems' of apprentice training is governed through negotiations between social partner bodies balancing different interests in each sector. Central governments in federal states typically have overall responsibility for the apprenticeship system, but the design and licensing of apprentice programmes may occur through a national body that represents the social partners. The central state often pays for the provision of general and vocational education in school-based part of apprenticeship provision, while employers for the most part pay for the work-based training. Sectoral agreements frequently stipulate the qualifications required for different occupations in the sector as well as pay bands; sectoral pay bands reduce the danger of firms using pay premia to 'poach' employees trained by another firm. Both the Works Councils in larger firms and the Chambers of Commerce have statutory rights to monitor the quality of training, and the Chambers may be involved in the assessment of the apprentices' skills for the purposes of certification.

Adult continuing training in the social partner-led systems tends to be less regulated than initial training; left mostly to individual employers, it stands not especially high. Employee interests are typically represented in Works Councils and on Company Boards in the larger firms, providing a forum for employees to lobby for the maintenance of skills levels with the requisite training.

One element of system coherence derives from the match between the apprenticeship system and employers' strategic preference for operating at the high value-added end of product markets, where workers are generally required to have broad skills, capable of adapting frequently to new and niche product lines with complex production processes.[16] Another element comes from incentive compatibility, wherein the pay and training regulation ensures that both employers and young people derive demonstrable benefits.

In addition to the comparatively high deployment of intermediate skills, the social partner-led skills system produces, by international comparative standards, a relatively even distribution of skills among the workforce, contributing alongside pay regulation to lower wage differentials than in Liberal Market Economies. The broad occupational training combined with ongoing learning in core areas of general education increases the facility with which workers can switch to new lines of skilled work as firms innovate with new designs.

Because they involve substantial levels of cooperation and trust among employers, and between employers and unions, the generation and persistence of intermediate-level skill formation institutions have attracted the close interest of political science. The contemporary constellation of institutions is the product of historical alliances and subsequent paths of development that can be partly explained by the functions they serve in supporting the interests of employers and workers in skill-intensive industries. A key feature of the emergence of Germany's apprenticeship system at the start of the twentieth century, for example, is that evolving class conflict between employers and workers did not entail a contest along a line of skill (unlike in the United Kingdom and the United States). Moreover, the authoritarian state actively supported the organization of artisans, and the formation of the modern apprenticeship system that emerged from traditional craft guilds. Differences among the CME countries in the evolution of skill systems are an ongoing focus of research.[17]

The social partner-led skills system, particularly its apprenticeship component, came under some strain in the late 1990s.[18] Apprentice places have declined, as employers rely more on graduate trainees and as young people increasingly gravitate towards higher education. Emerging high-tech economic sectors have not always found the apprenticeship system well adapted to their needs. More firms are opting out of the sectoral agreements that underpin social partnership, and the globalization of companies increasingly creates anomalies in training practices between home and abroad. Yet apprenticeship systems have adapted through the broadening of the content of training programmes and by offering dual certification routes that allow apprentices to gain both vocational and school qualifications. Such reforms, and the persistence of occupational labour markets, have helped to maintain dual systems as the primary bridge between school and work for the majority of young people. In Germany, there is evidence that the dual system has been revitalized, and that the advantages and attractions of dual training for many young people relative to university have been retained.[19]

STATE-LED SOCIAL PARTNERSHIP SKILL SYSTEMS

The other type of CME skill system is the state-led social partnership systems, associated with the Nordic countries. Here the government plays a greater role in the funding and regulation of adult education and training, and school systems also have a distinctive institutional structure. Overall, governments spend every year a significantly larger fraction of GDP on education than in other countries.

One significant feature is that pre-school education is universally provided by the state at a low cost to parents, making it easier for mothers of young children to supply their skilled labour. Compulsory education is provided in 'all-through' non-selective, mixed ability, comprehensive schools, which combine primary and lower secondary levels, and limit ability grouping to a minimum throughout the system. Initial training is predominantly school based or college based, with additional school-led hybrid apprenticeships in some countries. Adult learning is also substantially state led, with central and local authorities providing an exceptionally wide array of adult learning opportunities, both in the form of traditional adult general education, as with the Folk High Schools, and through labour market programmes for up-skilling and re-skilling of the workforce. The social partners are substantially involved in the latter provision and particularly with the Active Labour Market programmes, which seek to re-skill adults for new employment when their skills have become obsolescent owing to structural changes in the workplace.

These skills formation systems utilize substantial degrees of state and social partner regulation to facilitate the coordination of skills supply and demand. Late subject specialization in schooling and breadth in initial training are designed to maximize the acquisition of transferable skills and contribute to individual mobility and flexibility in the workforce. Meanwhile, the highly centralized, concerted, and solidaristic collective bargaining processes contribute towards the coordination of national efforts to articulate skills supply and demand, while acting to reduce wage differentials.[20]

The most distinctive outcome of state-led social partnership skill systems is their relatively equal distribution of skills and skilled work, consistent with the strong welfare state system. The egalitarian structure of schools systems, combined with the widely accessible adult learning opportunities, contribute to the wide distribution of skills in the workforce. They also show a strong emphasis on the broad, transferable skills required in high-skilled manufacturing and service sectors. Allied to the centralized trade union bargaining and coordinated wage setting procedures, the outcome is one where both wages and other aspects of job quality such as skill use, autonomy, and job prospects are more narrowly dispersed than in other capitalist nations.[21] However, for all their strengths, such systems have also faced difficulties. For instance, motivation and learning among young people on the less prestigious programmes in upper secondary education have often been poor. Increasingly, learning programmes, particularly for the lower achievers, have become more individualized in order to cater for the skills needs and learning preferences of individual students.

Liberal Market Economy (LME) skill systems

Liberal Market Economies are distinguished by relatively little industrial or economy-wide coordination, in either product or labour markets, a preference for minimal regulation except where competition policy or public health dictates, and a relatively low orientation to inclusiveness in the regulation of employment. Unions play a role, but bargaining usually takes place at firm or industry level. LME skills formation systems, typically associated with the United States, the United Kingdom, Australia, and other English-speaking countries, tend to be characterized by institutional diversity and a market-led approach to the coordination of skills supply and demand.

The state school systems are formally largely comprehensive in structure during the compulsory years but are increasingly characterized by policies for school choice and diversity. Private schooling for elites tends to be of high quality and cost. Setting and streaming policies increasingly differentiate students by ability groups at the secondary level. Schools have a high degree of managerial autonomy, with devolved budgets and powers of hire and fire, and are encouraged to compete with each other. The curricula allow for relatively early subject specialization, so that students are already taking elective subjects in lower secondary school, in preparation for an upper secondary system characterized by a high level of subject choice. Post-compulsory education and training also tend to be highly diverse. Universities display a substantial range of quality and cost, and a wide spread of vocational training qualifications is available. Courses and qualifications are often designed in modular fashion to allow flexible credit accumulation and speedy revision. There are complex structures with multiple transition routes into work, so that students are required to make frequent choices.

Adult education and training in LMEs is also diverse and market led. 'Second-chance' education is provided in publicly funded institutions as well as, in some countries, through national programmes for the enhancement of adult basic skills. However, most learning opportunities are provided by employers. Joint social partner regulation is rare: in the main, it is the market that determines how the supply of training meets demand.

The demand for skilled labour in LMEs is also subject to little governmental influence outside the public sector itself, except indirectly through minimum pay regulation. Technology and skills transfer between firms within sectors is typically facilitated by flexible labour markets and the circulation of high-skilled employees between firms, rather than through the plethora of technology transfer institutions typically found in more coordinated systems. The value of industrial and regional clusters (such as Silicon Valley) is especially salient. Another indirect influence in LMEs is the predominant mode of corporate governance and of financing linked to share capital, which are sometimes argued to discourage a long-term strategic orientation.

LME skill systems tend to generate a plentiful supply of highly skilled and qualified individuals, as well as a substantial proportion of less-qualified adults, responding to skills demands in labour markets where skills distribution have become more polarized. Participation in adult training has tended to be quite high but is unevenly distributed, so that it exacerbates the inequalities in skills that are evident among school leavers. The plentiful supply of highly skilled individuals supports the high skills, high value-added sectors, which are often well developed in these countries. However, at the same time, the 'long tail' of under-achievers in the education and training systems feeds into the substantial low skills segment of the labour force, depressing wage levels and encouraging firms in some sectors to compete on price rather than quality with low value-added products and services.

Developmental Economy (DE) skill systems

Developmental Economy skill systems are associated with the developmental states (particularly in East Asia), which pursue more interventionist programmes of state-led economic and social development. States are characterized as developmental when they make an absolute priority of rapid economic development and use a wide range of government powers to this end.[22]

Education provision in developmental states grew rapidly to meet the increase in the demand for skills as these countries pursued export-led industrialization. Substantial initial public investment, later supplemented by considerable private family investment in secondary and post-secondary schooling, financed rising participation, first in primary, and subsequently in secondary and post-secondary education. Some public education systems were exceptionally egalitarian in their compulsory phases, with entirely unstreamed, mixed-ability classes in non-selective, neighbourhood comprehensive schools. Others, while remaining strongly meritocratic, were more stratified. In all cases, however, the developmental education systems were highly centralized, using the powers of the state to achieve consistent standards across schools and to universalize the acquisition of the skills demanded by newly industrializing economies.

The dominant forms of adult training have varied in developmental skills formation systems. In countries like Singapore with economies dominated by foreign multinational firms, governments have provided wide-ranging adult training programmes, while cajoling large firms to invest in training through incentive schemes, including taxes on low-paid jobs to encourage employers to up-skill their workforces. By contrast, in a large country like Japan, with its economy dominated by home-grown multinationals, governments have been able to limit their interventions mostly to training for the small firm and artisanal sectors, since large employers have been willing to invest in training without external pressure. Policies of long-term employment in the large firms are accompanied by substantial investments in developing their staff. Large firms have thus expected public education systems to deliver recruits with high levels of general education and good learning abilities, rather than specific vocational skills.

In DE skill systems, industrial policies and related skills policies are more interventionist than in other systems, shaping employer demand for skills. Industrial policies are adopted that promote certain economic sectors and discourage others. It is here that the nation state motive for intervention in skill systems is most transparent. What is distinctive about the skills matching process in the DE skill systems is that, where governments have implemented policies for the long-term development of particular sectors, they have also analysed the likely effects of these policies on future skills demand and put in place measures to ensure that such skills demands will be met. They have been able to organize this skills matching through systems of government that have evolved to allow a more coordinated and strategic approach to skills planning than is found elsewhere. Such an approach results in the development of new vocational courses in public provider institutions in anticipation of future demand, and the use of quotas on programmes to match the flow of those trained in particular areas to perceived demand at each stage of development.

DE skill systems have thus been very effective in supporting economic growth in newly industrializing countries. Skills policy has often been used in a proactive fashion, not only to meet immediate employer demands, but also to shape employer strategies towards skills, encouraging firms to move to more skilled, higher value-added areas of manufacturing and service provision. However, they have been less successful hitherto in developing the creative talents demanded in the growing knowledge economy sectors. Also, in recent years there has been less centralized control over higher education, with the result that the link between the supply and demand for college labour is weakened and more dependent on market forces.

The role for skills interventions in an institutionally constrained environment

Models of national institutional regimes have proved quite helpful for understanding the development of skills institutions in various national settings. Yet they should not be used as a substitute for an understanding of country-specific institutions affecting skills. The four national regime models are contested abstractions, with some analysts finding that 'hybrid' models are more revealing and emphasizing the ways that the models are themselves evolving under external and internal pressures. The terms 'system' and 'regime' may thus oversell the extent to which national institutions and relationships are coherent. It is generally agreed, however, that the national institutional environment should be the starting point for addressing the question motivating this chapter—namely: what principles can democratic governments follow when devising an approach or strategy to help resolve the problems of national skill systems?

The motivation to develop a skills strategy arises because the skill needs of modern societies are changing and education systems are expanding. The pace of these changes implies that piecemeal, ad hoc, adjustments to vocational education and training systems, and normal business evolutions, risk the creation of skills mismatches and inefficiencies in the system that can be greatly detrimental to economic and social well-being. Several problematic skills outcomes were illustrated in the previous chapter. The advocated response is not a universal strategy or even a common list of policies, but a set of guidelines for designing and assessing nationally specific policies relevant to each national institutional environment. Though nationally specific, the intervening agency will often be sub-national, based on region or industry. Following the arguments of this chapter, four general guidelines may be stated.

(i) Address the reason for getting involved

First, governments should assess what they do against the principles for intervention reviewed earlier this chapter:

- The conventional case for intervention is built on the prevalence of failures in the market for skill formation services. Governments should identify and assess the importance of externalities and public goods. After considering whether it has the capacity to rectify private deficiencies, bearing in mind its own imperfections, the government should intervene where appropriate with tax/subsidy incentives or through regulation, or support the interventions of other social actors.

- When not blinded by the neo-liberal blanket proscription against all forms of intervention with private employment relations, governments can consider whether there exist areas or sectors where employers lack capacity or ambition to choose a high-skill route. A government may consider that its own capacities and resources are not sufficient even to provide advice services (in which case it could consider developing this capacity). Alternatively it may consider that it has a longer-term perspective and superior strategic capacity, and hence legitimately decide on policies to persuade and enable some employers to make better use of employees' capacities to learn, using incentives or other means.

- Governments should also legitimately intervene to assist individuals in their choices with proper advice and guidance services, avoiding paternalism and refraining from compulsion; they should also monitor the structures of work and learning options, and attempt to minimize learning barriers.

- Governments oriented towards reducing inequality may legitimately consider education and training policies to intervene in cycles of cumulative disadvantage; Active labour market policy for retrenched employees is a common example. In general, governments should assess such education and training interventions against alternative redistributive mechanisms.

- It may also seem appropriate before their own citizens for national governments to do whatever they can to ensure that both skills and skilled work are located in their own countries. Included under this principle are skill-oriented migration policies, and skill-oriented inward investment and trade policies. Yet, such policies may be neither legitimate nor efficient from a supra-national perspective, if they redistribute skills and skilled work away from countries where these are relatively scarce.

(ii) *Take account of the institutional environment*

Second, whatever policies are considered under the above general principles, they need to be assessed in the context of the institutional environment for which they are proposed. Two principles emerge, coherence and national specificity:

- Policies need to respect institutional coherence where it exists. Occasionally, policies may reasonably be considered in isolation, but often there are connections that, if ignored, lead to failure. For example, a policy of providing subsidies for training low-paid workers may not succeed if other policies and institutions (such as reducing the minimum wage) limit demand for the skills they acquire. The machineries in the education and training ministries need to be articulated with each other, and with industrial and trade ministries. Moreover, policies suitable in one model of skill system may not work so well in another. For example, a classic issue is the challenge of generating a mass apprenticeship programme in an LME skill system that lacks a major role for the social partners in their planning and support.[23]
- From this stems also the principle of national specificity: that each government, even though it should learn from the successes and failures of policies in other countries, has to devise policies that are suitable for its own economy and institutional environment. Of course, the coherence of skill system models is limited, so this principle is not a proscription against pulling in individual policies from abroad. The rule should be: benchmark against others to help assess skills deficits, but evaluate others' policies in their institutional context.

(iii) *Always evaluate*

Because policies must always be country specific, even though similar ones may have been tried and tested in other countries, their efficacy is always likely to be in question. An obvious, if often neglected, principle, therefore, is that policies should be evaluated, rather than assumed to work, even if there is supportive evidence from other countries. Preferably, an independent evaluation plan should be built into all skills policy implementation strategies. Evaluations should be premised upon the above intervention criteria.

(iv) *Consider the case for institutional development*

Bearing in mind the detrimental effects of poorly functioning institutions, governments may have to embark on a path of institutional reform and development. The skills tactics of the different branches and ministries must be coordinated within government, and it is important that the incentives instilled with new institutions are compatible with each other. For example, if the strategy is to stimulate more firms to engage in high value-added production through industrial policies, such a policy should be coordinated with the plans of education and training ministries to ensure against skill shortages. Or policies to stimulate a high-quality apprenticeship system should be accompanied by a programme to incentivize partnership behaviour by unions, who can both help to certify apprenticeship quality and raise the supply of potential apprentices.

An ambitious agenda of institutional development for a skill system, however, will need to take cognisance of the limits and possibilities for such a reform programme within the context of a feasible variety of capitalism. To what extent does the skills agenda provide a way forward for institutional development, rather than a disguising of older fundamental contradictions and conflicts that remain as potent as ever? This question and other fundamental debates, are highlighted in Chapter 11; before that, Chapter 10 takes as its premise that there are many potential policies that governments may legitimately consider in contemporary capitalism, but that these need to be based on an adequate empirical understanding of skills and skilled work in each country. Its focus is on the analytical tools now becoming available for this task.

10

Skills Analysis for Modern Economies

Auditing skills

When in 1709 thousands of people from the Palatinate and neighbouring territories arrived in London, escaping the aftermath of war, famine, and religious persecution, pastors George Ruperti and John Tribbeko came to their assistance. These two pleaded the case for government support to help the German refugees on their way to the colonies in America. They also made a list of each man's name along with his occupation, and whether he was accompanied by a wife and children. In stating the occupation the list assigned each man an identity, and a mark of what he could do, which was important given that most had lost their wealth. Among them were carpenters, tanners, joiners, coopers, husbandmen, herdsmen, wheelwrights, smiths, saddlers, bakers, brewers, butchers, weavers, tailors, shoemakers, masons, bookbinders, and miners. Though the pastors' list came to be used later for different purposes—it was to become invaluable to historians and genealogists—it was, in part, an early form of 'skills audit'.

In the present day knowledge economy the skills audit has become a general tool for the planning of individuals' access to skilled work and for employers' management of their human resources. It has also broadened out into a method by which governments can become more strategic in their support for skill formation. If, as discussed in the previous chapter, there are contingent and complex reasons for state intervention in skills markets, adopted policies should be preceded and accompanied by adequate analyses. This chapter aims to explain and illustrate several kinds of skills analyses, and how they can be used to support evidence-based policy-making.

At the individual level, the skills audit is a self-help device in support of a thoughtful approach to deciding what courses to take or jobs to aspire to. It can be put to use in specific communities—for example, among immigrant workers who may have many skills but whose educational qualifications are not recognized in a host country. Its essential objective is to establish and clarify the skills that a person has. In itself an accounting of one's skills is insufficient for planning; the audit is then accompanied by some form of future analysis that entails, on the one hand, identifying the skills that the individual aspires to obtain, and, on the other, identifying the learning and training processes through which the gap between the present and desired future skills is to be bridged.

Skills audits are most commonly carried out, however, by employers, as preludes to their own attempt at rationally planning the development of the human resources of their overall workforce—a 'training needs analysis'. Together, the skills audit and training needs analyses should lead to an understanding of the skills available to the organization, the skills needed to fulfil the organization's goals, and the training and recruitment needed to fill the gaps—the same threefold construct as for an individual skills audit. In some organizations the process can become highly formalized. Skills gap identification, for example, might entail full surveys of the whole workforce, or focus groups, or appraisal meetings. In the latter context a skills gap analysis might also become evaluative and contested—a direct illustration of the social construction of skill. Comprehensive skill needs and training needs analyses typically result in training and development plans, as well as systematic succession and recruitment strategies. There is some evidence of an increasing use of a formal approach to skills planning in organizations, reflecting an evolution of human resource management.[1]

At regional and national levels, skills audits have a wider purpose. Skills audits of particular regions and localities are sometimes carried out, not only to help local state institutions plan provision of tertiary courses, but also to inform and impress businesses enquiring about investment in the region. In more recent years, skills audits have become important in national and supra-national strategies for skills development, and in so doing their purpose and content have broadened still further. Wherever a government has adopted a long-term framework for instilling growth and development, skills audits aim to inform about the prospects for, and progress of, required skills development and utilization. Sometimes, audits entail assessing progress towards targets that may be set to generate and coordinate higher aspirations among multiple actors in society, including government agencies. A supra-national instance is the EU's Europe 2020 targets to reduce school drop-outs below 10 per cent and have at least 40 per cent of 30–34-year-olds having completed tertiary education. National targets tend to be more detailed and entail benchmarking against other countries. National skills audits also try to give an early warning about developing imbalances, whether overall—for example, in the market for tertiary educated labour—or in particular sectors. Detailed skills forecasts aim to inform providers and employers who wish to plan for their long term, as well as policy-makers' decisions for the allocation of funds to state provision.

In short, modern-day skills audits are being developed in the belief that making the right choices can affect both skills supply and utilization, hence also growth and development, and that better choices stem from better analysis. How far this promise is fulfilled remains, however, to be determined.

A full national skills audit could amount to a thorough analysis of the skills markets across a nation. It could comprise a description and projection of skills supply, a similar forecast of skills demand including an understanding of newly emerging skills, an analysis of the social and private returns to the acquisition of skills, and an analysis of skills mismatches. Let us see how well these things can be done.

Describing and projecting skills supply

To capture the skills of a regional or national workforce, analysts will usually have no alternative to taking educational attainment as their measure of skill, though this will change when adult skills tests become widely available (Chapter 4). A typical audit will record the proportions qualified to various levels, and in each subject. Since qualifications measures are quite widely available, and have been for some time in many countries, it is also relatively easy to describe past changes. More challenging is to forecast the future supply of qualifications. A rough-and-ready approach to framing the future is to break down educational attainment by age group. Older people typically have lower attainment, since this is an era of educational expansion. As time passes, young adults retain their levels of achievement, and come to replace retiring workers in the labour supply. The attainment differences between the age groups is, then, an indication of how rapidly the supply of qualifications is rising.

The OECD regularly provides a cross-national comparison that deploys this method, which is illustrated for a selection of countries in Figure 10.1, with a range of levels of tertiary education attainment and strikingly varying dynamics. In France, and even more so in Japan and South Korea, the younger age group has especially high tertiary attainment, compared to its older compatriots. Even if there were no further expansion of attainment for the next generation of young adults—a conservative assumption—the average attainment of the workforce in these countries is set to rise rapidly as the older, less-educated, cohorts retire. In stark contrast, there is very little expansion to be expected in Estonia or the United States, since their older cohorts are almost as highly educated as their younger ones. In Israel, even a small decline is envisaged by this method. In between are the majority of countries: Sweden, the Netherlands, and Canada are typical, with substantive rises in the supply of skills expected, Canada starting from an already high level of tertiary

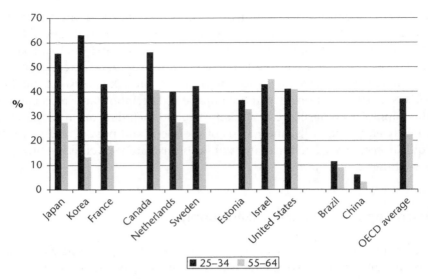

Figure 10.1. Proportion of the population that has attained tertiary education, 2009
Source: OECD (2011: table A1.3a).

educational attainment. Finally, Brazil and China start from low levels of tertiary attainment, but are just beginning a period of expansion.

Yet this simple approach to forecasting future skills supply is imprecise and ignores several factors: the proportion of people with different qualifications who participate in the labour market, the rate at which people acquire further qualifications during their adult life, and the levels of inward and outward migration of skilled workers. The alternative is formally to model the future supply of qualifications, taking such factors into account.

Many governments now develop such models building on demographic forecasts of the population. The two key ingredients are the projection of the future labour force, and data for the education and skill attainments of existing age cohorts by sex. The more sophisticated models incorporate estimates of how people respond to economic factors in their decisions about participation in the labour force and in further skill formation, building on existing macroeconomic models of the economy and the labour market. Where there are insufficient data available for this approach, future behaviours are extrapolated from how people have participated in the recent past. Forecasts are made of the future qualification achievement of each group, then aggregated to yield predictions of the overall supply of qualified people. As one illustration, using this method the prediction is that the supply of workers in the twenty-seven countries of the European Union with high qualifications (ISCED 5–6) will have risen from 67.2 million in 2010 to 82.5 million in 2020; in the same period, those with low qualifications (ISCED 0–2) will have fallen from 54.5 down to 39.5 million, while those with intermediate qualifications (ISCED 3–4) will have remained fairly static, changing from 121.1 to 123.9 million.[2] In principle, the same method is applicable to alternative measures of skill; however, with skills measures serious consideration has to be given to how skills are augmented or deteriorate through the life course.

The uses to which such projections are put include national benchmarking and the achievement of qualifications targets, and a comparison with demand projections. For benchmarking, the same method for forecasting the stock of qualifications is applied to other countries at similar stages of development, or sometimes to a broad range of countries. Then the country's qualifications supply can be compared with those elsewhere, providing it is assumed that mass migration does not significantly alter the picture. For the latter, it is necessary to have projections of the demand for workers at various levels of educational attainment, to which I now turn.

Describing and projecting skills demand

In contrast to supply, forecasting the demand for skills and qualifications derives, not from the logic of cohorts and their education, but from expectations about the future trajectory of the economy. Technological and organizational changes, the global reorganizations of labour, and evolving consumer demands for services are the driving factors (Chapter 5).

A rough-and-ready forecast of skills demand is essentially an extrapolation of recent trends. Several governments prefer, however, formally to model the future demand, typically for a period of a decade or so. The two key ingredients of this exercise are an economic model of industrial demand, and an occupation–industry matrix that converts the prediction into a demand for occupations. The economic projections make assumptions about macroeconomic growth and stability, and about changing demand, which lend one domain of uncertainty about the forecasts.

The links between occupations and industry are a second source of uncertainty. In the more sophisticated models—such as that used by the US Bureau of Labor Statistics—the links are projected by extrapolating historical trends, but attempts are also made to allow for specific factors in each industry, including technological and organizational change, new products, and government policies; sometimes these are inserted using industry specific knowledge and judgement.[3] Although the principles behind such projections are simple, the breadth of their data requirements from industry and employment statisticians, including the need to combine data sources that may be inconsistent, makes for a complex operation. The requirements are magnified when the forecasts are multinational, as is the case with pan-European projections of

Table 10.1. Projections of the occupation structure in Europe (m.)

Occupation	2010	2020	Change	Replacement	Openings
Legislators, senior officials, and managers	19.1	20.6	1.4	8.5	9.9
Professionals	32.4	35.1	2.7	12.4	15.0
Technicians and associate professionals	38.3	32.8	−4.5	10.4	14.8
Clerks	23.9	22.7	−1.2	6.1	4.9
Service and sales workers	32.1	34.3	2.2	7.9	10.1
Skilled agricultural and fishery workers	9.7	7.7	−2.0	2.1	0.1
Craft and related trade workers	28.7	26.5	−2.1	12.5	10.3
Plant and machine operators, assemblers	18.6	18.5	−0.1	5.4	5.3
Elementary occupations	25.1	23.1	−2.0	8.0	9.9
ALL	227.3	234.5	7.2	73.1	80.3

Note: All EU member states plus Norway and Switzerland.
Source: CEDEFOP (2010: annexe II, tables 6 and 7).

occupational structure, developed in part response to the 'new skills for new jobs' resolution of the European Council in 2007.[4]

The chief output is a projection of future change in the numbers employed in each occupation, as illustrated in Table 10.1. As can be seen, high-skilled occupations are expanding. It is these figures that underpin Figure 8.3, which forms part of the evidence base for rising skills demand.

In some cases, projections of the occupational structure are transformed into projections of the 'demand for qualifications'. Unfortunately, this extension tends to be limited only to a very high level of aggregation, and it is debatable whether it adds much insight to the projection. The basis for this conceptual leap is an implicit assumption that the qualifications of current job-holders in each occupation indicate the demand for qualifications of these same occupations in the future. This assumption is questionable. In several occupations there may be found job-holders with high qualifications that are not being utilized (over-education), so the current stock of qualifications held is a biased proxy for qualifications required to do the job.

More promising are studies that aim to develop occupational skill profiles, derived from direct data on qualification requirements and other skills needs. Until recently there have been no available cross-national data on occupational skill and qualification requirements, so analysts have generalized from national studies—chiefly the O*NET from the United States, with additional help from national surveys in Britain, the Czech Republic, Germany, and Italy, and from Europe as a whole.[5] Occupational skill profiles can be used as an input into projections of future skills demand. This approach is conceptually superior to inferring qualification requirements from educational attainment, though for generating cross-national projections relies on assuming that qualification and other skill requirements are the same across countries for the same occupation. It is reasonable to assume, for example, that professional workers would require degree-level qualifications in most countries. Yet, given that qualification requirements may be affected by credentialism, and that there is abundant space for even well-defined occupations to be pursued in different ways across different cultures, the validity of this method remains to be fully assessed, and is unlikely to be fully accepted until adequate harmonized data are available. A high correlation across nations in the average qualification requirements for major occupational groups is to be expected, and has been found; but whether this holds for other skills and for detailed occupational groups remains to be examined.

Whether we look at occupational projections, or at their extension and transformation into projections of qualifications demand, the method assumes that the required skills in each occupation are fixed. This means that occupational projections are not fully indicators of overall changes in job skill, because the skills required within each occupation change over time. Past changes in generic skills demand are only partially accounted for by changes in occupational structure; hence one must also expect future changes in skills demand within each occupation.[6] Thus projections based on the changing occupational structure are likely to understate the extent of the change in skills demand. Successive worker-level surveys of skills utilization can establish patterns of change in a range of generic skills usage. Occupational forecasts could then in principle be adapted to incorporate the changing link between skills and occupations.

An additional problem with using occupational projections to capture skills demand is that the method, since it is rooted in historical categories, fails to capture some of the effects of innovation, which may require newly emerging skills. Some new skills could be anticipated, such as those associated with addressing environmental issues of growing importance, including climate change; others are unforeseen.[7] New skills demands can develop within occupations or, from time to time, give rise to quite new occupations that do not fit into pre-existing classifications. The effects of innovation are recognized only at long intervals with occasional reconstruction of occupational code systems. For example, the 1988 international classification system ISCO88 was replaced only in 2008 by ISCO08.

The importance of changes within occupations and of newly emerging skills needs not otherwise captured suggests that other means of projection are required. A promising way of seeing into the future is through detailed studies of particular sectors of industry. Such studies are typically expert based, where the experts for an industry can be either senior employees from the leading or trend-setting companies, or representatives from industry-wide bodies such as sectoral councils made up of employers, trade union representatives, and government officers.[8] Starting with a review of consumer trends, and of underlying changes in technology, such studies can identify which occupation-specific and generic skills are in increasing demand, and identify newly emerging skills. Bespoke studies are sometimes used to inform training institutions where there are strong sectoral bodies in place. Typically, such studies are largely qualitative. Typically, such studies are largely qualitative and can be effective instruments for skills planning in particular contexts. The disadvantage of detailed studies lies in their cost, and in the difficulty of generalizing their findings for the rest of the economy.

Using survey methods, a broader economy-wide approach to anticipating the changing demand for skills over the near future, by studying the views of employers, is also possible in principle. Managers have good knowledge of ongoing changes taking place in workplaces, even if they do not take a long-term perspective of where their company is likely to be several years ahead. They are able to report on what task domains are changing for particular occupational groups, and on what new tasks are emerging.[9]

The balance between supply and demand

For governments to assess whether, from a labour market perspective, they are putting enough into education and training to meet the demands of the future, they must make some kind of comparison with the projected supplies and demands of workers at the various levels of attainment. That comparison might be very approximate, or implicit in an overall intuitive and political judgement. But, if the government desires to be more systematic and strategic in its education planning, it will need to take projections of supply and demand seriously. The extent to which they are supporting today's children will affect the qualification level of the national workforce for many decades to come.

From the perspective of the whole economy it is possible to compare the current supplies of people in the labour force with each level of qualification, with the numbers of jobs requiring each level of qualification. However, for such an analysis one needs data on the qualification requirements of jobs, independent of the qualifications actually held by workers. Hitherto these datea have been available for only a few countries. For example, from successive Skills Surveys in the United Kingdom, it is found that there has been a developing broad imbalance between the supply of people with high-level qualifications and the numbers of jobs for which a high level is required, where the qualification requirement has been reported by the job-holders.[10] A problem with this kind of analysis is that the estimates of the demand for qualifications are survey based and rest on the reliability of job-holders' reports.

The problems multiply when it comes to forward projections. The fundamental difficulty stems from the conundrum noted above—namely, how to turn occupational projections into projections of demand for qualifications. Some analyses have used the current match between qualifications and occupations as the basis for the future projection. Using this method, the forecast made in 2010 for the European Union's twenty-seven member states is for a predicted increase of ten million jobs demanding people with high-level qualifications between 2010 and 2020. This rise can be contrasted with the forecast that the supply of people with high-level qualifications (with tertiary education, that is, at ISCED levels 5 and 6) would increase by approximately fifteen million.[11] Thus there is some indication that in aggregate the supply of highly educated workers across the European Union is more than keeping up with demand.

Analyses using an alternative approach try to pick up the fact that higher-educated workers will be doing jobs that did not previously require higher education. This method accepts that more educated workers will displace those with less education in such jobs and assumes that they will still receive an education premium in those jobs above those with less education in the same jobs; this assumption is used (sometimes implicitly) to justify reclassifying these jobs as requiring higher education. Unsurprisingly, the method finds an overall balance between supply and demand. This alternative method is unsatisfactory, however, since it is not based on evidence about the transformation of those jobs that are reclassified as high-qualification jobs. In a recent controversy in the United States, one group of analysts predicted a coming shortfall of tertiary-educated workers, while critics responded by pointing out that such a shortfall was premised on an assumed reclassification of jobs as high-qualification jobs, without properly taking into account the possibility of over-education. The controversy hinged partly on the measurement of skills requirements in the jobs that are being reclassified as college jobs: while critics called for no reclassification, the labour economists predicting the shortfall held that any job where there was a positive return, however small, to holding a college degree could be reclassified as a college job.[12] These and similar controversies about supply–demand imbalances for qualifications are properly to be resolved only by evidence on the changing qualifications requirements of jobs.

One aspect of the supply–demand imbalance is, however, more straightforward to compute—namely, 'replacement demand'. With a combination of the occupational employment data and data on the age structure of those employed, by making assumptions about the age at which the job-holders retire and about mortality, one can estimate the numbers exiting from each occupation—in effect, the negative element to supply. Moreover, unlike other components of supply, this element has the same units as the demand—namely, the numbers employed per occupation. Thus, to project the flow of new workers to fill the jobs, the overall change in occupational demand should be supplemented by the replacement demand. The 2010–20 projection for Europe, for example, is for a replacement demand of 10.4 million Technicians and Associated professionals, a high proportion (70 per cent) of the total number of new job openings (see Table 10.1).

It will be equally useful for governments to monitor individual skills mismatches. Some interventions may well be centred on better adjustment of labour markets—that is, on directly reducing the extent of mismatch. Information, advice, and guidance services, for example, contribute to better-informed decisions, and hopefully better matches. Skill gaps and shortages can give early notice of training courses that may need to be provided, while indicators of skills under-utilization or over-education may, with careful analyses, give early warning of changes in either the mean level or the dispersion (and hence the risk) of the returns to investment in education courses. Neither the presence of mismatches nor their effects are likely to remain unchanged, so the monitoring should be regular, at suitable intervals. It is probably of less use, however, to attempt to project future levels of individual mismatch.

Measuring the private and social benefits of becoming more skilled

Along with analysis of skill supplies and demands, there is a place for regular estimates of the benefits to and costs of skill acquisition.

Informing private choices

For private individuals the prospective return to the investment—an accounting of the future monetary and non-monetary benefits net of the cost—is the key criterion variable. As discussed in Chapter 7, skill formation decisions are typically taken in a framework of deep uncertainty. Knowledge of the average expected skills premium can help to reduce, though not remove, the uncertainty over some parameters of the decision. To learn about prospective returns from multiple education choices would normally impose prohibitive costs for an individual. In most cases people have only a rough, often biased, impression of the earnings to be expected in each occupation. Yet information on the skills premium is non-rival: one person's use of it does not stop someone else benefiting. This makes a classic efficiency argument for states to provide the information. It is reinforced by the equity argument: those from a socially advantaged background tend to have less restricted horizons and to be better informed about the financial and wider consequences of educational choices; public information provision is likely to be of most use to those who receive least private guidance.

What kinds of analyses of private benefits and costs should states produce and publicize, and how should they be done? Answers will differ according to the specificities of each nation's education and skill system, but some general principles apply:

1. Be careful to analyse and disseminate *causal* effects. Analyses of returns to educational and training courses need to control as far as possible for conflating factors so that the estimates reflect the causal influence of an investment. The art of estimating returns has been well advanced in recent years, through the use of quasi-experimental methods, non-parametric methods of estimating internal rates of return, 'propensity score' matching methods (that allow comparisons with control groups similar to those being 'treated' with skills acquisition), instrumental variables methods (that derive effects of an exogenous trigger for skills acquisition), the study of sets of siblings and twins, and data improvements that allow better controls for previously attained skills.[13] Sometimes it is especially important to control for the selection of individuals into particular courses: if a training programme is designed for workers who have failed in some way to find good jobs, the evaluation must take this into account. While no method is perfect, where an accepted procedure can be routinely and consistently followed, with regularly renewed labour market data, this should become a function of national statistical offices, with relevant benefits and returns data published annually.

2. In view of the uncertainty affecting skills decisions it is important that the information is *timely*. Estimated benefits are derived from past observations; they rarely, if ever, incorporate information about future conditions and benefits. Therefore, it is incumbent on government to keep its estimates as up to date as possible to ensure no lag in capturing changing labour markets and to incorporate as much current information as possible.

3. Useful information can be provided about the premiums associated with broad levels of education, about particular subject choices in education, and about occupational choices. To assist occupational choice—which may have implications for prior education and training choices—it will also be useful to publish information about the earnings from following various occupations, even though people do not stay all their lives in the same occupation. Other information about occupations, especially the kind of work involved, is also relevant to the choices made, and may be especially hard for private individuals to learn about. Without social

assistance, the narrow gaze that can be the private heritage of young persons becomes the vector for the cross-generation entrenchment of social class.

A further tempting possibility may be to supply information about the benefits of attending different educational institutions, but here the risks of misinformation about causal effects are especially high: one cannot infer the benefits of, say, a Harvard or a Sorbonne education without somehow controlling for the fact that it is a rather special cohort that gets to attend in the first place.

4. Where possible the published information should include the wider benefits of education and training, such as through improved health, which are potentially of equal or greater magnitude than the monetary benefits.[14]

5. To assist employers' decisions surrounding training, estimates of benefits, preferably on a sectoral basis, should be provided.

Informing public policies

Whenever governments choose to support education or training, where possible they should consider regularly measuring and disseminating the net social benefits. Their spending needs to be accountable, and a full rendering will also help governments to make more rational decisions about allocating resources between competing budgets.

The private net benefits, just discussed, form a large component of the social net benefits. To these should be added estimates of the external benefits of skill acquisition. The efficiency rationale for public intervention in skill acquisition rests in part on these externalities, the differences between the social and private benefits. There are external market benefits, driving the endogenous growth of economies, through education's effects on several non-private outcomes (innovation, health, fertility, civic engagement, crime reduction, lower inequality, and better environmental management) and the effects of these on economic development. Many of these outcomes also encompass non-market benefits that are less easily quantified, such as public health, political stability, and security. Estimates put the social rate of return as averaging 55 per cent for primary education in Africa, and still as much as 18 per cent for higher education in OECD countries. These figures are much larger than private monetary returns to education, because they also include both externalities and non-market private benefits.[15]

Since such estimates vary across countries, it makes sense for national governments where possible to be in possession of the best estimates of social returns and of external benefits. Yet the data requirements are almost certainly too high to permit this to take place in all countries. Moreover, the externality assessments for education typically depend on long-run projections and are therefore unlikely to change much over time. Where possible the full calculation of net social returns to education should form the backdrop to discourse on education policy. Where this is difficult, components that can be measured should be included, with appropriate concern for the problem of causation. Estimates of external and non-monetary effects now available at country level should be incorporated in the national discourse on public expenditure.[16]

Analyses to be done

The case has been argued, in this chapter, that, in support of social interventions in skill systems, governments have informational and analytical needs that it is increasingly possible to meet, at least partially, as data collection and integration methods are evolving. Analysing skills is a developing art. It seems appropriate that governments should now be assessing their presented and projected skills supplies, skills demands, and mismatches; they should also be estimating the private and social benefits of skills formation. The types of analyses to be done will be expected to vary across the levels of government. Hitherto, skills analyses for these purposes have been confined to fairly broad skill types determined by the qualifications data. In future, some more detailed analyses will become possible using data on particular skill domains. It should not be the intention, however, to develop disaggregated occupational supply and demand forecast for the purposes envisaged in detailed 'manpower planning' objectives during the 1960s. The skills analyses should be used to inform and justify their own policies and those of regional, local, and sectoral agencies. The relevant and appropriate analyses should also be publicized and made available to people making their choices in schools and universities.

Finally, because of the uncertainties and the absence of universal empirical truths surrounding skills, analyses of governments' own actions are of more than usual importance. Where they intervene in education or training decisions, whether through regulations or subsidies, they also have an obligation regularly to evaluate their interventions, both the processes of intervention (whether and how far policies were successfully implemented) and its outcomes (whether its efficiency or equity objectives were being met). Too often, for political and cost reasons, evaluations are either avoided or focused only on implementation, ignoring the outcomes in relation to objectives.

11

Threads and Limits

Threads

Part III has been broadly positive, though also wary, about the potential for a skills-oriented policy and research agenda that might achieve some good in this world. There are, however, some cogent reasons to remain sceptical, and this final chapter considers the critical discussion on two fronts. First, it asks whether 'over-education' warrants serious concern by policy-makers. Second, it examines debate about the limitations to what can be achieved through skills policies.

To set the scene it is worth revisiting some key lines of argument through the book. While incentives—for skill formation and for skill supply and deployment—have formed a constant ingredient of the analysis, these have not been treated as they would in a neoclassical treatise. Rather, what has been emphasized, both for employers and for workers, are the nature and the depth of uncertainty encountered in responding to incentives and making decisions about skills formation and deployment. The embeddedness of beliefs, capacities, and dispositions about skills incentives has also meant that it would be seriously unscientific to adopt uncritically a rational-behaviour model of how people make their skills choices. Moreover, it has been maintained that the main actors should be treated seriously, neither as ciphers for an abstract motive of profit maximization, nor as mere class representatives. It is important to study what employers and workers do, which is why their behaviours have been set in the core of the book.

Inevitably, this approach makes for a degree of complexity in how one should frame these issues. From the perspectives of workers, skills are formed and used through a life course, during which large and usually irreversible decisions are being made, in which there is little space for learning from one's own experiences and starting again in the light of that knowledge. Through the life course workers' preferences and dispositions evolve alongside the opportunities faced, as the world about them is changing. The framing of opportunities, resources, and dispositions by social class and institutional environment must be accounted for, as well as the reflexive possibilities for rational decision-making. For employers, their demands for skilled labour, and their demands for and supplies of skill formation services, emerge from their aim to make profit, but their decisions are subject to their beliefs about future pay-offs, which are also conditioned by their uncertain outlooks and variable strategic capacities.

Although the complexity does not permit a full theory of skills and skilled work, with scientific predictions and a core of accepted theorems, a framework has been developed in which supplies and demands, within two interlocking markets, can be located and analysed; key theories and evidence in these areas have been described, spanning multiple disciplines. To help facilitate further progress, the PES concept of skill developed in Chapter 2 introduces possibilities for communication between the main social science disciplines that wonder about skills, without taking away from their differences.

The analytical framework has also led to a normative one that provides a way of thinking about social interventions in skill formation and use that includes but extends beyond the conventional rule that balances the costs of market failures against the imperfections of government. The extended criteria, grounded in managerial theories and evidence, provide a realistic and sophisticated additional normative basis for understanding and advising on government behaviour. They ask questions about management capabilities, learning barriers, a nationalist approach to influencing skills location, and the importance of the demand side of the economy (see Chapter 9)—all of which are likely to occupy the time of skills researchers and policy-advisers in coming years.

Should governments worry about over-education?

The demand side of the economy is prominent in much of the critical discourse about the possibilities for skills policy, the debate on over-education being no exception. Should governments worry about the spectacle of shelf-packers with advanced high-school diplomas, secretaries with bachelor degrees, sales staff with Ph.D.s? The phenomenon of over-education has been examined for some time in academic discourse but is rarely discussed by policy-makers. It is, perhaps, the pejorative feel to the term that has inhibited debate. Official indifference to over-education owes something to an understandable embarrassment and fear that it could be construed by treasury ministers as implying that education budgets are too high. Silence, however, is also risky if it hinders debate about the significance of over-education, which arguably goes to the heart of education's purpose. The aim of this section is to note the arguments on both sides.

There will be always be some degree of mismatch between education achievements and job requirements, because there are mobility restrictions and other rigidities in labour markets, and because educational qualifications compete in importance with other criteria for employee selection. Even if such restrictions are weak, temporary mismatches can occur. People may study a subject in college that bears no direct relation to the knowledge base of the occupation subsequently followed. Both over-education and under-education are found to be prevalent in several countries, and should be regarded as normal.[1] The potential concern about over-education lies in these findings:

- The prevalence of over-education is almost certainly growing in many countries. In the two countries for which there is reliable evidence of trends (Germany and Great Britain, see Chapter 10), over-education has been increasing over recent decades. There is no reason to think that these countries are alone: education achievements are now expanding rapidly in most countries; while the demand for skills has been rising (Chapter 5) and will probably continue to do so, it is likely that rising proportions of younger college graduate cohorts will find themselves, when employed, in lesser jobs than earlier generations of graduates. These trends presage greater diversity in the skills premia from education.

- Even though there is evidence that those with higher ability (on some measures) are somewhat less likely to become over-educated, no piece of evidence has come anywhere near refuting that a substantial proportion of over-educated workers would be able to pursue a more skilled job.[2]

- It can be optimal that some individuals should be over-educated and under-utilizing their skills in the short run: workers may take jobs with low education requirements while they are searching for a better match; over-education therefore may be temporary in the life of some. Yet the balance of high-quality evidence suggests that, for the majority of over-educated and overskilled workers, this state is persistent over a long time.[3]

There are two main reasons for concern about these developments. At the individual level, the outcome of the transition between education and work leading to over-education may come as a surprise and a delusion, depending on young people's foresight and expectations. It will almost certainly occasion significantly more job dissatisfaction and lower average pay for over-educated workers than for those who find employment at the same level as their education achievement.[4] If education continues to be sold as the means to better jobs, increasing proportions of each cohort may feel and resent being let down. The other cause for concern, both at the individual level and for the government, is whether the expense of the education may have been wasted. From the individual's perspective, the fees and effort may be resented; for governments, the cost of provision and any student subsidy can be substantial.

Set against these concerns there are also some reasons to be relaxed about the potential further growth of over-education. First, at least until recently over-educated workers have been found to earn somewhat more than others doing the same job, suggesting that their jobs might be differentiated in otherwise unobserved ways owing to their extra capabilities. Second, an increase in the supply of qualified workers is arguably beneficial for economic growth, even if it generates an excess supply, since it stimulates innovation and generates a subsequent growth in skills demand. The basic idea is that, when there is a larger pool of skilled workers available in the economy, skilled workers are cheaper to hire and innovators have a greater incentive to develop technologies that intensively utilize their skills. It has been suggested that part of the reason for the successful innovation and diffusion of computer-based technologies in the United States has been the abundance of educated labour.[5] Yet it would be a bold step confidently to base a supply-driven policy strategy on such a model. The problem is that any policy of raising skills supply in order to raise skills demand would have to have a long-term perspective— possibly decades. The horizon for such a policy is lengthened to the extent that managerial classes are inhibited from reorganizing work to make use of a more educated workforce. The supply-side policies would need to be accompanied by policies further to encourage the take-up of skills by employers.

Third, a complementary comfort is the possibility that formal statistical evidence on the economic benefits of education is seriously misleading, because it fails to capture the very long-term effects of education on societal development, not least through the external benefits of education that are rarely captured in econometric research. If education's effects are subject to long and uncertain lags, researchers had better direct their attention to these, and policy-makers should adopt a longer-term perspective in planning the nation's education system.

Taking a longer-term view sits well with the final, arguably the most telling, reason for downplaying concern about over-education—namely that it is only a problem in so far as education is conceived as serving the economic system and generating only economic outcomes. However, evidence is also accumulating about the many non-pecuniary benefits of education, and about the large magnitude of education's externalities.[6] Among other things, better-educated workers are found to have higher levels of well-being, enjoy better health, live longer, have more stable marriages, commit fewer crimes, and contribute to better development of their children. Those dissatisfied at work because their jobs are not utilizing their skills gain some consolation elsewhere in life. Education's cultural benefits might be even greater for those not in work, since they have more time to enjoy them. According to this line of argument, then, concern about growing over-education should be replaced by renewed debate about the purposes and functions of education, and a contestation of the widespread tendency to orient education and training narrowly to the purposes of employment.

If as expected there is an increasing over-education in many countries in the coming decades, policy-makers will be obliged to discuss the issue more openly. Whether or not this raises concerns, there remains a case for developing policies to improve the interface between education and work, including previously discussed strategies for stimulating employers' demand for skills, and the further development of information, advice, and guidance policies to improve the chances of workers finding jobs to which they are better matched.

Limits of skills policies

Concern about over-education is one element of a wider scepticism about the effectiveness of supply-side skills policies in bringing about significant changes in modern economic and social life. To return full circle to the claims described at the start of this book, expectations have been raised that movements to increase skills and broaden access to skilled work would span the class divide, both raising economic growth and lowering inequality, giving people jobs that were more meaningful and better paid, raising productivity and profits for companies, gaining more tax revenues for governments—in other words, all things to all.

An expansion in the volume and spread of interesting and rewarding jobs would add immensely to human welfare in any country that was successful in achieving it, and the idea that raising skills is a necessary condition for these social and private benefits to accrue is built into the framework of this book. What is questioned, however, by those with a proper scepticism, is the notion that skills policies might also be sufficient. Two types of objections can be raised, related in their concern about the demand side.

First, not all jobs can become highly skilled and meaningful, and not all people can expect to be lucky enough to gain fulfilment through paid work. Many jobs are likely to persist in any real economy for the foreseeable future that, while they may involve non-routine labour and are therefore less likely to be substituted by a computerized machine or to be relocated to another country, are nevertheless less than fulfilling. If policy-makers want to improve the quality of such jobs, imaginative policies can be devised that address other aspects of intrinsic job quality such as autonomy and social support, and extrinsic aspects of job quality such as wages and security.[7]

Second, to achieve some of the hoped-for gains, a skills strategy needs to incorporate both the supply and demand sides. Even though they will ultimately respect both their fiscal boundaries and the autonomy of capital, governments should pay attention to the demand side of the skill system, rather than focus exclusively (as they commonly do) on skill formation policies. Strategies should consider policies to raise the demand for skilled labour, either through industrial and regional policies or through policies of engagement, persuasion, and incentives; policies in related areas can be included— for example, altering the minimum wage and migration policies so as to reduce employers' incentives to adopt low-skill production methods. Supply-side policies to match increases in the demand for skills could then be expected to be more successful. The requirement to influence demand may be more of a limitation in some countries than others, depending on government capabilities and powers. In all countries, governments' skills policies are differentially conditioned by their position in the world economy, through macroeconomic and fiscal constraints and through the political boundaries demanded by neoliberalism.

Around the world governments have increasingly come to treat education and training policy as economic policy, hoping that this will deliver on the promise of sustained economic growth. It is far from clear, however, whether in the light of the above objections, national-level policies can bear the weight of expectations that are sometimes placed upon them.[8] Just because other avenues for governments to affect economic growth may be narrowed by international constraints, this is no guarantee that the high skills road is any wider, especially if the private economy is mired in a low-skills ecosystem. A failure to recognize these and other limitations can lead governments to 'over-claiming', an unwarranted raising of expectations for what skills policies can hope to achieve in the realms of economic efficiency and of a more just distribution of rewards. Especially if the demand-side policies are absent, skills supply policies are severely limited, and will not be able to resolve the problems of low-wage work as policy designers might have hoped.

While the apparent innocence of over-claiming only risks exposure in the fullness of time as policies fail to have their claimed effects—and, even then, the short-termism of political life often permits an escape from blame—it becomes more cynical when it is used as a substitution, even a distraction, from debating the need for the social transformations that would enable a broader expansion of skilled work, which the government is not willing to espouse. Cynicism can also involve a blaming of individuals for their failures to commit to gaining skills, a hand-washing of any social responsibility to create a positive environment for learning. The scope for making individuals feel their own shortcomings is greater where they perceive that they have a broader range of choice.[9]

Yet drawing attention to the potential for over-claiming can attract the opposite risk of an excess scepticism, a kind of negative utopianism, in effect encouraging the view that nothing beneficial can be achieved through skills policies without a radical social transformation. This may be a defensible position, but if so it is one that invokes a far deeper historical debate about reform and revolution, in the absence of which one is still left with the need for a reasoned approach to skills policies. The arguments about the principles for social intervention, set out in Chapter 9, can yet serve as guidelines for policy design, as long as over-claiming is avoided. This book has advocated that a multidisciplinary approach can help to frame a proper understanding of the distribution of skills and skilled work in society. It is hoped that the framework developed here, building on an already large literature, can help to encourage the flourishing of a successful sub-field devoted to skills research and guide the consideration of skills policies of democratic governments in capitalist economies.

Notes

Chapter 1

1. F. Green (2006); Smith et al. (2008); Green and Mostafa (2012).

Chapter 2

1. Attewell (1990); Spenner (1990); Vallas (1990).
2. Felstead et al. (2007a); Handel (2008); National Research Council (2010); Green and Keese (2012).
3. Becker (1964); Mincer (1974).
4. Hashimito (1982); Stevens (1994, 1999); Acemoglu and Pischke (1999).
5. Avineri (1968).
6. F. Green (1992); Ashton and Green (1996: ch. 2); Rees et al. (2006).
7. McGuiness (2006); Mavromaras et al. (2007).
8. Tversky and Kahnemann (1986)
9. Lave and Wenger (1991).
10. Attewell (1990).
11. Attewell (1990: 443).
12. Marx (1976: ch. 7); Sayers (2005).
13. See Braverman (1974).
14. Cockburn (1983); Attewell (1990); Steinberg (1990); Wajcman (1991).
15. Steinberg (1990).
16. Wajcman (1991).
17. Welford (1968).
18. Attewell (1990).
19. National Research Council (2010: 32).
20. Gaudart and Weill–Fassina (1999); Clarke and Winch (2006); Brockmann et al. (2011); Méhaut (2011).
21. Oliver and Turton (1982).
22. Bowles and Gintis (1976, 1988, 2002).
23. <http://www.onetcenter.org/content.html> (accessed 16 November 2012); Green and Keese (2012).
24. Blanden et al. (2008); Heckman (2008); Martins (2010); Heckman and Kautz (2012).
25. Bowles (1998).
26. Himmelweit (1999).

27. Adnett and Davies (2002).
28. Rychen (2003).
29. Game (2007).
30. Felstead et al. (2009).
31. Steinberg and Figart (1999); Hamermesh et al. (2002); Warhurst and Nickson (2007).
32. Autor et al. (2003a, b).
33. Jensen and Kletzer (2010).
34. Payne (2000).

Chapter 3

1. UKCES (2010: 60).
2. Green and McIntosh (2007).
3. Acemoglu and Autor (2011).
4. Bassanini et al. (2005).
5. Culpepper (2003).
6. Tversky and Kahneman (1992).
7. Knight (1921).
8. Collier et al. (2011).
9. Culpepper (2003); Thelen (2004).
10. Wajcman (1991); Acemoglu (1998).
11. Mayer and Solga (2008: 6).

Chapter 4

1. Attewell (1990: 426).
2. Barro and Lee (1996, 2001).
3. Mincer (1974).
4. Hanushek and Woessman (2010).
5. OECD (2010).
6. Steedman and McIntosh (2001).
7. http://www.ehea.info/ (accessed 16 November 2012).
8. http://ec.europa.eu/education/lifelong-learning-policy/doc44_en.htm   (accessed 16 November 2012).
9. Brockmann et al. (2008, 2011).
10. Steedman and McIntosh (2001).
11. Hanushek and Kimko (2000); Hanushek and Woessman (2010).
12. Attewell (1990); Stasz (2001).
13. Finnie and Meng (2005).
14. Blanden et al. (2008); Borghans et al. (2008); Heckman (2008); Ter Weel (2008).
15. F. Green (2012).
16. Spence (1973); Chevalier et al. (2004).
17. Jones and Chiripanhura (2010).
18. F. Green (2012).

19. Banks (1988).
20. National Research Council (2010); Wilson (2010).
21. Rohrbach-Schmidt and Tiemann (2011).
22. Handel (2008, 2013); Klynge (2011); Sung and Loke (2011); Green and Keese (2013); Green et al. (2013); Mane and Miravet (2013); Rohrbach-Schmidt and Tiemann (2013).
23. <http://www.oecd.org/> (accessed 16 November 2012).
24. http://www.ilo.org/public/english/bureau/stat/isco/index.htm (accessed 16 November 2012).
25. Felstead et al. (1997).
26. Dearden et al. (2006).
27. De Grip and van Loo (2002).
28. http://www.cedefop.europa.eu/EN/about-cedefop/projects/employers-surveys/index.aspx (accessed 16 November 2012).
29. Dolton and Marcenaro-Gutierrez (2009).

Chapter 5

1. Hamermesh (1993).
2. Manning (2003).
3. Classic studies were Akerlof (1982) and Shapiro and Stiglitz (1984).
4. Lazear (1999).
5. Simon (1955).
6. Bloom and van Reenen (2007, 2010).
7. Boxall and Purcell (2011).
8. Wright et al. (1994); Mueller (1996).
9. Eisenhardt and Martin (2000); Teece (2007).
10. Boudreau and Ramstad (2005).
11. Prais (1995); Redding (1996); Finegold and Mason (1999); Green et al. (2003b); Mason (2010).
12. F. Green (2008).
13. Gallie et al. (2012).
14. MacDuffie (1995); Appelbaum et al. (2000); Godard (2004); Wall and Wood (2005).
15. F. Green (2012).
16. Brynjolfsson and Hitt (2000); Caroli and van Reenen (2001); Greenan (2003); Piva et al. (2005).
17. Van Reenen (2011).
18. Maskell and Malmberg (1999, 2007).
19. Felstead et al. (2009); Erez (2010).
20. Dobbin and Boychuk (1999); Gallie (2003); Bloom and van Reenen (2010); Lloyd and Payne (2010).
21. Christen et al. (2008).
22. Ferris et al. (2001); Hochwarter et al. (2006); Blickle et al. (2008).
23. Peterson et al. (2008); Wasunna et al. (2010).

24. Mason and van Ark (1993); Black and Lynch (1996); Carmeli (2006); Zwick (2006); Colombo and Stanca (2008); Grugulis and Stoyanova (2011).
25. Bartel (1995, 2000); Krueger and Rowse (1998); Collier et al. (2005, 2011).
26. Sianesi and van Reenen (2003).
27. Hanushek and Woessman (2010).
28. Goldin and Katz (2008).
29. E.g., Howell and Wolff (1991); Fernández-Macías and Hurley (2008).
30. Cappelli (1993); Spitz-Oener (2006); F. Green (2012).
31. F. Green (2012).
32. Berman et al. (1998); Machin (2003).
33. Autor et al. (1998).
34. Card and DiNardo (2002).
35. Felstead et al. (2007b).
36. Machin and van Reenen (1998, 2007).
37. Chusseau et al. (2008).
38. Blauner (1964); Braverman (1974); Friedman (1977); Edwards et al. (1982); Piore and Sabel (1984); Gallie et al. (1998: 2–5).
39. Reich (1992: 177).
40. Ricardo (1971: 384).
41. Autor et al. (1998).
42. Berman et al. (1998).
43. Machin and van Reenen (1998); Autor et al (1998); Haskel and Heden (1999); Green et al. (2003a).
44. Spitz-Oener (2006); F. Green (2012).
45. Reich (1992); Autor et al. (2003a, b); Wright and Dwyer (2003); Spitz-Oener (2006); Goos and Manning (2007); Fernández-Macías and Hurley (2008); Goos et al. (2009).
46. Acemoglu (1998).
47. Wajcman (1991, 2010).
48. F. Green (2012).
49. Wood and Bryson (2009).
50. Gallie et al. (2004); Kalleberg (2011).
51. CEDEFOP (2010b); the methods are reviewed in Chapter 9.
52. Ashton et al. (1999); Green et al. (1999a).
53. Curry (2010).
54. Hamermesh (1993).

Chapter 6

1. Lave and Wenger (1991).
2. MEADOW Consortium (2010: 28–30).
3. Fuller and Unwin (2004); Felstead et al. (2009).
4. The 5th European Working Conditions Survey <www.eurofound.europa.eu/surveys/ewcs/2010/index.htm> and the US General Social Survey http://www3.norc.org/GSS+Website/ (both accessed 16 November 2012); author's analyses.

5. Felstead et al. (2002).
6. Official Statistics of Finland (OSF) (2005).
7. Booth (1991); F. Green (1993); Osterman (1995); Bartel and Sicherman (1998); Whitfield (2000).
8. Collier et al. (2005).
9. Freeman and Medoff (1984); Booth and Chatterji (1998); Green et al. (1999b); Almeida-Santos and Mumford (2004); Boheim and Booth (2004).
10. Hashimoto (1982).
11. Stevens (1994, 1999).
12. Acemoglu and Pischke (1999).
13. Dustmann and Schoenberg (2008, 2009).
14. Streeck (1989).
15. Fuller and Unwin (2011).
16. Macduffie and Kochan (1995); Osterman (1995); Whitfield (2000); Felstead et al. (2010).
17. Collier et al. (2011).
18. Bassi and McMurrer (2004).
19. Ichniowski et al. (1997); Ichniowski and Shaw (1999).
20. Tversky and Kahneman (1992: 297).
21. European Social Statistics (2002); Parent-Thirion et al. (2007: 49).
22. James et al. (2012).
23. Gospel and Foreman (2006); Cooney and Gospel (2008); Unwin (2012).
24. Culpepper (2003).
25. Crouch et al. (1999).
26. Bosch (2010).

Chapter 7

1. Jevons (1871).
2. Saget (1999); Ashenfelter et al. (2010).
3. Gallie et al. (1998); F. Green (2006).
4. Karasek (1979).
5. Bratti (2003); Laplagne et al. (2007).
6. Dustmann and Schoenberg (2008); Ollo-Lopez et al. (2010).
7. F. Green (1993); Oosterbeek and Webbink (1995); Lauer (2002); Fersterer and Winter-Ebmer (2003); Mastekaasa (2003); Bedi et al. (2004); Renaud et al. (2004); Dearden et al. (2009); Flannery and O'Donoghue (2009); Neidell and Waldfogel (2009); Neill (2009); Spiess and Wrohlich (2010); Attanasio et al. (2012).
8. Schoon and Silbereisen (2009).
9. Bowles and Gintis (1976, 1988, 2002).
10. Schneider (2009).
11. Zimmerman (2000).
12. Greenhalgh and Mavrotas (1994); Schoon and Duckworth (2010); Chowdry et al. (2011).
13. Bosch and Charest (2010).

14. Miller et al. (2001); Reay et al. (2001); Gutman and Akerman (2008); Jones (2009).
15. Cieslik (2006); Walther (2009); Evans and Waite (2010); Biesta et al. (2011: 91–2, 47–8).
16. Rees et al. (2006).
17. Evans (2002); Evans et al. (2010).
18. Ecclestone et al. (2010); Field (2010).
19. Wolfe and Zuvekas (1997); Harmon et al. (2003); McMahon (2004); Schuller et al. (2004).
20. Hartog et al. (2001); Selz and Thelot (2004).
21. Green and Zhu (2010).
22. Harmon et al. (2003).
23. Chevalier et al. (2004).
24. Loewenstein and Spletzer (1999); Parent (1999); Goux and Maurin (2000); Vignoles et al. (2004); O'Connell and Byrne (2012).
25. Murnane et al. (1995); McIntosh and Vignoles (2001); Leuven et al. (2004); Tyler (2004); Kuhn and Weinberger (2005).
26. Wolfe and Zuvekas (1997); Silles (2009); Kemptner et al. (2011); Seo and Senauer (2011).
27. Schoon and Silbereisen (2009); Ecclestone et al. (2010).
28. Bynner (2005); Arnett (2006); Côté and Bynner (2008).
29. Schoon et al. (2009); Serracant (2012).
30. Walther (2009).
31. Ryan (2001); Christopoulou and Ryan (2009).
32. OECD <http://www.oecd.org/home/;%20statistics%20tab> (accessed 1 June 2012).
33. White and Green (2011).

Chapter 8

1. Field (2006).
2. Lucio et al. (2007); Dustmann and Schoenberg (2009); Bosch (2010).
3. Ashton et al. (1999).
4. Haskel and Martin (1993).
5. Doeringer and Piore (1971); Edwards et al. (1982); Estevez-Abe (2005).
6. Browning and Heinesen (2012).
7. Gregg and Tominey (2005).
8. Hutton (1996); Conway et al. (2008).
9. Grissmer (2000).
10. Wail et al. (2011).
11. A. Green (2011).
12. OECD (2005: 39–41).
13. Allen and Van der Velden (2001); McGuiness (2006); Green and McIntosh (2007); Dolton and Marcenaro-Gutierrez (2009).
14. Shury et al. (2010: 96).
15. Department of Education Employment and Workplace Relations (2011).

16. Neumark et al. (2011).
17. OECD (2011).
18. Australian Bureau of Statistics (2006).
19. Felstead et al. (2012).
20. Shields and Price (1999); Gibson (2002); Forrier and Sels (2003).
21. Simpson and Stroh (2002); Evertsson (2004); Jones et al. (2007).
22. Author's calculation using the 2006 UK Skills Survey (Felstead et al. 2007a).

Chapter 9

1. Centre for Educational Research and Innovation (2007).
2. Barr (2012).
3. Murphy et al. (2008).
4. Keep (2006).
5. Bassanini et al. (2005).
6. Bassanini et al. (2005).
7. Crouch et al. (1999).
8. Erez (2010).
9. Dobbin and Boychuk (1999); Gallie (2003); Bloom and van Reenen (2010); Lloyd and Payne (2010).
10. Buchanan et al. (2010).
11. OECD (2012: 48–52).
12. Veblen (1899).
13. Finegold and Soskice (1988); Froy and Giguère (2010).
14. Finegold (1999); Buchanan et al. (2009).
15. Esping-Andersen (1990); Hall and Soskice (2001); Green et al. (2006); Bosch et al. (2007); Gallie (2011); Green and Janmaat (2011).
16. Streeck (1991); Dustmann and Schoenberg (2008).
17. Culpepper (2003); Thelen (2004); Trampusch (2010); Busemeyer and Trampusch (2011).
18. Culpepper and Thelen (2008).
19. Bosch (2010).
20. Wiborg and Court (2010).
21. Green et al. (2013).
22. Ashton et al. (1999); A. Green (1999).
23. Ryan (2000).

Chapter 10

1. Shury et al. (2010: 153–61).
2. CEDEFOP (2010b: 86–7).
3. Bureau of Labor Statistics (2011: ch. 13).
4. CEDEFOP (2010b).
5. Dickerson and Wilson (2012); Koucký et al. (2012).
6. F. Green (2012).

7. CEDEFOP (2010a).
8. CEDEFOP (2009: chs 9 and 10).
9. <http://www.cedefop.europa.eu/EN/identifying-skills-needs/index.aspx> (accessed 17 November 2012). a, b).
10. Felstead et al. (2007a).
11. CEDEFOP (2010b: 43, 61).
12. Carnevale et al. (2010); Harrington and Sum (2010a, b); Neumark et al. (2011).
13. Harmon et al. (2003); Heckman et al. (2006).
14. Centre for Educational Research and Innovation (2007).
15. McMahon (2004: 244).
16. OECD (2011, and other years).

Chapter 11

1. Groot and Maassen van den Brink (2000); Quintini (2011).
2. Green et al. (2002).
3. Battu et al. (1999); Dolton and Vignoles (2000); Mavromaras and McGuinness (2012).
4. Green and Zhu (2010); Brown et al. (2011).
5. Acemoglu (1998).
6. Oreopoulos and Salvanes (2011).
7. Lloyd et al. (2008); Kalleberg (2011).
8. Keep and Mayhew (2010).
9. Evans (2002).

References

Acemoglu, D. (1998). 'Why do New Technologies Complement Skills? Directed Technical Change and Wage Inequality', *Quarterly Journal of Economics*, 113/4: 1055–89.

Acemoglu, D., and Autor, D. (2011). 'Skills, Tasks and Technologies: Implications for Employment and Earnings', in O. Ashenfelter and D. E. Card (eds), *Handbook of Labor Economics Volume 4*. Amsterdam: Elsevier.

Acemoglu, D., and Pischke, J.-S. (1999). 'The Structure of Wages and Investment in General Training', *Journal of Political Economy*, 107/3: 539–72.

Adnett, N., and Davies, P. (2002). 'Education as a Positional Good: Implications for Market-Based Reforms of State Schooling', *British Journal of Educational Studies*, 50/2: 189–205.

Akerlof, G. A. (1982). 'Labor Contracts as Partial Gift Exchange', *Quarterly Journal of Economics*, 97 (November): 543–69.

Allen, J., and van der Velden, R. (2001). 'Educational Mismatches versus Skill Mismatches: Effects on Wages, Job Satisfaction, and On-the-Job Search', *Oxford Economic Papers*, 53/3: 434–52.

Allen, J., and van der Velden, R. (2007) (eds), *The Flexible Professional in the Knowledge Society: General Results of the REFLEX Project*. Maastricht: The Netherlands: Research Centre for Education.

Almeida-Santos, F., and Mumford, K. A. (2004). 'Employee Training in Australia: Evidence from AWIRS', *Economic Record*, 80 (Special Issue, September): S53–64.

Appelbaum, E., Bailey, T., Berg, P., and Kalleberg, A. L. (2000). *Manufacturing Advantage: Why High-Performance Work Systems Pay Off*. Ithaca, NY, and London: Cornell University Press.

Arnett, J. J. (2006). 'Emerging Adulthood in Europe: A Response to Bynner', *Journal of Youth Studies*, 9/1: 111–23.

Ashenfelter, O., Doran, K., and Schaller, B. (2010). 'A Shred of Credible Evidence on the Long-Run Elasticity of Labour Supply', *Economica*, 77/308: 637–50.

Ashton, D., and Green, F. (1996). *Education, Training and the Global Economy*. Cheltenham: Edward Elgar.

Ashton, D., Green, F., James, D., and Sung, J. (1999). *Education and Training for Development in East Asia: The Political Economy of Skill Formation in East Asian Newly Industrialised Economies*. London and New York: Routledge.

Attanasio, O. P., Meghir, C., and Santiago, A. (2012). 'Education Choices in Mexico: Using a Structural Model and a Randomized Experiment to Evaluate PROGRESA', *Review of Economic Studies*, 79/1: 37–66.

References

Attewell, P. (1990). 'What Is Skill?', *Work and Occupations*, 17/14: 422–48.

Australian Bureau of Statistics (2006). *Education and Training Experience, Australia*. Canberra: Australian Bureau of Statistics.

Autor, D. H., Katz, L. F., and Krueger, A. B. (1998). 'Computing Inequality: Have Computers Changed the Labour Market?' *Quarterly Journal of Economics*, 113/4: 1169–214.

Autor, D. H., Levy, F., and Murnane, R. J. (2003a). 'The Skill Content of Recent Technological Change: An Empirical Exploration', *Quarterly Journal of Economics*, 118/4: 1279–333.

Autor, D. H., Levy, F., and Murnane, R. J. (2003b). 'Computer-Based Technological Change and Skill', in E. Appelbaum, A. Bernhardt, and R. J. Murname (eds), *Low-Wage America*. New York: Russell Sage Foundation.

Avineri, S. (1968). *The Social and Political Thought of Karl Marx*. Cambridge: Cambridge University Press.

Banks, M. (1988). 'Job Components Inventory', in S. Gael (ed.), *The Job Analysis Handbook for Business, Industry, and Government*. New York: Wiley, ii. 960–74.

Barr, N. (2012). *Economics of the Welfare State*. 5th edn. Oxford: Oxford University Press.

Barro, R. J., and Lee, J. W. (1996). 'International Measures of Schooling Years and Schooling Quality', *American Economic Review, Papers and Proceedings*, 86/2: 218–23.

Barro, R. J., and Lee, J. W. (2001). 'International Data on Educational Attainment: Updates and Implications', *Oxford Economic Papers*, 53/3: 541–63.

Bartel, A. P. (1995). 'Training, Wage Growth, and Job Performance: Evidence from a Company Database', *Journal of Labour Economics*, 13/3: 401–25.

Bartel, A. P. (2000). 'Measuring the Employer's Return on Investments in Training: Evidence from the Literature', *Industrial Relations*, 39/3: 502–24.

Bartel, A. P., and Sicherman, N. (1998). 'Technological Change and the Skill Acquisition of Young Workers', *Journal of Labor Economics*, 16/4: 718–55.

Bassanini, A., Booth, A., Brunello, G., De Paola, M., and Leuven, E. (2005). 'Workplace Training in Europe', IZA, June, Discussion Paper No. 1640.

Bassi, L., and McMurrer, D. (2004). 'How's Your Return on People?', *Harvard Business Review*, 82/3: 18.

Battu, H., Belfiel, C. R., and Sloane, P. (1999). 'Overeducation among Graduates: A Cohort View', *Education Economics*, 7/1: 21–38.

Becker, G. S. (1964). *Human Capital*. New York: National Bureau of Economic Research.

Bedi, A. S., Kimalu, P. K., Mandab, D. K., and Nafula, N. (2004). 'The Decline in Primary School Enrolment in Kenya', *Journal of African Economies*, 13/1: 1–43.

Berman, E, Bound, J., and Machin, S. (1998). 'Implications of Skill-Biased Technological Change: International Evidence', *Quarterly Journal of Economics*, 113: 1245–79.

Biesta, G. J. J., Field, J., Hodkinson, P., Macleod, F. J., and Goodson, I. F. (2011). *Improving Learning through the Lifecourse*. London: Routledge.

Black, S., and Lynch, L. (1996). 'Human Capital Investments and Productivity', *American Economic Review*, 86 (May): 263–8.

Blanden, J., Gregg, P., and Macmillan, L. (2008). 'Accounting for Intergenerational Persistence: Non-Cognitive Skills, Ability and Education', *Economic Journal*, 117: C43–C60.

Blauner, Robert (1964). *Alienation and Freedom*. Chicago: University of Chicago Press.

Blickle, G., Meurs, J. A., Zettler, I., Solga, J., Noethen, D., Kramer, J., and Ferris, G. R. (2008). 'Personality, Political Skill, and Job Performance', *Journal of Vocational Behavior*, 72/3: 377–87.

Bloom, N., and J. van Reenen (2007). 'Measuring and explaining management practices across firms and countries.' *Quarterly Journal of Economics*, 122 (4): 1351–408.

Bloom, N., and van Reenen, J. (2010). 'Why Do Management Practices Differ across Firms and Countries?', *Journal of Economic Perspectives*, 24/1: 203–24.

Boheim, R., and Booth, A. L. (2004). 'Trade Union Presence and Employer-Provided Training in Great Britain', *Industrial Relations*, 43/3: 520–45.

Booth, A. (1991). 'Job-Related Formal Training: Who Receives It and What Is It Worth?', *Oxford Bulletin of Economics and Statistics*, 53: 281–94.

Booth, A. L., and Bryan, M. L. (2005). 'Testing Some Predictions of Human Capital Theory: New Evidence from Britain', *Review of Economics and Statistics*, 87/2: 391–4.

Booth, A. L., and Chatterji, M. (1998). 'Unions and Efficient Training', *Economic Journal*, 108/447: 328–43.

Borghans, L., Duckworth, A. L., Heckman, J. J., and ter Weel, B. (2008). 'The Economics and Psychology of Personality Traits', *Journal of Human Resources*, 43/4: 972–1059.

Bosch, G. (2010). 'The Revitalization of the Dual System of Vocational Training in Germany', in G. Bosch and J. Charest (eds), *Vocational Training: International Perspectives*. London: Routledge, 136–61.

Bosch, G., and Charest, J. (2010) (eds). *Vocational Training: International Perspectives*. London: Routledge.

Bosch, G., Rubery, J., and Lehndorff, S. (2007). 'European Employment Models under Pressure to Change', *International Labour Review*, 146/3–4: 253–77.

Boudreau, J. W., and Ramstad, P. M. (2005). 'Talentship, Talent Segmentation, and Sustainability: A New HR Decision Science Paradigm for a New Strategy Definition', *Human Resource Management*, 44/2: 129–36.

Bowles, S. (1998). 'Endogenous Preferences: The Cultural Consequences of Markets and Other Economic Institutions', *Journal of Economic Literature*, 36/1: 75–111.

Bowles, S., and Gintis, H. (1976). *Schooling in Capitalist America*. London: Routledge and Kegan Paul.

Bowles, S., and Gintis, H. (1988). 'Schooling in Capitalist America: Reply to our Critics', in M. Cole (ed.), *Bowles and Gintis Revisited*. London: Falmer Press, 235–45.

Bowles, S., and Gintis, H. (2002). 'Schooling in Capitalist America Revisited', *Sociology of Education*, 75/1: 1–18.

Boxall, P., and Purcell, J. (2011). *Strategy and Human Resource Management*. 3rd edn. Basingstoke: Palgrave Macmillan.

Bratti, M. (2003). 'Labour Force Participation and Marital Fertility of Italian Women: The Role of Education', *Journal of Population Economics*, 16/3: 525–54.

Braverman, H. (1974). *Labor and Monopoly Capital*. New York: Monthly Review Press.

Brockmann, M., Clarke, L., and Winch, C. (2008). 'Knowledge, Skills, Competence: European Divergences in Vocational Education and Training (VET): The English, German and Dutch Cases', *Oxford Review of Education*, 34/5: 547–67.

References

Brockmann, M., Clarke, L., Winch, C., Hanf, G., Méhaut, P., and Westerhuis, A. (2011). 'Introduction: Cross-National Equivalence of Skills and Qualifications across Europe?', in M. Brockmann, L. Clarke, and C. Winch (eds), *Knowledge, Skills and Competence in the European Labour Market*, Abingdon: Routledge, 1–21.

Brown, P., Lauder, H., and Ashton, D. (2011). *The Global Auction*. Oxford: Oxford University Press.

Browning, M., and Heinesen, E. (2012). 'Effect of Job Loss Due to Plant Closure on Mortality and Hospitalization', *Journal of Health Economics*, 31/4: 599–616.

Brynjolfsson, E., and Hitt, L. M. (2000). 'Beyond Computation: Information Technology, Organizational Transformation and Business Performance', *Journal of Economic Perspectives*, 14/4: 23–48.

Buchanan, J., Yu, S., Marginson, S., and Wheelahan, L. (2009). *Education, Work and Economic Renewal*. Southbank: Australian Education Union.

Buchanan, J., Scott, L., Yu, S., Schutz, H., and Jakubauskas, M. (2010). 'Skills Demand and Utilisation: An International Review of Approaches to Measurement and Policy Development'. Paris, OECD Local Economic and Employment Development (LEED) Working Papers 2010/04.Bureau of Labor Statistics (2011). *BLS Handbook of Methods*. Washington: Office of Publications and Special Studies <http://www.bls.gov/opub/hom> (accessed 17 November 2012).

Busemeyer, M. R., and Trampusch, C. (2011). 'Introduction: The Comparative Political Economy of Collective Skill Formation', in M. R. Busemeyer and C. Trampusch (eds), *The Political Economy of Collective Skill Formation* (Oxford: Oxford University Press).

Bynner, J. (1994). *Skills and Occupations: Analysis of Cohort Members' Self-Reported Skills in the Fifth Sweep of the National Child Development Study*. London: Social Statistics Research Unit, City University.

Bynner, J. (2005). 'Rethinking the Youth Phase of the Life-Course: The Case for Emerging Adulthood?', *Journal of Youth Studies*, 8/4: 367–84.

Cappelli, P. (1993). 'Are Skill Requirements Rising? Evidence from Production and Clerical Jobs', *Industrial and Labor Relations Review*, 46/3: 515–30.

Card, D., and DiNardo, J. E. (2002). 'Skill-Biased Technological Change and Rising Wage Inequality: Some Problems and Puzzles', *Journal of Labor Economics*, 20/4: 733–83.

Carmeli, A. (2006). 'The Managerial Skills of the Top Management Team and the Performance of Municipal Organisations', *Local Government Studies*, 32/2: 153–76.

Carnevale, A. P., Smith, N., and Strohl, J. (2010). *Help Wanted: Projections of Jobs and Education Requirements through 2018*. Washington: Center on Education and the Workforce, Georgetown University.

Caroli, E., and van Reenen, J. (2001). 'Skill-Biased Organizational Change? Evidence from a Panel of British and French Establishments', *Quarterly Journal of Economics*, 116/4: 1449–92.

CEDEFOP (2009). *Skills for Europe's Future: Anticipating Occupational Skill Needs*. Luxembourg: Office for Official Publications of the European Communities.

CEDEFOP (2010a). *Skills for Green Jobs: European Synthesis Report*. Luxembourg: Publications Office of the European Union.

CEDEFOP (2010b). *Skills Supply and Demand in Europe: Medium-Term Forecast up to 2020*. Luxembourg: Publications Office of the European Union.

Centre for Educational Research and Innovation (2007). *Understanding the Social Outcomes of Learning*. Paris: OECD.

Chevalier, A., Harmon, C., Walker, I., and Zhu, Y. (2004). 'Does Education Raise Productivity, or Just Reflect It?', *Economic Journal*, 114/499: F499–F517.

Chowdry, H., Crawford, C., and Goodman, A. (2011). 'The Role of Attitudes and Behaviours in Explaining Socio-Economic Differences in Attainment at Age 16', *Longitudinal and Life Course Studies*, 2/1: 59–76.

Christen, R. N., Alder, J., and Bitzer, J. (2008). 'Gender Differences in Physicians' Communicative Skills and their Influence on Patient Satisfaction in Gynaecological Outpatient Consultations', *Social Science & Medicine*, 66/7: 1474–83.

Christopoulou, R., and Ryan, P. (2009). 'Youth Outcomes in the Labour Markets of Advanced Economies: Decline, Deterioration, and Causes', in I. Schoon and R. K. Silbereisen (eds), *Transitions from School to Work*. Cambridge: Cambridge University Press, 67–94.

Chusseau, N., Dumont, M., and Hellier, J. (2008). 'Explaining Rising Inequality: Skill-Biased Technical Change and North-South Trade', *Journal of Economic Surveys*, 22/3: 409–57.

Cieslik, M. (2006). 'Reflexivity, Learning Identities and Adult Basic Skills in the United Kingdom', *British Journal of Sociology of Education*, 27/2: 237–50.

CIPD (2011). *Meeting the UK's People Management Skills Deficit*. London: CIPD.

Clarke, L., and Winch, C. (2006). 'A European Skills Framework?: But what Are Skills? Anglo-Saxon versus German Concepts', *Journal of Education and Work*, 19/3: 255–69.

Cockburn, C. (1983). *Brothers: Male Dominance and Social Change*. London: Pluto Press.

Collier, W., Green, F., and Peirson, J. (2005). 'Training and Establishment Survival', *Scottish Journal of Political Economy*, 52/5: 710–35.

Collier, W., Green, F., Kim, Y.-B., and Peirson, J. (2011). 'Education, Training and Economic Performance: Evidence from Establishment Survival Data', *Journal of Labor Research*, 32/4: 336–61.

Colombo, E., and Stanca, L. (2008). 'The Impact of Training on Productivity: Evidence from a Large Panel of Firms'. Milan, University of Milan-Bicocca, Department of Economics, Working Paper No. 134.

Conway, N., Deakin, S., Konzelmann, S., Petit, H., Rebérioux, A., and Wilkinson, F. (2008). 'The Influence of Stock Market Listing on Human Resource Management: Evidence for France and Britain', *British Journal of Industrial Relations*, 46/4: 631–73.

Cooney, R., and Gospel, H. (2008). 'Interfirm Cooperation in Training: Group Training in the UK and Australia', *Industrial Relations Journal*, 39/5: 411–27.

Côté, J., and Bynner, J. M. (2008). 'Changes in the Transition to Adulthood in the UK and Canada: The Role of Structure and Agency in Emerging Adulthood', *Journal of Youth Studies*, 11/3: 251–68.

Crouch, C., Finegold, D., and Sato, M. (1999). *Are Skills the Answer? The Political Economy of Skill Creation in Advanced Industrial Countries*. Oxford: Oxford University Press.

References

Cully, M., van den Heuvel, A., Wooden, M., and Curtain, R. (2000). 'Participation in, and Barriers to, Training: The Experience of Older Adults', *Australasian Journal on Ageing*, 19/4: 172–9.

Culpepper, P. D. (2003). *Creating Cooperation*. Ithaca, NY: Cornell University Press.

Culpepper, P. D., and Thelen, K. (2008). 'Institutions and Collective Actors in the Provision of Training: Historical and Cross-National Comparisons', in K. U. Mayer and H. Solga (eds), *Skill Formation: Interdisciplinary and Cross-National Perspectives*. New York: Cambridge University Press.

Curry, A. (2010). *The World in 2020: The Business Challenges of the Future*. London: Futures Company.

Davies, B., Gore, K., Shury, J., Vivian, D., Winterbotham, M., and Constable, S. (2011). *UK Commission's Employer Skills Survey 2011: UK Results*. Wath-upon-Dearne: UK Commission for Employment and Skills.

De Grip, A., and van Loo, J. (2002). 'The Economics of Skills Obsolescence: A Review', *Research in Labor Economics: A Research Annual*, 21: 1–26.

Dearden, L., Reed, H., and van Reenen, J. (2006). 'The Impact of Training on Productivity and Wages: Evidence from British Panel Data', *Oxford Bulletin of Economics and Statistics*, 68/4: 397–421.

Dearden, L., Emmerson, C., Frayne, C., and Meghir, C. (2009). 'Conditional Cash Transfers and School Dropout Rates', *Journal of Human Resources*, 44/4: 827–57.

Department of Education Employment and Workplace Relations (2011). *Skill Shortages Australia*, Commonwealth of Australia <http://www.deewr.gov.au/employment/lmi/skillshortages> (accessed 17 November 2012).

Dickerson, A., and Green, F. (2004). 'The Growth and Valuation of Computing and Other Generic Skills', *Oxford Economic Papers*, 56/3: 371–406.

Dickerson, A., and Wilson, R. (2012). *Developing Occupational Skills Profiles for the UK: A Feasibility Study*. London: UK Commission for Employment and Skills, Evidence Report 44.

Dobbin, F., and Boychuk, T. (1999). 'National Employment Systems and Job Autonomy: Why Job Autonomy is High in the Nordic Countries and Low in the United States, Canada and Australia', *Organization Studies*, 20/2: 257–92.

Doeringer, Peter B., and Piore, Michael J. (1971). *Internal Labor Markets and Manpower Analysis*. Massachusetts: D. C. Heath and Company.

Dolton, P., and Marcenaro-Gutierrez, O. (2009). 'Overeducation across Europe', in P. Dolton, R. Asplund, and E. Barth (eds), *Education and Inequality across Europe*. Cheltenham: Edward Elgar.

Dolton, P., and Vignoles, A. (2000). 'The Incidence and Effects of Overeducation in the UK Graduate Labour Market', *Economics of Education Review*, 19: 179–98.

Dustmann, C., and Schoenberg, U. (2008). 'Why Does the German Apprenticeship System Work?', in K. U. Mayer and H. Solga (eds), *Skill Formation: Interdisciplinary and Cross-National Perspectives*. Cambridge: Cambridge University Press, 85–108.

Dustmann, C., and Schoenberg, U. (2009). 'Training and Union Wages', *Review of Economics and Statistics*, 91/2: 363–76.

Ecclestone, K., Biesta, G., and Hughes, M. (2010). 'Transitions in the Lifecourse: The Role of Identity, Agency and Structure', in K. Ecclestone, G. Biesta and M. Hughes (eds), *Transitions and Learning through the Lifecourse*. London: Routledge, 1–15.

Edwards, R. C., Gordon, D. M., and Reich, M. (1982). *Segmented Work, Divided Workers: The Historical Transformation of Labor in the United States*. Cambridge: Cambridge University Press.

Eisenhardt, K., and Martin, J. (2000). 'Dynamic Capabilities: What Are They?', *Strategic Management Journal*, 21: 1105–21.

Erez, M. (2010). 'Culture and Job Design', *Journal of Organizational Behavior*, 31/2–3: 389–400.

Esping-Andersen, G. (1990). *The Three Worlds of Welfare Capitalism*. Cambridge: Polity Press.

Estevez-Abe, G. (2005). 'Gender Bias in Skills and Social Policies: The Varieties of Capitalism Perspective on Sex Segregation', *Social Politics*, 12/2: 180–215.

European Social Statistics (2002). *Continuing Vocational Training Survey (CVTS2)*. Luxembourg: Office for Official Publications of the European Communities.

Evans, K. (2002). 'Taking Control of their Lives? Agency in Young Adult Transitions in England and the New Germany', *Journal of Youth Studies*, 5/3: 245–69.

Evans, K., and Waite, E. (2010). Adults Learning in and through the Workplace', in K. Ecclestone, G. Biesta, and M. Hughes (eds), *Transitions and Learning through the Lifecourse*. London: Routledge, 162–81.

Evans, K., Schoon, I., and Weale, M. (2010). 'Life Chances, Learning and the Dynamics of Risk throughout the Life Course'. London, Centre for Learning and Life Chances in Knowledge Economies and Societies (LLAKES), Research Paper 9 <http:www.llakes. org> (accessed 17 November 2012).

Evertsson, M. (2004). 'Formal on-the-Job Training: A Gender-Typed Experience and Wage-Related Advantage?', *European Sociological Review*, 20/1: 79–94.

Felstead, A., Green, F., and Mayhew, K. (1997). *Getting the Measure of Training*. Leeds: Centre for Industrial Policy and Performance, University of Leeds.

Felstead, A., Gallie, D., and Green, F. (2002). *Work Skills in Britain 1986–2001*. Nottingham: DfES Publications.

Felstead, A., Gallie, D., Green, F., and Zhou, Y. (2007a). *Skills at Work, 1986 to 2006*. Oxford: University of Oxford, SKOPE.

Felstead, A., Fuller, A., Jewson, N., Kakavelakis, K., and Unwin, L. (2007b). 'Grooving to the Same Tunes? Learning, Training and Productive Systems in the Aerobics Studio', *Work, Employment and Society*, 21/2: 189–208.

Felstead, A., Fuller, A., Jewson, N., and Unwin, L. (2009). *Improving Working as Learning*. Abingdon: Routledge.

Felstead, A., Gallie, D., Green, F., and Zhou, Y. (2010). 'Employee Involvement, the Quality of Training and the Learning Environment: An Individual-Level Analysis', *International Journal of Human Resource Management*, 21/10: 1667–88.

Felstead, A., Green, F., and Jewson, N. (2012). 'An Analysis of the Impact of the 2008–09 Recession on the Provision of Training in the UK', *Work, Employment and Society*, 26/6: 968–86.

References

Fernández-Macías, E., and Hurley, J. (2008). *More and Better Jobs: Patterns of Employment Expansion in Europe*. Dublin: European Foundation for the Improvement of Living and Working Conditions.

Ferris, G. R., Witt, L. A., and Hochwarter, W. A. (2001). 'Interaction of Social Skill and General Mental Ability on Job Performance and Salary', *Journal of Applied Psychology*, 86/6: 1075–82.

Fersterer, J., and Winter-Ebmer, R. (2003). 'Smoking, Discount Rates, and Returns to Education', *Economics of Education Review*, 22/6: 561–6.

Fersterer, J., Pischke, J. S., and Winter-Ebmer, R. (2008). 'Returns to Apprenticeship Training in Austria: Evidence from Failed Firms', *Scandinavian Journal of Economics*, 110/4: 733–53.

Field, J. (2006). *Lifelong Learning and the New Educational Order*. Stoke on Trent: Trentham.

Field, J. (2010). 'Preface', in K. Ecclestone, G. Biesta, and M. Hughes (eds), *Transitions and Learning through the Lifecourse*. London: Routledge, pp. xvii–xxiv.

Finegold, D. (1999). 'Creating Self-Sustaining, High-Skill Ecosystems', *Oxford Review of Economic Policy*, 15/1: 60–81.

Finegold, D., and Mason, G. (1999). 'National Training Systems and Industrial Performance: US-European Matched-Plant Comparisons', *Research in Labor Economics*, 8: 331–58.

Finegold, D., and Soskice, D. (1988). 'The Failure of British Training: Analysis and Prescription', *Oxford Review of Economic Policy*, 4/3: 21–53.

Finegold, D., Wong, P. K., and Cheah, T. C. (2004). 'Adapting a Foreign Direct Investment Strategy to the Knowledge Economy: The Case of Singapore's Emerging Biotechnology Cluster', *European Planning Studies*, 12/7: 921–41.

Finnie, R., and Meng, R. (2005). 'Literacy and Labour Market Outcomes: Self-Assessment versus Test Score Measures', *Applied Economics*, 37/17: 1935–51.

Flannery, D., and O'Donoghue, C. (2009). 'The Determinants of Higher Education Participation in Ireland: A Micro Analysis', *Economic and Social Review*, 40/1: 73–107.

Forrier, A., and Sels, L. (2003). 'Temporary Employment and Employability: Training Opportunities and Efforts of Temporary and Permanent Employees in Belgium', *Work Employment and Society*, 17/4: 641–66.

Freeman, R., and Medoff, J. L. (1984). *What Do Unions Do?* New York: Basic Books.

Freeman, R., and Schettkatt, R. (2001). 'Skill Compression, Wage Differentials and Employment: Germany vs the US', *Oxford Economic Papers*, 53/3: 583–603.

Friedman, A. L. (1977). *Industry and Labour*. London: Macmillan.

Froy, F., and Giguère, S. (2010). *Putting in Place Jobs that Last*. Paris: OECD.

Fuller, A., and Unwin, L. (2004). 'Expansive Learning Environments: Integrating Personal and Organisational Development', in H. Rainbird, A. Fuller, and A. Munro (eds), *Workplace Learning in Context*. London: Routledge.

Fuller, A., and Unwin, L. (2011). 'Workplace Learning and the Organization', in M. Malloch, L. Cairns, K. Evans, and B. N. O'Connor (eds), *The Sage Handbook of Workplace Learning*. London: Sage.

Gallie, D. (2003). 'The Quality of Working Life: Is Scandinavia Different?', *European Sociological Review*, 19/1: 61–79.

Gallie, D. (2011). 'Production Regimes, Employee Job Control and Skill Development, Centre for Learning and Life Chances in Knowledge Economies and Societies'. London, Centre for Learning and Life Chances in Knowledge Economies and Societies (LLAKES), Research Paper 31 <http://www.llakes.org> (accessed 17 November 2012).

Gallie, D., White, M., Cheng, Y., and Tomlinson, M. (1998). *Restructuring the Employment Relationship*. Oxford: Clarendon Press.

Gallie, D., Felstead, A., and Green, F. (2004). 'Changing Patterns of Task Discretion in Britain', *Work Employment and Society*, 18/2: 243–66.

Gallie, D., Zhou, Y., Felstead, A., and Green, F. (2012). 'Teamwork, Skill Development and Employee Welfare', *British Journal of Industrial Relations*, 50/1: 23–46.

Game, A. M. (2007). 'Workplace Boredom Coping: Health, Safety, and HR Implications', *Personnel Review*, 36/5–6: 701–21.

Gaudart, C., and Weill-Fasina, A. (1999). 'L'Évolution des compétences au cour de la vie professionelle: Une approche ergonomique', *Formation Emploi*, 67: 47–62.

Gibson, J. (2002). 'Decomposing Ethnic Differences in the Incidence of Employer-Provided Training in New Zealand', *Applied Economics Letters*, 9/2: 121–6.

Giret, J. F., and Masjuan, J. M. (1999). 'The Diffusion of Qualifications in the Spanish Labour Market', *Journal of Education and Work*, 12/2: 179–99.

Godard, J. (2004). 'A Critical Assessment of the High-Performance Paradigm', *British Journal of Industrial Relations*, 42/2: 349–78.

Goldin, C., and Katz, L. F. (2008). *The Race between Education and Technology*. Cambridge, MA: Harvard University Press.

Goos, M., and Manning, A. (2007). 'Lousy and Lovely Jobs: The Rising Polarization of Work in Britain', *Review of Economics and Statistics*, 89/1: 118–33.

Goos, M., Manning, A., and Salomons, A. (2009). 'Job Polarization in Europe', *American Economic Association*, 99/2: 58–63.

Goos, M., Manning, A., and Salomons, A. (2010). 'Explaining Job Polarization in Europe: The Roles of Technology, Globalization and Institutions'. London School of Economics, CEP Discussion Paper No 1026.

Gospel, H., and Foreman, J. (2006). 'Inter-Firm Training Co-Ordination in Britain', *British Journal of Industrial Relations*, 44/2: 191–214.

Goux, D., and Maurin, E. (2000). 'Returns to Firm-Provided Training: Evidence from French Worker–Firm Matched Data', *Labour Economics*, 7/1: 1–19.

Green, A. (1999). 'East Asian Skill Formation Systems and the Challenge of Globalisation', *Journal of Education and Work*, 12/3: 253–79.

Green, A. (2011). 'Lifelong Learning, Equality and Social Cohesion', *European Journal of Education*, 46/2: 228–48.

Green, A., and Janmaat, J. G. (2011). *Regimes of Social Cohesion: Societies and the Crisis of Globalisation*. Basingstoke: Palgrave.

Green, A., Preston, J., and Janmaat, J. G. (2006). *Education, Equality and Social Cohesion*. Basingstoke: Palgrave Macmillan.

Green, C., Kler, P., and Leeves, G. (2007). 'Immigrant Overeducation: Evidence from Recent Arrivals to Australia', *Economics of Education Review*, 26/4: 420–32.

Green, F. (1992). 'On the Political Economy of Skill in the Advanced Industrial Nations', *Review of Political Economy*, 4/4: 413–35.

References

Green, F. (1993). 'The Determinants of Training of Male and Female Employees in Britain', *Oxford Bulletin of Economics and Statistics*, 55/1 (February): 103–22.

Green, F. (2006). *Demanding Work: The Paradox of Job Quality in the Affluent Economy*. Woodstock: Princeton University Press.

Green, F. (2008). 'Leeway for the Loyal: A Model of Employee Discretion', *British Journal of Industrial Relations*, 46/1: 1–32.

Green, F. (2012). 'Employee Involvement, Technology and Evolution in Job Skills: A Task-Based Analysis', *Industrial and Labor Relations Review*, 65/1: 35–66.

Green, F., and Keese, M. (2013) (eds). *Job Tasks, Work Skills and the Labour Market*. Paris: OECD.

Green, F., and Mcintosh, S. (2007). 'Is there a Genuine Underutilisation of Skills amongst the Over-Qualified?', *Applied Economics*, 39/4: 427–39.

Green, F., and Mostafa, T. (2012). *Trends in Job Quality in Europe: A Report Based on the Fifth European Working Conditions Survey*. Dublin: Eurofound.

Green, F., and Zhu, Y. (2010). 'Overqualification, Job Dissatisfaction, and Increasing Dispersion in the Returns to Graduate Education', *Oxford Economic Papers*, 62/2: 740–63.

Green, F., Ashton, D., James, D., and Sung, J. (1999a). 'The Role of the State in Skill Formation: Evidence from the Republic of Korea, Singapore, and Taiwan', *Oxford Review of Economic Policy*, 15/1: 82–96.

Green, F., Machin, S., and Wilkinson, D. (1999b). 'Trade Unions and Training Practices in British Workplaces', *Industrial and Labor Relations Review*, 52/2: 175–95.

Green, F., McIntosh, S., and Vignoles, A. (2002). 'The Utilization of Education and Skills: Evidence from Britain', *Manchester School*, 70/6: 792–811.

Green, F., Felstead, A., and Gallie, D. (2003a). 'Computers and the Changing Skill-Intensity of Jobs', *Applied Economics*, 35/14: 1561–76.

Green, F., Mayhew, K., and Molloy, E. (2003b). *Employers' Perspectives Survey*. Nottingham: Department for Education and Skills.

Green, F., Felstead, A., and Gallie, D. (2013). 'Skills and Work Organisation in Britain', in F. Green and M. Keese (eds), *Job Tasks, Work Skills and the Labour Market*. Paris: OECD.

Green, F., Mostafa, T., Parent-Thirion, A., Vermeylen, G., Houten, G. V., Biletta, I., and Lyly-Yrjanainen, M. (2013). 'Is Job Quality Becoming More Unequal?', *Industrial and Labor Relations Review*.

Greenan, N. (2003). 'Organisational Change, Technology, Employment and Skills: An Empirical Study of French Manufacturing', *Cambridge Journal of Economics*, 27/2: 287–316.

Greenhalgh, C. and G. Mavrotas (1994). 'The Role Of Career Aspirations And Financial Constraints In Individual Access To Vocational Training.' *Oxford Economic Papers* 46 (4): 579–604.

Gregg, P., and Tominey, E. (2005). 'The Wage Scar from Male Youth Unemployment', *Labour Economics*, 12/4: 487–509.

Gregory, M., Zissimos, B., and Greenhalgh, C. (2001). 'Jobs for the Skilled: How Technology, Trade, and Domestic Demand Changed the Structure of UK Employment, 1979–90', *Oxford Economic Papers*, 53/1: 20–46.

Grissmer, D. W. (2000). 'The Continuing Use and Misuse of SAT Scores', *Psychology, Public Policy and Law*, 6/1: 223–32.

Groot, W., and Maassen van den Brink, H. (2000). 'Overeducation in the Labour Market: A Meta-Analysis', *Economics of Education Review*, 19/2: 149–58.

Grugulis, I., and Stoyanova, D. (2011). 'Skill and Performance', *British Journal of Industrial Relations*, 49/3: 515–36.

Gutman, L. M., and Akerman, R. (2008). 'Determinants of Aspirations'. London, Institute of Education, Centre for Research on the Wider Benefits of Learning, Research Report 27.

Hall, P., and Soskice, D. (2001). 'An Introduction to Varieties of Capitalism', in P. Hall and D. Soskice (eds), *Varieties of Capitalism*. Oxford: Oxford University Press, 1–70.

Hamermesh, D. (1993). *Labor Demand*. Princeton: Princeton University Press.

Hamermesh, D. S., Meng, X., and Zhang, J. S. (2002). 'Dress for Success: Does Primping Pay?' *Labour Economics*, 9/3: 361–73.

Handel, M. J. (2008). 'Measuring Job Content: Skills, Technology, and Management Practices'. Institute for Research on Poverty, Discussion Paper 1357-08.

Handel, M. (2013). 'What Do People Do at Work'?, in F. Green and M. Keese (eds), *Job Tasks, Work Skills and the Labour Market*. Paris: OECD.

Hanushek, E. A., and Kimko, D. D. (2000). 'Schooling, Labor-Force Quality, and the Growth of Nations', *American Economic Review*, 90/5: 1184–208.

Hanushek, E. A., and Woessman, L. (2010). 'The Economics of International Differences in Educational Achievement'. National Bureau of Economic Research, Working Paper 15949.

Harmon, C., Oosterbeek, H., and Walker, I. (2003). 'The Returns to Education: Microeconomics', *Journal of Economic Surveys*, 17/2: 115–55.

Harrington, Paul E., and Sum, Andrew M. (2010a). 'College Labor Shortages in 2018?', *New England Journal of Higher Education*, November <http://www.nebhe.org/thejournal/college-labor-shortages-in-2018/> (accessed 18 November 2012).

Harrington, Paul E., and Sum, Andrew M. (2010b). 'College Labor Shortages in 2018? Part Deux', *New England Journal of Higher Education*, December <http://www.nebhe.org/thejournal/college-laborshortages-in-2018-part-two/> (accessed 18 November 2012).

Hartog, J., Pereira, P. T., and Vieira, J. A. C. (2001). 'Changing Returns to Education in Portugal during the 1980s and Early 1990s: OLS and Quantile Regression Estimators', *Applied Economics*, 33/8: 1021–37.

Hashimoto, M. (1982). 'Firm-Specific Human-Capital as a Shared Investment', *American Economic Review*, 71/3: 475–82.

Haskel, J., and Martin, C. (1993). 'Do Skill Shortages Reduce Productivity: Theory and Evidence from the United Kingdom', *Economic Journal*, 103/417: 386–94.

Haskel, J., and Heden, Y. (1999). 'Computers and the Demand for Skilled Labour: Industry- and Establishment-Level Panel Evidence for the UK', *Economic Journal*, 109 (March): C68–79.

Heckman, J. J. (2008). 'Schools, Skills, and Synapses', *Economic Inquiry*, 46/3: 289–324.

Heckman, J. J., and Kautz, T. (2012). 'Hard Evidence on Soft Skills', *Labour Economics*, 19/4: 451–64.

References

Heckman, J., Lochner, L. and Todd, P. (2006). 'Earnings Functions, Rates of Return and Treatment Effects: The Mincer Equation and Beyond', *Handbook of the Economics of Education*. Amsterdam: North Holland, i, ch. 7.

Himmelweit, S. (1999). 'Caring Labor', *Annals of the American Academy of Political and Social Science*, 561: 27–38.

Hochwarter, W. A., Witt, L. A., Treadway, D. C., and Ferris, G. R. (2006). 'The Interaction of Social Skill and Organizational Support on Job Performance', *Journal of Applied Psychology*, 91/2: 482–9.

Holzer, H. J. (1998). 'Employer Skill Demands and Labor Market Outcomes of Blacks and Women', *Industrial and Labor Relations Review*, 52/1: 82–98.

Hoque, K., and Bacon, N. (2011). 'Assessing the Impact of Union Learning Representatives on Training: Evidence from a Matched Sample of ULRs and Managers', *Work Employment and Society*, 25/2: 218–33.

Howell, D., and Wolff, E. (1991). 'Trends in the Growth and Distribution of Skill in the US Workplace, 1960–1985', *Industrial and Labor Relations Review*, 44/3: 481–501.

Hutton, W. (1996). *The State We're In*. London: Vintage.

Ichniowski, C., and Shaw, K. (1999). 'The Effects of Human Resource Management Systems on Economic Performance: An International Comparison of US and Japanese Plants', *Management Science*, 45/5: 704–21.

Ichniowski, C., Shaw, K., and Prennushi, G. (1997). 'The Impact of Human Resource Management Practices on Productivity', *American Economic Review*, 87 (June): 291–313.

James, L., Guile, D., and Unwin, L. (2012). 'From Learning for the Knowledge-Based Economy to Learning for Growth: Re-Examining Clusters, Innovation and Qualifications'. London, Centre for Learning and Life Chances in Knowledge Economies and Societies (LLAKES), Research Paper 29 <http: www.llakes.org> (accessed 18 November 2012).

Jensen, J. B., and Kletzer, L. G. (2010). 'Measuring Tradable Services and the Task Content of Offshorable Services Jobs', in K. Abraham, M. Harper, and J. Spletzer (eds), *Labor in the New Economy*. Chicago: University of Chicago Press.

Jevons, W. S. (1871). *The Theory of Political Economy*. London: Macmillan.

Jones, G. (2009). 'From Paradigm to Paradox: Parental Support and Transitions to Independence', in I. Schoon and R. K. Silbereisen (eds), *Transitions from School to Work*. Cambridge: Cambridge University Press, 145–64.

Jones, M. K., Latreille, P. L., and Sloane, P. J. (2007). 'Crossing the Tracks? Trends in the Training of Male and Female Workers in Great Britain', *British Journal of Industrial Relations*, 46/2: 268–82.

Jones, R., and Chiripanhura, B. (2010). 'Measuring the UK's Human Capital Stock', *Economic & Labour Market Review*, 4/11: 36–63.

Kalleberg, A. L. (2011). *Good Jobs, Bad Jobs*. New York: Russell Sage Foundation.

Karasek, R. A. (1979). 'Job Demands, Job Decision Latitude, and Mental Strain: Implications for Job Design', *Administrative Science Quarterly*, 24: 285–308.

Keep, E. (2006). *Market Failure in Skills*. Wath-upon-Dearne: SSDA Catalyst Series, No. 1, Sector Skills Development Agency.

Keep, E., and Mayhew, K. (2010). 'Moving beyond Skills as a Social and Economic Panacea', *Work Employment and Society*, 24/3: 565–77.

Kemptner, D., Juerges, H., and Reinhold, S. (2011). 'Changes in Compulsory Schooling and the Causal Effect of Education on Health: Evidence from Germany', *Journal of Health Economics*, 30/2: 340–54.

Klynge, A. H. (2011). 'The Returns to the Multiple Abilities'. University of Copenhagen, Ph.D. thesis.

Knight, F. H. (1921). *Risk, Uncertainty, and Profit*. Boston and New York: Houghton Mifflin Co., Riverside Press.

Koucký, J., Kovařovic, J., and Lepič, M. (2012). *Forecasting Skill Supply and Demand in Europe to 2020. Occupational Skills Profiles: Methodology and Application*. Luxembourg: CEDEFOP, Publications Office of the European Union, January.

Krueger, A., and Rouse, C. (1998). 'The Impact of Workplace Education on Earnings, Turnover and Job Performance', *Journal of Labour Economics*, 16 (January): 61–94.

Kuhn, P., and Weinberger, C. (2005). 'Leadership Skills and Wages', *Journal of Labor Economics*, 23/3: 395–436.

Laplagne, P., Glover, M., and Shomos, A. (2007). 'Effects of Health and Education on Labour Force Participation'. Melbourne, Staff Working Paper, Australian Government Productivity Commission.

Lauer, C. (2002). 'Participation in Higher Education: The Role of Cost and Return Expectations', *International Journal of Manpower*, 23/5: 443–57.

Lave, J., and Wenger, E. (1991). *Situated Learning: Legitimate Peripheral Participation*. Cambridge: Cambridge University Press.

Lazear, E. (1999). 'Personnel Economics: Past Lessons and Future Directions', *Journal of Labor Economics*, 17/2: 199–236.

Leuven, E., Oosterbeek, H., and van Ophem, H. (2004). 'Explaining International Differences in Male Skill Wage Differentials by Differences in Demand and Supply of Skill', *Economic Journal*, 114/495: 466–86.

Lindley, J. (2012). 'The Gender Dimension of Technical Change and the Role of Task Inputs', *Labour Economics*, 19/4: 516–26.

Liu, X. M., and Batt, R. (2007). 'The Economic Pay-Offs to Informal Training: Evidence from Routine Service Work', *Industrial & Labor Relations Review*, 61/1: 75–89.

Lloyd, C., and Payne, J. (2010). '"We have Got the Freedom": A Study of Autonomy and Discretion among Vocational Teachers in Norway and the UK'. Cardiff, Centre on Skills, Knowledge and Organisational Performance, July, Research Paper No. 95,

Lloyd, C., Mason, G., and Mayhew, K. (2008) (eds). *Low-Wage Work in the United Kingdom*. New York: Russell Sage Foundation.

Loewenstein, M. A., and Spletzer, J. R. (1999). 'Dividing the Costs and Returns to General Training', *Journal of Labor Economics*, 16/1: 142–71.

Lucio, M. M., Skule, S., Kruse, W., and Trappmann, V. (2007). 'Regulating Skill Formation in Europe: German, Norwegian and Spanish Policies on Transferable Skills', *European Journal of Industrial Relations*, 13/3: 323–40.

MacDuffie, J. P. (1995). 'Human Resource Bundles and Manufacturing Performance: Organizational Logic and Flexible Production Systems in the World Auto Industry', *Industrial and Labor Relations Review*, 48/2: 197–221.

References

Macduffie, J. P., and Kochan, T. A. (1995). 'Do US Firms Invest Less in Human Resources? Training in the World Auto Industry', *Industrial Relations*, 34/2: 147–68.

McGuinness, S. (2006). 'Overeducation in the Labour Market', *Journal of Economic Surveys*, 20/3: 387–418.

Machin, S. (2003). 'Wage Inequality since 1975', in R. Dickens, P. Gregg and J. Wadsworth (eds), *The Labour Market under New Labour*. Basingstoke: Palgrave Macmillan.

Machin, S., and van Reenen, J. (1998). 'Technology and Changes in Skill Structure: Evidence from Seven OECD Countries', *Quarterly Journal of Economics*, 113/4: 1215–44.

Machin, S., and van Reenen, J. (2007). 'Changes in Wage Inequality'. LSE, Centre for Economic Performance, Special Paper No. 18.

McIntosh, S., and Vignoles, A. (2001). 'Measuring and Assessing the Impact of Basic Skills on Labour Market Outcomes', *Oxford Economic Papers*, 53/3: 453–81.

McMahon, W. M. (2004). 'The Social and External Benefits of Education', in G. Johnes and J. Johnes (eds), *International Handbook on the Economics of Education*. Cheltenham: Edward Elgar, 211–59.

Mane, F., and Miravet, D. (2013). 'Using the Job Requirement Approach and Matched Employer–Employee Data to Investigate on the Content of Individual's Human Capital', in F. Green and M. Keese (eds), *Job Tasks, Work Skills and the Labour Market*. Paris: OECD.

Manning, A. (2003). *Monopsony in Motion: Imperfect Competition in Labor Markets*. Princeton: Princeton University Press.

Manning, A. (2004). 'We Can Work It Out: The Impact of Technological Change on the Demand for Low-Skill Workers', *Scottish Journal of Political Economy*, 51/5: 581–608.

Martins, P. (2010). 'Can Targeted, Non-Cognitive Skills Programs Improve Achievement? Evidence from EPIS'. Seminars in Quantitative Social Science, Institute of Education, 6 October.

Marx, K. (1976). *Capital, Volume 1*, trans. B. Fowkes. Harmondsworth: Penguin.

Maskell, P., and Malmberg, A. (1999). 'Localised Learning and Industrial Competitiveness', *Cambridge Journal of Economics*, 23: 167–85.

Maskell, P., and Malmberg, A. (2007). 'Myopia, Knowledge Development and Cluster Evolution', *Journal of Economic Geography*, 7/5: 603–18.

Mason, G. (2010). *Product Strategies, Skill Shortages and Skill Updating Needs in England: New Evidence from the National Employers Skills Survey*. London: UK Commission for Employment and Skills.

Mason, G., and van Ark, B. (1993). 'Productivity, Machinery and Skills In Engineering: An Anglo-Dutch Comparison', National Institute of Economic and Social Research Discussion Paper, No. 36.

Mastekaasa, A. (2003). 'The Best and the Brightest?', *Tidsskrift for Samfunnsforskning*, 44/3: 331–66.

Mavromaras, K., and McGuinness, S. (2012). 'Overskilling Dynamics and Education Pathways', *Economics of Education Review*, 31/5: 619–28.

Mavromaras, K., McGuinness, S., and Wooden, M. (2007). 'Overskilling in the Australian Labour Market', *Australian Economic Review*, 40: 307–12.

Mayer, K. U., and Solga, H. (2008). 'Skill Formation: Interdisciplinary and Cross-National Perspectives', in K. U. Mayer and H. Solga (eds), *Skill Formation: Interdisciplinary and Cross-National Perspectives*. Cambridge: Cambridge University Press.

MEADOW Consortium (2010). *The MEADOW Guidelines* <http://www.meadow-project.eu/index.php?option=com_frontpage&Itemid=1> (accessed 18 November 2012).

Méhaut, P. (2011). '*Savoir*: The Organizing Principle of French VET', in M. Brockmann, L. Clarke, and C. Winch (eds), *Knowledge, Skills and Competence in the European Labour Market*, Abingdon: Routledge, 36–49.

Miller, L., Kellie, D., and Acutt, B. (2001). 'Factors Influencing the Choice of Initial Qualifications and Continuing Development in Australia and Britain', *International Journal of Training and Development*, 5/3: 196–222.

Mincer, J. (1974). *Schooling, Experience and Earnings*. New York: NBER.

Ministry of Education, Youth and Sports (2007). *The Strategy of Lifelong Learning in the Czech Republic*. Prague: Ministry of Education, Youth and Sports.

Moser, C. (1999). *Improving Literacy and Numeracy: A Fresh Start*. London: DfEE.

Mueller, F. (1996). 'Human Resources as Strategic Assets: An Evolutionary Resource-Based Theory', *Journal of Management Studies*, 33/6: 757–85.

Murnane, R. J., Willet, J. B., and Levy, F. (1995). 'The Growing Importance of Cognitive Skills in Wage Determination', *Review of Economics and Statistics*, 77: 251–66.

Murphy, P., Latreille, P. L., Jones, M., and Blackaby, D. (2008). 'Is There a Public Sector Training Advantage? Evidence from the Workplace Employment Relations Survey', *British Journal of Industrial Relations*, 46/4: 674–701.

National Research Council (2010). *A Database for a Changing Economy*. Washington: National Academies Press.

Neidell, M., and Waldfogel, J. (2009). 'Program Participation of Immigrant Children: Evidence from the Local Availability of Head Start', *Economics of Education Review*, 28: 704–15.

Neill, C. (2009). 'Tuition Fees and the Demand for University Places', *Economics of Education Review*, 28/5: 561–70.

Neumark, D., Johnson, H., and Mejia, M. C. (2011). 'Future Skill Shortages in the US Economy?'. National Bureau of Economic Research, Working Paper No. 17213'.

O'Connell, P. J., and Byrne, D. (2012). 'The Determinants and Effects of Training at Work: Bringing the Workplace Back In', *European Sociological Review*, 28/3: 283–300.

OECD (2000). *Literacy in the Information Age: Final Report of the International Adult Literacy Survey*. Paris: OECD.

OECD (2005). *Learning a Living: First Results of the Adult Literacy and Life Skills Survey*. Paris: OECD.

OECD (2010). *Education at a Glance 2010*. Paris: OECD.

OECD (2011). *Education at a Glance 2011: OECD Indicators*. Paris: OECD Publishing.

OECD (2012). *Better Skills, Better Jobs, Better Lives: A Strategic Approach to Skills Policies*. Paris: OECD.

OECD, Human Resources Development Canada and Statistics Canada (1997). *Literacy Skills for the Knowledge Society: Further Results from the International Adult Literacy Survey*. Paris: OECD.

OECD and Statistics Canada (1995). *Literacy, Economy and Society, Results of the First International Adult Literacy Survey*. Paris and Ottawa: OECD.

Official Statistics of Finland (OSF) (2005). *CVTS, Continuing Vocational Training Survey* [e-publication]. Helsinki: Statistics Finland.

Oliver, J. M., and Turton, J. R. (1982). 'Is there a Shortage of Skilled Labour?', *British Journal of Industrial Relations*, 20: 195–200.

Ollo-Lopez, A., Bayo-Moriones, A., and Larraza-Kintana, M. (2010). 'The Relationship between New Work Practices and Employee Effort', *Journal of Industrial Relations*, 52/2: 219–35.

Oosterbeek, H., and Webbink, D. (1995). 'Enrollment in Higher-Education in the Netherlands', *Economist*, 143/3: 367–80.

Oreopoulos, P. and K. G. Salvanes (2011). 'Priceless: The Nonpecuniary Benefits of Schooling.' *Journal of Economic Perspectives* 25/1: 159–84.

Osterman, P. (1995). 'Skill, Training, and Work Organization in American Establishments', *Industrial Relations*, 34/2: 125–46.

Parent, D. (1999). 'Wages and Mobility: The Impact of Employer-Provided Training', *Journal of Labor Economics*, 17/2: 298–317.

Parent-Thirion, A., Fernandez Macias, E., Hurley, J., and Vermeylen, G. (2007). *Fourth European Working Conditions Survey*, Luxembourg: Office for Official Publications of the European Communities <http://www.eurofound.europa.eu/publications/htmlfiles/ef0698.htm> (accessed 18 November 2012).

Payne, J. (2000). 'The Unbearable Lightness of Skill: The Changing Meaning of Skill in UK Policy Discourses and Some Implications for Education and Training', *Journal of Education Policy*, 15/3: 353–69.

Peterson, M. D., Dodd, D. J., Alvar, B. A., Rhea, M. R. and Favre, M. (2008). 'Undulation Training for Development of Hierarchical Fitness and Improved Firefighter Job Performance', *Journal of Strength and Conditioning Research*, 22/5: 1683–95.

Piore, P., and Sabel, C. (1984). *The Second Industrial Divide: Possibilities for Prosperity*. New York: Basic Books.

Piva, M., Santarelli, E., and Vivarelli, M. (2005). 'The Skill Bias Effect of Technological and Organisational Change: Evidence and Policy Implications', *Research Policy*, 34/2: 141–57.

Prais, S. (1995). *Productivity, Education and Training: An International Perspective*. Cambridge: Cambridge University Press.

Quintini, G. (2011). 'Over-Qualified or Under-Skilled: A Review of Existing Literature'. OECD Publishing, OECD Social, Employment and Migration Working Papers, No. 121.

Reay, D., Davies, J., David, M., and Ball, S. J. (2001). 'Choices of Degree or Degrees of Choice? Class, "Race" and the Higher Education Choice Process', *Sociology*, 35/4: 855–74.

Redding, S. (1996). 'The Low-Skill, Low-Quality Trap: Strategic Complementarities between Human Capital and R&D', *Economic Journal*, 106 (March): 458–70.

Rees, G., Fevre, R., Furlong, J., and Gorard, S. (2006). 'History, Biography and Place in the Learning Society: Towards a Sociology of Life-Long Learning', in H. Lauder, P. Brown, J.-A. Dillabough, and A. H. Halsey (eds), *Education, Globalization and Social Change*. Oxford: Oxford University Press.

Reich, R. B. (1992). *The Work of Nations: Preparing Ourselves for 21st Century Capitalism*. New York: Vintage Books.

Renaud, S., Lakhdari, M., and Morin, L. (2004). 'The Determinants of Participation in Non-Mandatory Training', *Relations Industrielles–Industrial Relations*, 59/4: 724–43.

Ricardo, D. (1971). *On the Principles of Political Economy and Taxation*. Harmondsworth: Penguin Books.

Rohrbach-Schmidt, D., and Tiemann, M. (2011). 'Mismatching and Job Tasks in Germany: Rising Over-Qualification through Polarization?', *Empirical Research in Vocational Education and Training*, 3/1: 39–53.

Rohrbach-Schmidt, D., and Tiemann, M. (2013). 'Qualification- and Skill-Based Mismatching in Germany', in F. Green and M. Keese (eds), *Job Tasks, Work Skills and the Labour Market*. Paris: OECD.

Ryan, P. (2000). 'The Institutional Requirements of Apprenticeship: Evidence from Smaller EU Countries', *International Journal of Training and Development*, 4/1: 42–65.

Ryan, P. (2001). 'The School-to-Work Transition: A Cross-National Perspective', *Journal of Economic Literature*, 39/1: 34–92.

Rychen, D. S. (2003). 'Key Competencies: Meeting Important Challenges in Life', in D. S. Rychen and L. H. Salganik (eds), *Key Competencies for a Successful Life and a Well-Functioning Society*. Göttingen: Hogrefe and Huber, 63–108.

Saget, C. (1999). 'The Determinants of Female Labour Supply in Hungary', *Economics of Transition*, 7/3: 575–91.

Sayers, S. (2005). 'Why Work? Marx and Human Nature', *Science & Society*, 69/4: 606–16.

Schneider, B. (2009). 'Challenges of Transitioning into Adulthood', in I. Schoon and R. K. Silbereisen (eds), *Transitions from School to Work*. Cambridge: Cambridge University Press, 265–92.

Schoon, I., and Duckworth, K. (2010). 'Leaving School Early—and Making It! Evidence from Two British Birth Cohorts', *European Psychologist*, 15/4: 283–92.

Schoon, I. and R. K. Silbereisen (2009). 'Conceptualising School-to-Work Transitions in Context', in I. Schoon and R. K. Silbereisen (eds), *Transitions from School to Work*. Cambridge: Cambridge University Press, 3–29.

Schoon, I., Ross, A., and Martin, P. (2009). 'Sequences, Patterns, and Variations in the Assumption of Work and Family-Related Roles: Evidence from Two British Birth Cohorts', in I. Schoon and R. K. Silbereisen (eds), *Transitions from School to Work*. Cambridge: Cambridge University Press, 219–42.

Schuller, T., Preston, J., Hammond, C., Brassett-Grundy, A., and Bynner, J. (2004). *The Benefits of Learning: The Impacts of Formal and Informal Education on Social Capital, Health and Family Life*. London: RoutledgeFalmer.

Selz, M., and C. Thelot (2004). 'The Returns to Education and Experience: Trends in France over the Last Thirty-Five Years', *Population*, 59/1: 11–50

Seo, B., and Senauer, B. (2011). 'The Effect of Education on Health among US Residents in Relation to Country of Birth', *Health Economics*, 20/1: 45–55.

Serracant, P. (2012). 'Changing Youth? Continuities and Ruptures in Transitions into Adulthood among Catalan Young People', *Journal of Youth Studies*, 15/2: 161–76.

Shapiro, C., and Stiglitz, J. E. (1984). 'Equilibrium Unemployment as a Worker Discipline Device', *American Economic Review*, 74/3: 433–44.

Shields, M. A., and Price, S. W. (1999). 'Ethnic Differences in the Incidence and Determinants of Employer-Funded Training in Britain', *Scottish Journal of Political Economy*, 46/5: 523–51.

Shury, J., Winterbotham, M., Davies, B., Oldfield, K., Spilsbury, M., and Constable, S. (2010). *National Employer Skills Survey 2009*. Wath-Upon-Dearne: UK Commission for Employment and Skills.

Sianesi, B., and van Reenen, J. (2003). 'The Returns to Education: Macroeconomics', *Journal of Economic Surveys*, 17/2: 157–200.

Silles, M. A. (2009). 'The Causal Effect of Education on Health: Evidence from the United Kingdom', *Economics of Education Review*, 28/1: 122–8.

Simon, H. A. (1955). 'A Behavioral Model of Rational Choice', *Quarterly Journal of Economics*, 69: 99–118.

Simpson, P. A., and Stroh, L. K. (2002). 'Revisiting Gender Variation in Training', *Feminist Economics*, 8/3: 21–53.

Smith, M., Burchell, B., Fagan, C., and O'Brien, C. (2008). 'Job Quality in Europe', *Industrial Relations Journal*, 39/6: 586–603.

Spence, M. (1973). 'Job Market Signalling', *Quarterly Journal of Economics*, 87/3: 355–74.

Spenner, K. I. (1990). 'Skill: Meanings, Methods and Measures', *Work and Occupations*, 17/4: 399–421.

Spiess, C. K., and Wrohlich, K. (2010). 'Does Distance Determine who Attends a University in Germany?', *Economics of Education Review*, 29/3: 470–9.

Spitz-Oener, A. (2006). 'Technical Change, Job Tasks, and Rising Educational Demands: Looking outside the Wage Structure', *Journal of Labor Economics*, 24/2: 235–70.

Stasz, C. (2001). 'Assessing Skills for Work: Two Perspectives', *Oxford Economic Papers*, NS 53/3: 385–405.

Steedman, H., and McIntosh, S. (2001). 'Measuring Low Skills in Europe: How Useful Is the ISCED Framework?', *Oxford Economic Papers*, 53/3: 564–81.

Steinberg, R. J. (1990). 'Social Construction of Skill', *Work and Occupations*, 17/4: 449–82.

Steinberg, R. J., and Figart, D. M. (1999). 'Emotional Labor since the Managed Heart', *Annals of the American Academy of Political and Social Science*, 561: 8–26.

Stevens, M. (1994). 'An Investment Model for the Supply of Training by Employers', *Economic Journal*, 104 (May): 556–70.

Stevens, M. (1999). 'Human Capital Theory and UK Vocational Training Policy', *Oxford Review of Economic Policy*, 15/1: 16–32.

Streeck, W. (1989). 'Skills and the Limits of Neoliberalism: The Enterprise of the Future as a Place of Learning', *Work, Employment and Society*, 3/1: 89–104.

Streeck, W. (1991). 'On the Institutional Conditions of Diversified Quality Production', in E. Matzner and W. Streeck (eds), *Beyond Keynesianism: The Socio-Economics of Production and Full Employment*. Cheltenham: Edward Elgar.

Strietska-Ilina, O. (2004). 'Skill Shortages Enquiry by a Combined Method', in S. L. Schmidt, O. Strietska-Ilina, M. Tessaring, and B. Dworschak (eds), *Identifying*

Skill Needs for the Future. Luxembourg: Office for Official Publications of the European Communities, 76–86.

Sung, J., and Loke, F. (2011). *You and your Work: Skills Utilisation in Singapore*. Singapore: Institute for Adult Learning.

Sussman, D. (2002). 'Barriers to Job-Related Training', *Perspectives on Labour and Income*, 3/3: 5–12.

Teece, D. (2007). 'Explicating Dynamic Capabilities: The Nature and Microfoundations of (Sustainable) Enterprise Performance', *Strategic Management Journal*, 28: 1319–50.

Ter Weel, B. (2008). 'The Noncognitive Determinants of Labor Market and Behavioral Outcomes', *Journal of Human Resources*, 43/4: 729–37.

Thelen, K. (2004). *How Institutions Evolve: The Political Economy of Skills in Germany, Britain, The United States, and Japan*. Cambridge: Cambridge University Press.

Trampusch, C. (2010). 'Employers, the State and the Politics of Institutional Change: Vocational Education and Training in Austria, Germany and Switzerland', *European Journal of Political Research*, 49: 545–73.

Tsai, H. Y., Compeau, D., and Haggerty, N. (2007). 'Of Races to Run and Battles to be Won: Technical Skill Updating, Stress, and Coping of IT Professionals', *Human Resource Management*, 46/3: 395–409.

Tversky, A., and Kahneman, D. (1986). 'Rational Choice and the Framing of Decisions', *Journal of Business*, 59/4(2): S251–78.

Tversky, A., and Kahneman, D. (1992). 'Advances in Prospect Theory: Cumulative Representation of Uncertainty', *Journal of Risk and Uncertainty*, 5/4: 297–323.

Tyler, J. H. (2004). 'Basic Skills and the Earnings of Dropouts', *Economics of Education Review*, 23/3: 221–35.

UKCES (2009). *Ambition 2020: World Class Skills and Jobs for the UK*. London: UK Commission for Employment and Skills.

UKCES (2010). *Skills for Jobs: Today and Tomorrow*, ii. *The Evidence Report*. London: UK Commission for Employment and Skills.

Unwin, L. (2012). *Report of the Commission of Inquiry into the role of Group Training Associations*. London: Centre for Learning and Life Chances in Knowledge Economies and Societies (LLAKES) <http:www.llakes.org> (accessed 18 November 2012).

Vallas, S. P. (1990). ''The Concept of Skill: A Critical-Review', *Work and Occupations*, 17/4: 379–98.

Van Reenen, J. (2011). 'Does Competition Raise Productivity through Improving Management Quality?', *International Journal of Industrial Organization*, 29/3: 306–16.

Veblen, T. (1899). *The Theory of the Leisure Class: An Economic Study of Institutions*. New York: MacMillan.

Vignoles, A., Galindo-Rueda, F., and Feinstein, L. (2004). 'The Labour Market Impact of Adult Education and Training: A Cohort Analysis', *Scottish Journal of Political Economy*, 51/2: 266–80.

Wail, B., Hanchane, S., and A. Kamal (2011). 'A New Data Set of Educational Inequality in the World, 1950–2010: Gini Index of Education by Age Group' (July), SSRN <http://dx.doi.org/10.2139/ssrn.1895496> (accessed 18 November 2012).

Wajcman, J. (1991). 'Patriarchy, Technology, and Conceptions of Skill', *Work and Occupations*, 18/1: 29–45.

Wajcman, J. (2010). 'Feminist Theories of Technology', *Cambridge Journal of Economics*, 34/1: 143–52.

Wall, T. D., and Wood, S. J. (2005). 'The Romance of Human Resource Management and Business Performance, and the Case for Big Science', *Human Relations*, 58/4: 429–62.

Walther, A. (2009). ' "It Was Not My Choice, You Know?" Young People's Subjective Views and Decision-Making Processes in Biographical Transitions', in I. Schoon and R. K. Silbereisen (eds), *Transitions from School to Work*. Cambridge: Cambridge University Press, 121–44.

Warhurst, C., and Nickson, D. (2007). ' "Who's Got the Look?" Emotional, Aesthetic and Sexualized Labour in Interactive Services', *Gender, Work and Organisation*, 16/3: 385–404.

Wasunna, B., Zurovac, D., Bruce, J., Jones, C., Webster, J., and. Snow, R. W (2010). 'Health Worker Performance in the Management of Paediatric Fevers following In-Service Training and Exposure to Job Aids in Kenya', *Malaria Journal*, 9/261, September.

Welford, A.T. (1968). *Fundamentals of Skill*. London: Methuen and Co.

White, R. J., and Green, A. E. (2011). 'Opening up or Closing down Opportunities? The Role of Social Networks and Attachment to Place in Informing Young Peoples' Attitudes and Access to Training and Employment', *Urban Studies*, 48/1: 41–60.

Whitfield, K. (2000). 'High-Performance Workplaces, Training, and the Distribution of Skills', *Industrial Relations*, 39/1: 1–25.

Wiborg, S., and Court, P. (2010). 'The Vocational Training System in Denmark: Continuity and Change', in G. Bosch and J. Charest (eds), *Vocational Training: International Perspectives*. London: Routledge, 84–109.

Wilson, R. (2010). 'Lessons from America: A Research and Policy Briefing', UK Commission for Employment and Skills, Briefing Paper Series, November.

Wolfe, B., and Zuvekas, S. (1997). 'Non-Market Outcomes of Schooling', *International Journal of Educational Research*, 27/6: 491–501.

Wood, S. J., and Bryson, A. (2009). 'High Involvement Management', in W. Brown, A. Bryson, J. Forth, and K. Whitfield (eds), *The Evolution of the Modern Workplace*. Cambridge: Cambridge University Press.

Wooden, M., van den Heuvel, A., Cully, M., and Curtain, R. (2001). *Barriers to Training for Older Workers and Possible Policy Solutions*. Canberra: Australian Government, Department for Education, Employment and Work Relations.

Wright, Erik O., and Dwyer, R. E. (2003). 'Patterns of Job Expansions in the USA: A Comparison of the 1960s and 1990s', *Socio-Economic Review*, 1: 289–325.

Wright, P. M., McMahan, G. C., and McWilliams, A. (1994). 'Human Resources and Sustained Competitive Advantage: A Resource-Based Perspective', *International Journal of Human Resource Management*, 5/2: 301–26.

Zimmerman, B. J. (2000). 'Self-Efficacy: An Essential Motive to Learn', *Contemporary Educational Psychology*, 25: 82–91.

Zwick, T. (2006). 'The Impact of Training Intensity on Establishment Productivity', *Industrial Relations*, 45/1: 26–46.

Index

aesthetic skills 13, 22–3
agency
    employers' 35, 61–2, 65–6, 77, 90,
        145–6, 150
    employees' 4, 25, 101, 104–5
apprentices 36, 82, 85–6, 89, 96, 110, 151,
        154–6, 162–3
attitudes (non-cognitive skills) 6, 9, 11–24
        passim, 31, 41, 44, 81, 84, 86, 90, 93, 100,
        102, 104–5, 124, 146
autonomous work 13–14, 25, 47, 61, 64, 66,
        72, 87, 90, 57, 183

basic skills 23, 43, 103, 123, 127–8,
        135, 158
Becker 85, 143–4
bounded rationality 35, 61, 66, 90,
        102, 145
Braverman, Harry 14, 72
broad skill 24, 41, 129
    see also overall skill

chambers of commerce 36, 88, 151, 155
cognitive skills 17–18, 22–4, 68, 70, 75, 93,
        107–8
collective skill formation 88–90
communication skills 67, 70, 129
competence 4, 9, 15–22, 25, 31, 38, 42, 47,
        52, 130
complexity (skill definition) 11–25 *passim*, 39,
        42, 47
computing skills 42, 70, 82
credentialism 45–6, 171

deadweight loss 144, 146
deep uncertainty 6, 30, 34–5, 58, 77, 99–104,
        111, 113, 121, 150, 174
demand for learning, *see* skill formation
        services, demand for
deskilling 58, 70, 72, 74–7
    see also skilled labour, demand for
developmental economy 8, 154, 159–60
Dictionary of Occupational Titles 10, 47, 69

economic performance 4, 30, 48, 57–8, 67–9
education-to-work transition 93, 108–11

efficiency wages 61
elasticity
    of demand 59, 80
    of substitution 74, 79–80
    of supply 95
emotional skills 13, 22
employers' associations 36, 88–90
ethnicity 94, 103–5, 134
European Higher Education Area (EHEA) 42
European Qualifications Framework for
        Lifelong Learning (EQF) 41–2
externality 19–20, 88, 91, 108, 113,
        120, 142–4, 147, 153, 161,
        176–7, 182

firm-specific skills 12, 23, 49, 60, 85
Fordism 72

gender 14–15, 37, 40, 46, 76, 94, 99, 103–5,
        109, 123, 134
general skills 85
    see also transferable skills
generic skills 22–3, 41–7 *passim*, 64, 74, 126,
        128–9, 171–2
globalization 71–2, 75–6, 93, 156
grade inflation vi, 41–2

heterodox economics 12–13
High Involvement Work Practices 64, 76, 87,
        90, 145
higher education 42, 46, 98, 106, 108, 143,
        150, 156, 160, 173, 176
human
    capital theory 11–12, 17, 85, 142–9
        see also neoclassical approach
    resource management 16, 62, 65,
        143, 166

identity 35, 86, 93, 100, 108, 154, 165
industrial policy 77, 141, 148, 152, 159–60,
        163, 184
interactive skills 22, 64, 70, 75
International Adult Literacy Survey (IALS) 41,
        43, 126
International Standard Classification of
        Education (ISCED) 41–2

job
  requirement (task-based) approach 10, 17,
    47–8, 54, 74
  quality v, 5, 30, 57, 157, 183
  skill 11, 13–14, 17, 27, 40, 44–51, 69, 124,
    128–9, 133, 171

Knight, Frank 35
knowledge economy 72, 75, 133, 135, 160, 165

learning
  barrier 31–2, 36, 51–3, 105, 111–14, 134, 147
    see also training barrier, worker
  organization 27, 81, 87, 108
  at work v, 46, 81–3, 87, 90, 133, 150
liberal market economy 8, 119, 154, 157–9
life
  course 29, 35, 46, 94, 99, 101, 103, 108–9,
    111, 113, 147, 169, 179–80
  -cycle model 97–8
literacy 22, 41, 43, 65, 70, 108, 126–9, 138

marginal benefit of learning 98
marginal cost of learning 97–8
marginal product 46, 59–61, 67, 78–9, 83
market failure 8, 67, 86, 91, 142, 144–5,
    150, 180
Marxian thought 14, 72, 123
migration 123, 127, 132, 148–9, 162, 165,
    168–9, 184
minimum wage 66, 158, 162, 184
mismatch 6, 8, 13, 30–2, 40, 48, 51–2, 54,
    118–24 passim, 129–32, 161, 167, 172–4,
    177, 181
motivation 21, 101–5, 157, 160

negative skills 19–20
neoclassical approach 11–13, 18, 20–1, 25, 33,
    85, 95, 150, 175
numeracy 22, 41, 43, 70, 108, 126–9

O*NET 10, 13, 17, 45, 47, 170
occupation-specific skills 22–3, 41–2, 45,
    48, 172
omitted ability bias 106
optimal learning 111–12
overall skill 24, 40, 48, 70
over-education, 51–52, 131, 135, 147–8, 170,
    173–4, 179–83
  see also skills, under-utilization

pay, see wages
PES concept 9–13, 18, 21, 25–6, 37, 40, 43, 54,
    67, 180
physical skills 22, 70
planning process 119–20, 122
polarization 7, 58, 69, 75–6, 128

political economy 5, 10, 12–13, 81, 148
positional good 20, 149
preferences 12, 16, 18, 29, 94, 97, 99, 101–5,
    112, 147, 157, 179
  endogenous 34–5
price-signalling 118–20, 122
primary education 176
problem-solving skills 15, 22, 43, 70,
    73, 129
product specification 63
Programme for the International Assessment of
    Adult Competencies (PIAAC) 41, 43, 45,
    48, 51–2, 128
Programme for International Student
    Assessment (PISA) 41, 43

reflexivity 94, 105, 110, 180
  see also agency, employees'
regimes of capitalism 153–4, 160
rent-seeking skill 20
resource based view (RBV) 61–3
Ricardo, David 73
routine/non-routine skills 23, 47, 64, 70, 75,
    94, 183

secondary education 125, 134, 140, 157, 159
segmentation of labour markets 123–4, 134
segregation, gender and ethnic 123
self-efficacy 31, 99, 101–2, 113, 147
signalling model of education 107
skill
  acquisition, measurement of 49–50
  formation services 5–6, 27–8, 30, 34, 36–7,
    117–18, 132–5, 151, 161
  demand for vi, 3, 7, 21, 29–34, 36, 48, 53, 94,
    96–105, 112–14, 152, 180
  inequality in 122–3, 134
  supply of 29, 48, 57, 81–91, 180
  loss 28, 48–50, 90, 132
  obsolescence 30–1, 49–50, 132
  -biased technological change 25, 73–6, 80
skilled labour
  demand for 27, 44–8, 57–79, 90, 169–72
  supply of 28–9, 40–4, 93–6, 167–9, 184
skills
  audit 165–7
  ecosystem 36, 152–3, 184
  equilibrium 8, 30, 37, 53, 121, 152
  deficit 32, 52–3, 122, 132, 162
  gap 31, 51–3, 132, 166
  inequality 122–3, 126–9
  matching 117–20, 148
  poverty vi, 8, 23, 43, 121–3, 127–9
  premium 7, 67, 95, 97–8, 100, 105–8, 113,
    174–6
  shortage vi, 17, 28, 31, 44, 51–3, 122, 132,
    149, 163

under-utilization 31, 51–2, 87, 130–2,
147–8, 174
see also over-education
and values 5, 10–11, 18–21, 39–40, 58, 67,
78, 85–6, 97, 99–100, 102–3, 105, 108
see also skills, premium
social construction of skill 12, 14–15, 18, 20,
22, 25, 31, 42, 61, 67, 166
social intervention 6, 66–7, 81, 85–6, 88, 105,
121, 142–51 *passim*, 177, 180, 185
social partners 27, 36
social partner-led skill system 154–6
state-led partnership skill system 156–7
strategic management 60–6, 77, 145
stock of skills 29–31, 40, 46, 95, 118, 124–9,
167–9

tacit skill 13
talent 9, 23
task discretion, *see* autonomous work
Taylorism 14, 63, 70, 72
temporary work 111, 123, 134
time preference 97
training barrier
employer 32, 52

barrier, worker 31, 51–2, 134–5
deficit 32, 143
transferable skills 12, 23, 36, 60, 85–6, 89,
143, 157
Trends in International Mathematics and
Science Study (TIMSS) 41–2

under-education 51–2, 181
unions 6, 27, 36, 83–4, 89, 91, 103, 113, 151,
155, 157, 163

vocational education 16–17, 77, 155, 160
vocational training 82, 109, 140, 144, 158

wages 14, 19, 23, 28, 31, 33, 36–7, 40, 45–7, 49,
58–64, 66–73, 78–80, 82–3, 85, 95–6,
106–7, 110, 114, 118–19, 121–2, 124,
131, 143, 147, 155, 157, 181, 183
see also skills, premium
win-win strategy v, 4
workplace learning, *see* learning, at work
Works Councils 151, 155

youth transition, *see* education-to-work
transition